# Presentations For Du...

D0566027

## Preparing Your Presentation

- ✔ Don't get talked into making a presentation that you don't want to make.
- ✔ Organize your information in a simple pattern that the audience can easily recognize.
- ✔ Use various types of material — examples, stories, statistics, quotes — to maintain audience interest.
- ✔ Have a special conclusion ready that you can go right into if you run out of time. Never omit a conclusion.
- ✔ Anticipate the questions you'll be asked and have answers ready.
- ✔ Practice out loud.

## Perfecting Your Delivery

- ✔ Try to establish eye contact with your entire audience.
- ✔ Vary the rate, pitch, and volume of your voice, as well as its tone.
- ✔ Don't stand with your hands clasped in front of your crotch.
- ✔ Look at the audience more than your notes.
- ✔ Don't pace back and forth, jingle change in your pocket, or play with your hair.
- ✔ If standing behind a podium makes you feel more comfortable, do it.
- ✔ Convey enthusiasm for your subject. It's contagious.

## Heading Off Problems

- ✔ Anticipate things that can go wrong — the lights go out, the microphone squeals — and have a funny line ready.
- ✔ Repeat any questions you receive to make sure everyone in the audience hears them.
- ✔ If an audience member is sending your presentation off track with a long question or comment, offer to talk with him one-on-one after you're finished presenting.
- ✔ Check your visual aids to ensure they can be seen clearly by the entire audience.
- ✔ Get to the room early and make sure it's set up the way you want it to be.
- ✔ Find out exactly where you're presenting and how long it takes you to get there.

## Using PowerPoint

- ✔ Don't make slides that are difficult to read. Avoid too many words per line, too many colors, and designs that are too busy or too small.
- ✔ Check text for spelling errors.
- ✔ Take advantage of PowerPoint templates that help you design your presentation.
- ✔ Use animation and other special effects sparingly. Too many effects distract from your message.
- ✔ Don't read your slides to the audience.
- ✔ You can't check the working condition of your laptop and projector too many times.
- ✔ Bring an extension cord and adapter.

*For Dummies: Bestselling Book Series for Beginners*

# Presentations For Dummies®

**Cheat Sheet**

## Using Humor

- Make sure that your humor relates to a point in your presentation.
- Avoid sexist, ethnic, racist, and off-color humor.
- If you can't tell a joke well, use humor that doesn't require comic delivery: a personal anecdote, a funny quotation, or an amusing analogy.
- Build rapport by poking fun at yourself — appropriately.

## Managing Stage Fright

- Alcohol and pills don't work. If they wear off before you speak, you'll be even more nervous. If they don't, you'll be incoherent.
- Channel nervous tension into your performance — use broader gestures, more movement, and more excitement in your voice.
- Work through nervous energy by taking a few deep breaths.
- Leave time to go to the bathroom shortly before you speak.
- Remember that the audience wants you to succeed.

## Helpful Web Sites

| Site | URL | Description |
|------|-----|-------------|
| Kushner & Associates | www.kushnergroup.com | Loaded with great links for public speakers (if I say so myself). |
| The Virtual Reference Desk | www.refdesk.com | Researching something? Start here. |
| WebRing | www.webring.com | Tired of traditional search engines? Try a Web ring. |
| The Museum of Humor.com | www.museumofhumor.com | Lots of links to humorous material for presenters. |
| FedWorld | www.fedworld.gov | A gold mine of government information. |
| The Lycos Image Gallery | www.multimedia.lycos.com | Find a visual aid. |
| RealNetworks | www.real.com | Go here to download the Real Player. Then listen to presentations on your computer. |

## For Dummies: Bestselling Book Series for Beginners

**Presentations For Dummies®**

Published by
**Wiley Publishing, Inc.**
111 River St.
Hoboken, NJ 07030-5774
www.wiley.com

WILEY

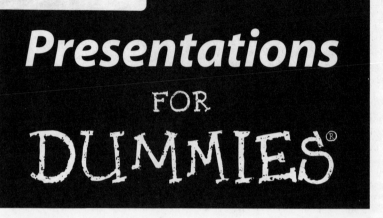

# Presentations FOR DUMMIES®

## by Malcolm Kushner

WILEY

Wiley Publishing, Inc.

# About the Author

Malcolm Kushner, "America's favorite humor consultant," is an internationally acclaimed expert on humor and communication and a professional speaker. Since 1982, he has trained thousands of managers, executives, and professionals how to gain a competitive edge with humor. His clients include IBM, Hewlett-Packard, AT&T, Chevron, Aetna, Motorola, and Bank of America.

A popular speaker, his Leading With Laughter® presentation features rare video clips of U.S. presidents using humor intentionally and successfully. He has performed the speech at many corporate and association meetings, as well as at the Smithsonian Institution.

Kushner has also written presentations for some of the nation's leading corporate executives. His work has included everything from remarks at annual shareholder meetings to commencement addresses and Congressional testimony.

A Phi Beta Kappa graduate of the University of Buffalo, Kushner holds a B.A. in Speech-Communication. His M.A. in Speech-Communication is from the University of Southern California, where he taught freshman speech. He also has a J.D. from the University of California Hastings College of the Law. Prior to becoming a humor consultant, he practiced law with a major San Francisco law firm.

Kushner is the author of *The Light Touch: How to Use Humor for Business Success* (Simon & Schuster) and *Vintage Humor for Wine Lovers* (Malcolm Kushner & Associates). He is also a cocreator of the humor exhibit at the Ronald Reagan Presidential Library.

Frequently interviewed by the media, Kushner has been profiled in *Time Magazine*, *USA Today*, *The New York Times,* and numerous other publications. His television and radio appearances include CNN, National Public Radio, CNBC, *Voice of America,* and *The Larry King Show.* His annual "Cost of Laughing Index" has been featured on *The Tonight Show* and the front page of *The Wall Street Journal*.

Need a great speaker for your next meeting or event? Contact Malcolm at P.O. Box 7509, Santa Cruz, CA 95061, call 831-425-4839, or e-mail him at mk@ kushnergroup.com. Visit his Web site at www.kushnergroup.com.

# Dedication

In memory of John Cantu, a comedy teacher, writer, and legend in his own mind — and a lot of other people's too.

# Author's Acknowledgments

"You love me. You really love me." (Oops, I thought this was my Academy Awards speech.) This is actually the speech about people I love. Let's start with the people at Wiley. My thanks go to Marc Mikulich for talking me into writing this book and to Kathy Cox for making it happen. Thanks also to Georgette Beatty, who provided superb editing and due-date reminders, as well as copy editor Jennifer Bingham and technical editor Susan Clark Lawson.

Speaking of special thanks, I must shower praise upon my wife, Christine Griger, who put up with me while I was writing. And I must thank my son, Sam, for his encouragement.

Special thanks go to the late San Francisco comedy coach John Cantu. He was a good friend and teacher who is greatly missed by everyone who knew him. Loyd Auerbach, Allatia Harris, and N.R. Mitgang also received repeated calls to tap into their expertise — and came through every time. And John Gallagher's computer expertise was invaluable.

I also want to thank all the other people who were interviewed for this book. They include Kare Anderson, Neil Baron, Martin Gonzales Bravo, Rachael Brune, Joe DiNucci, Scott Fivash, James Harris III, David Haussler, Barbara Howard, Rich Johnson, Willy Keats, Charles Lax, Marcia Lemmons, Jim Lukaszewski, Steven Resnick, Paula Swanson, Allen Weiner, Patty White, and Les Wright. (I've probably forgotten somebody, and if I did, I apologize.)

Thanks for support and encouragement go to Rich Herzfeld, Bob Reed, Jack Burkett, Stu Silverstein, Debra DeCuir, Karen Kushner, Barbara Nash, Emily and Elizabeth "Woodge" Stover, the DuFau family, and Arthur, Karen, Heather, and Amy Tamarkin. Special thanks go to Tom Daly IV at Vital Speeches for granting permission to use so many of the quotes contained in the book.

I love you. I really love you all.

## Publisher's Acknowledgments

We're proud of this book; please send us your comments through our Dummies online registration form located at www.dummies.com/register/.

Some of the people who helped bring this book to market include the following:

*Acquisitions, Editorial, and Media Development*

**Project Editor:** Georgette Beatty

**Acquisitions Editor:** Kathy Cox

**Copy Editor:** Jennifer Bingham

**Technical Editor:** Susan Clark Lawson

**Editorial Manager:** Jennifer Ehrlich

**Editorial Assistants:** Courtney Allen, Melissa S. Bennett

**Cartoons:** Rich Tennant, www.the5thwave.com

*Composition*

**Project Coordinator:** Adrienne Martinez

**Layout and Graphics:** Andrea Dahl, Lauren Goddard, Stephanie D. Jumper

**Proofreaders:** Andy Hollandbeck, Carl Pierce, Dwight Ramsey, Brian H. Walls, TECHBOOKS Production Services

**Indexer:** TECHBOOKS Production Services

***Special Help*** Carmen Krikorian, Elizabeth Rea, Chad R. Sievers

---

**Publishing and Editorial for Consumer Dummies**

    **Diane Graves Steele,** Vice President and Publisher, Consumer Dummies

    **Joyce Pepple,** Acquisitions Director, Consumer Dummies

    **Kristin A. Cocks,** Product Development Director, Consumer Dummies

    **Michael Spring,** Vice President and Publisher, Travel

    **Brice Gosnell,** Associate Publisher, Travel

    **Kelly Regan,** Editorial Director, Travel

**Publishing for Technology Dummies**

    **Andy Cummings,** Vice President and Publisher, Dummies Technology/General User

**Composition Services**

    **Gerry Fahey,** Vice President of Production Services

    **Debbie Stailey,** Director of Composition Services

# Contents at a Glance

# Table of Contents

## *Part II: Creating a Presentation: The Basics* ..................*67*

### Chapter 6: Building the Body with Stories, Statistics, and Other Good Stuff . . . . . . . . . . . . . . . . . . . . . . . . . . . . . . . . . . . . . . . . . .69

# Introduction

· · · · · · · · · · · · · · · · · · · · · · · · · · · · · · · · · · · · · · · · · · · · · · ·

*W*elcome to *Presentations For Dummies,* the book that gives a new meaning to the term "influence peddling." No, I don't show you anything illegal, but you do figure out how to use basic presentation skills to influence your boss, coworkers, customers, vendors, butcher, baker, candlestick maker, and anyone else who matters in your career. You can even influence people who don't matter — like your senator.

This book provides all the tools you need to make a successful presentation. And that doesn't mean just formal presentations. Some of the most important presentations you give may not involve a PowerPoint show. What do you do when you need to give an impromptu talk about your strategy to customers, an answer that defuses a hostile question at a business meeting, or a pep talk to your morale-deprived coworkers? Success or failure in these situations, as well as in formal presentations, depends on how well you present.

That's why this book covers the full range of skills needed to give a successful presentation. You can discover everything from how to develop and deliver a presentation to how to think on your feet. An old philosopher once said, "Every time you open your mouth, your mind is on parade." This book ensures that your parade looks sharp, sounds smart, and dazzles your audience.

## About This Book

If you want to improve the full range of your presentation skills, then read the entire book. You can become an expert communicator.

Too busy to read a whole book? Don't worry. *Presentations For Dummies* is designed with your time constraints in mind. The book is divided into easy-to-read segments that cover very specific topics. Choose an area of interest, such as dealing with hecklers, and turn directly to it.

You can also use the book to accent the design of your home or office. Just put it on a bookshelf in full view. The bold yellow-and-black cover contrasts nicely with the muted brown tones of many bookcases. (And anyone seeing the book on your shelf will assume you read it and will think you're smart.)

# Conventions Used in This Book

So you can navigate through this book better, I use the following conventions:

- ✔ *Italic* is used for emphasis and to highlight new words or terms that are defined.
- ✔ **Boldfaced** text is used to indicate keywords in bulleted lists.
- ✔ `Monofont` is used for Web addresses.

# What You're Not to Read

Sidebars, which are shaded gray boxes with text enclosed in them, consist of information that is interesting to know but not necessarily critical to your understanding of the topic. Feel free to skip them. Of course, you may be missing some of the most interesting stuff in the book. But that's up to you.

# Foolish Assumptions

While writing this book, I made some assumptions about you and your knowledge of presentations. Here are the assumptions I've made about you:

- ✔ You may be fretting about your next presentation, because you don't understand how to engage the audience.
- ✔ You may know nothing about presentations but would like to be prepared in case you're ever asked to give one — impromptu or otherwise.
- ✔ Maybe you know quite a bit about presentations and have a lot of experience, but you want to polish your presentation development and delivery more.
- ✔ You may know how to give a formal presentation, but you would like to improve your presenting skills in special situations — question-and-answer sessions, panels, or roundtables.
- ✔ You may know the basics of giving a presentation, but you want to acquire some advanced techniques, like using humor successfully or adding some style.
- ✔ You may know that you shouldn't fear giving a presentation, but you fear it anyway — and you want to know how to overcome your anxiety.

# How This Book Is Organized

*Presentations For Dummies* has six major parts, each of which is divided into chapters covering specific topics. The chapters are self-contained units of brilliant insight, so you don't have to plow through them in sequence. You can read them separately or together in any order you wish. Don't worry about missing any gems of wisdom. The book is thoroughly cross-referenced and guides you to related items of information.

Each part covers a major area of presentation skills. The following is a brief tour of what you can find.

## Part 1: Presenting with Purpose

Getting started is probably the hardest aspect of developing a presentation, or doing anything else. In this part, I show you how to ease into the task. You discover all kinds of research resources, including some great Web sites. I also discuss what you need to find out about your audience and how to organize your presentation. And if you're anxious about presenting, don't worry — literally. You find some effective tips for handling stage fright.

## Part II: Creating a Presentation: The Basics

The key to success with presentations — as with so much else in life — is preparation. You have to find material to wow your audience: attention-grabbing quotes, stories, and statistics. Adding humor can also help. And you definitely want stunning visual aids. But all that's not even enough. You've got to choose your words wisely. They have to convey your message with impact — especially your introduction and conclusion. In this part, I tell you how to create a presentation that your audience will never forget.

## Part III: Giving Your Presentation with Ease

You have much more to think about when it comes to giving a presentation than your topic. You must decide whether you should use a podium, what you should wear, what gestures you should use, how fast you should speak, and how you should handle the audience and their questions. And these are just a few issues involved in transforming your written message into a masterful oral performance. In this part, I show you how to deliver a presentation that wows your audience. Simple, proven techniques guarantee success even if you're nervous, shy, or disorganized. But don't worry; you'll be great.

## Part IV: Mastering the Power of PowerPoint

Many people get sick at the thought of watching yet another PowerPoint presentation. But they won't feel that way about *your* presentations after you read this part of the book. I tell you how to make PowerPoint slides that are graphically appealing and easy to read. Want to do cool special effects? That's all here, too. I tell you how to use video, audio, and animation to make your slides stand out. You even get a crash course in avoiding the PowerPoint mistakes that really irritate people.

## Part V: Checking Out Tips and Tricks for Common Presentations

Have you ever had to talk "off the top of your head"? Or train someone how to do something? Or give financial information to an audience? Or make a presentation to people from another culture? All of these are common tasks in today's business world. And if you haven't had to make any of these presentations yet, the odds are that you will. In this part of the book, I give you some pointers on how to handle these situations. I also discuss sales, technical, and motivational presentations, as well as how to present a business plan, serve on a panel, and participate in virtual meetings.

## Part VI: The Part of Tens

In this part of the book, I throw in three chapters that didn't fit anywhere else. But you'll be glad I did — especially if you ever have to make a presentation at a public meeting. I cover that in one of the chapters. Another chapter covers what to check before you make a presentation, and the third chapter gives you snappy lines to say when you goof up.

# Icons Used in This Book

This icon signals important advice about how to maximize the effectiveness of your presentation.

An elephant never forgets, but people do. This icon alerts you to information you want to remember (unless you're subpoenaed by a Senate subcommittee).

This icon points to information that justifies your purchase of this book — brilliant advice that you can't readily find anywhere else. Most of it's based on the personal experience, knowledge, and insight of myself as well as several of my colleagues.

To indicate potential problems, I use this icon.

# Where to Go from Here

You hold in your hands a powerful tool — a guide to increasing your influence through the sheer force of your presentations. This tool can be used for good or evil. That's up to you. Consider yourself warned. To begin your journey, turn to the table of contents or index, pick a topic of interest, and turn to the page indicated. Good luck in your travels. You're now ready to dive into this book, unless you plan to wait for the movie version.

# Part I

# Presenting with Purpose

## The 5th Wave

### By Rich Tennant

"GET READY, I THINK THEY'RE STARTING TO DRIFT."

## In this part . . .

The toughest part of preparing a presentation (or doing anything) is getting started. In these chapters, I show you how to take the first steps toward doing what has to be done. Here you can discover what information you need to know about your audience in order to craft a successful presentation. I also cover how to get started researching what you're going to say, organizing your presentation, and overcoming performance anxiety.

# Chapter 1

# Presentations: One Key to Doing Business

So you have to give a presentation. That's the reason most people pick up this book. You've made a wise decision. Whether you're giving your first presentation or your five hundredth, this book can help you improve your presentation skills. It's crammed full of nuts-and-bolts ideas, techniques, and suggestions. Beginners will benefit just from discovering and avoiding basic mistakes. Experienced presenters will appreciate the expert tips and techniques sprinkled throughout these pages. This book isn't designed to be read from cover to cover. Of course, you can if you want to, but you can skip chapters and even sections within chapters, focusing only on the material that suits your needs. If you're looking for an idea of where to start or an idea of what chapters may benefit you the most, just check out the sections that follow to find out what each chapter has to offer.

## Finding Out What You Need to Know

Getting asked to present is the beginning of a process in which you'll make a lot of decisions. First, you have to decide exactly what to talk about, because even when you're assigned a topic, you often have room to shape it. For example, say you're asked to talk about trends in the economy. You can give a broad overview, you can talk about two or three specific trends, or you can do something in between.

What you do depends on what you feel like talking about and what you know about the audience that you're presenting to. In fact, finding out about your audience is one of your key research tasks as a presenter. You need to know as much about them as possible — even if they're just your colleagues from work. What are their attitudes toward you and your topic? What are their values and beliefs? All of these factors come into play as you develop your presentation. They affect what information you include, its level of difficulty, and your whole approach to your subject.

And finding out about your audience is just the beginning of your research. After you finish that, you must gather facts and data to put in your presentation. One of the world's best-kept secrets is how you can get other people to do this for you — free of charge. Hint: It's their job. Reference librarians, government public information officers, corporate archivists — all of them are paid to answer your questions. These folks are a tremendous and often-overlooked resource for helping you research business presentations.

Of course, I have to mention the Web. This is the greatest thing for presentation research since sliced bread. Actually, it's better than sliced bread, unless you're giving a presentation about sandwiches. The information resources of the Web are almost beyond imagination. You can get data from government, corporate, and nonprofit organizations — a veritable cornucopia of facts and figures for any topic you're presenting. But the Web is useful for obtaining much more than dry data. It's a treasure trove of quotations, stories, and humor that you can use to make your presentations memorable and distinctive — if you get the necessary permissions to use the material.

So what's the secret of successful research? Discover that in Chapters 2 and 3. You find out when to ask whom about what. And you find some incisive questions to ask — questions that can produce information to make your presentations stand out. You can also find some lists of really cool Web sites to help turn your talk into a polished gem. I also discuss resources such as *Vital Speeches of the Day,* trade publications, and *The Wall Street Journal.*

But research is only the beginning of the process that leads to you standing in front of people and delivering your words of wisdom. Does that frighten you? Don't worry. You've got plenty of company. Numerous surveys have found that many people are more frightened of giving a presentation than dying. Fortunately, many ways exist to handle such anxiety. These range from psychological approaches like positive self-talk to physical approaches like stress-busting exercises. Besides, your audience *wants* you to succeed. You have knowledge that they want. That's why you're presenting! Odds are, they don't even realize you're afraid. Plus, you can use a whole bunch of tricks to make it seem like you're not nervous even when you are. You find out about all this and more in Chapter 5.

Overcoming your fear is something that you need to work on throughout the presentation process. Just thinking about presenting makes some people nervous. They worry that their whole talk will be disjointed and incomprehensible. One way to deal with that fear head-on is to make sure that your talk is well organized and easy to follow. How does it flow? That's the subject of Chapter 4. You find out how to create an outline that makes sense for your topic and conforms to your time limits. (One tip: Pick the right number of points.) I offer simple organizational patterns to choose among: problem and solution; past, present, and future; cause and effect. After you pick one, your presentation will start to write itself — sort of.

# Developing Your Presentation

You've done your research, and you've created an outline. That was a lot of work. You should be almost done, right? Not even close. You've still got to write the presentation. This is the part that many people find oppressive — figuring out exactly what to say to keep an audience interested. Hey, it's really not that bad. After you know what points you're making (see your outline), all you have to do is put some meat on those bones. (Or leaves, if you're a vegetarian.)

In fact, viewed from the right perspective, writing is actually the fun part. This is when you get to flesh out your message — add stories, quotes, and statistics — anything that will make your presentation more effective. It's like a puzzle. How can you assemble the pieces of your talk to give it the maximum impact on your audience? Well, it depends. What effect are you trying to achieve? Knowing this helps you determine the types of material to use. If you're talking to left-brained, rational, engineering types, you may want to use a logical appeal with lots of statistics and practical examples. If you're talking to right-brained, creative, graphic-artist types, you may do better with an emotional appeal, using stories that tug at the heartstrings. Or sometimes it's best to mix the two approaches — get them in the head *and* the heart. You can find out how to use a wide array of material in Chapter 6.

And we can't talk about material without discussing humor. So let me dispose of two myths right now:

✔ **Myth one:** You must begin your presentation with a joke.

 Baloney. If you can't tell a joke, don't even try. You'll spare yourself and your audience a lot of embarrassment.

✔ **Myth two:** You can't use humor if you can't tell a joke.

 Baloney again. Many simple types of humor can be used whether you can tell a joke or not. Look for some examples in Chapter 8. From anecdotes and analogies to bumper stickers and cartoons, many easy-to-use types of humor are often overlooked. They may not get you a comedy career, but they can make your presentation sparkle.

Okay, sparkle isn't a word often associated with business presentations. Dull. Boring. Deadly. Maybe those are more familiar. But it doesn't have to be that way. Go ahead and add some style. Traditional rhetorical tricks can add punch to a business presentation and make you stand out from the crowd. It all comes down to the words. Some words are more powerful than others. Some word combinations have different effects. For example, just starting a few sentences in a row with the same phrase can make your presentation seem more important. In Chapter 7, I go over some simple stylistic devices that can really jazz up your presentation.

Worried that fancy words aren't enough to make a big splash? You want fancy visual aids, right? One picture is worth a thousand words and all that sort of thing. I hear you. And I've got you covered. In Chapter 10, I discuss eye candy that can take your presentation to the next level. Now, this is a complicated area. Presenters make a lot of mistakes. They use visual aids that are cluttered, distracting, and unreadable — and I'm just warming up. So just by avoiding these mistakes, you can put yourself way ahead of the crowd. I show you exactly what *not* to do — whether you're using overheads, slides, flip charts, or whatever. I also give you tips for making your visuals more effective. For example, when using bar charts, don't make the bars three-dimensional. (No one can tell where they end or what numbers they represent.) I give you plenty of cool, practical tips like that as I cover everything you need to know about visual aids from start to finish.

And that reminds me — the start and finish of your presentation are its two most important points. Why? Those two parts are what the audience is most likely to remember. The introduction is especially important, because the start of your speech is when people decide if they want to listen to you. So how do you create an introduction that grabs them and doesn't let them go until your rousing conclusion? You've got lots of choices. You can start with a startling statistic and end with an inspirational quote. You can start with a rhetorical question and end with a personal story. You can start with a joke (if you can tell one) and end with a call to action. Like I said, you've got lots of choices. And I lay them out for you in Chapter 9.

Chapter 9 is also where I tell you how to use transitions — connective phrases that lead from one part of your talk to another. These are often overlooked when writing a presentation. But they're very important. They help the audience follow what you're saying, and they can generate excitement by previewing information that you give later in your talk.

## Delivering a Presentation

After you've written a brilliant, witty presentation that captures your message exactly, you've got to perform in front of an audience. For some people, performance is the hard part. Because even though your words are written perfectly, you've got to get your body to convey your message. The way you move, hold a microphone, make eye contact with the audience — all of these affect how your message is received. Not to mention the various qualities of your voice — pitch, timbre, volume, and so on. Then there's the whole issue of whether it's okay to "hide" behind a podium. The traditional wisdom says, "No." I, of course, disagree. The traditional thinking is that the podium is a barrier between you and your audience, so you're supposed to come out from behind it and let the audience see your full body. I say, "Bunk." If staying behind the podium makes you more comfortable and less frightened, then stay there, because fear is a much bigger barrier between a presenter and an audience than a podium is.

The body-language chapter — Chapter 11, for those who are keeping track — also covers how to avoid common mistakes. Like placing your hands over your crotch as you're talking, jiggling change in your pocket, or looking at your watch as an audience member asks a question.

In fact, answering audience questions is an art unto itself. What do you do if you don't know the answer? How do you respond to hostile questions? What if the questioners have no idea what they're talking about? I tell you how to handle all these situations and more in Chapter 13. One of the secrets is to spend some time anticipating audience questions before you give your presentation. Then you have answers ready when you're hit with the questions. Here's another tip: Repeat every question you receive. That allows everyone in the audience to hear the question and gives you a few more seconds to think about it. One more tip: If you don't know an answer, ask if anyone in the audience does. Quite often, someone will.

That's an example of an audience member helping you out. Sometimes, you're not so lucky. You get audience members who heckle you. Or fall asleep. Or — how dare they? — walk out of your presentation. How do you handle these people? That's the subject of Chapter 12. The key word here is "adapt." You can't keep doing what you were doing. If you get a tough audience, you've got to adapt to the situation. One technique is to get them involved. You can ask questions, take a survey, or do an audience-participation exercise — anything to change the energy flow. Sometimes, you can jolt nonresponsive audiences to attention just by telling them they can respond. Many audience members don't know that it's okay to laugh or take notes. You've got to give them permission in your presentation.

# Looking at PowerPoint Pointers

For better or worse, PowerPoint has become synonymous with business presentations around the globe. You can't go anywhere without seeing one. So you'd better know how to use it — properly.

We've all seen PowerPoint presentations with funky slides. The text is unreadable. The colors are ugly. And there are more bullets than at an annual meeting of the National Rifle Association. These slides probably conform to some design theory — just not one from Earth. Fortunately, I have simple rules to ensure that you don't make these mistakes. Don't put more than six bullets on a slide. Don't use all uppercase or lowercase text. Don't use several different fonts. Don't use too many colors. I tell you my rules in Chapter 14.

PowerPoint comes with built-in design templates that can take a lot of the guesswork out of creating attractive slides. If you pick a template and stick with it, you can create a decent-looking presentation. You can also create your own templates. Either way, using a template gives your slides a consistent look and feel.

But PowerPoint is much more than static slides. It's packed with all kinds of gee-whiz features that can spiff up your talk and make your audience go, "Wow." Want to make your text fly across the screen? Want to show a video-clip demo of your product actually working? Want to add sound effects to your presentation? You can do all this and more with PowerPoint. In Chapter 15, I give you a guided tour through PowerPoint's advanced features and show you some really easy, cool tricks. For example, you can link your slides to Web sites or documents. You can show your slides out of order. You can even use PowerPoint to keep track of action items discussed during your talk.

So if PowerPoint is so great, how come many people complain about it all the time? (The phrase you hear a lot is "Death by PowerPoint." It refers to the audience cringing as a presenter shows the hundredth slide — and he's not close to finished yet.) Here's my take on it. PowerPoint is a tool. Whether it works well depends on how it's used. The problem is that many people are using it very badly. They put full sentences on their slides instead of key words. They read their slides to the audience. They use too many special effects. They don't talk about what's on the slide. And the list goes on. I tell you how to avoid these mistakes in Chapter 16. Because if you use PowerPoint appropriately, it really does give your talk a lot more power.

# Sizing Up Special Presentation Situations

Although general rules are useful up to a point, certain presentation situations require more specific guidelines. In Part V, I give you some details about presentations that occur frequently in the business world.

Sales and motivational presentations (covered in Chapter 17) are a good example. I lump them together, because a sales presentation is really a specialized form of motivational talk — you want to motivate people to buy something. A key guideline that applies here is to talk about specifics. Customers want to know exactly what benefits they can get from your product or service.

And employees want to hear about concrete actions they can take to motivate themselves in their specific jobs. Don't just spout some feel-good platitudes about working *smarter, not harder.* Empathy is also crucial for these types of presentations. You really have to put yourself in the place of the customers or employees and understand what makes them tick. Then you can inspire them into action.

Two more common business presentations are the financial and technical presentations (see Chapter 18). Again, these are really the same thing. The financial presentation is a specialized form of technical presentation. The critical factor here is simplifying complex information — whether it's quarterly results or scientific research data. How do you do this? First, eliminate jargon and acronyms that nobody understands. Second, express your information in terms that are familiar to your audience. Use metaphors and analogies to put the unknown in terms of the known. And don't dump data on your audience. There's a real temptation to spew numbers — especially in financial presentations. Don't. Keep the numbers to a minimum. Just use the key indicators, and explain why they're important. Your audience doesn't need (or want) to know every last detail.

Speaking of numbers, another special situation involves presenting a business plan (see Chapter 20). Whether the funding comes from venture capitalists or top management of the company where you're employed, the drill is similar. You've got to give a talk that convinces them to fork over the funds. That means providing realistic financial assumptions and detailed feedback from prospective customers — two areas where presenters often screw up. You can't expect people to invest just because a technology seems cool to engineers. Your talk has to show them how much money investors need to contribute, when they'll get it back, and how much they'll make. You also have to be ready to answer rapid-fire questions and think on your feet.

In fact, thinking on your feet is a requirement of what is probably the most common presentation in the business world: the impromptu presentation (covered in Chapter 23). Have you ever been in a meeting when someone turned to you and asked, "What do you think about that?" Your answer was an impromptu presentation. Impromptu remarks also come up when you serve on a panel or participate in a roundtable discussion — two popular speaker formats at business conferences and conventions. So what do you do when you have to talk off the cuff? Stall for time while you organize your thoughts. One simple technique is to have an all-purpose quote ready. Then, no matter what you have to talk about, you always have an opening. That gives you more time to think about what else you will say.

The situation becomes even more complicated if your presentation isn't in your own country. And given today's global economy, with its rapidly growing multinational corporations, the odds are you'll eventually have to present before an international audience. That may mean working with an interpreter, because language differences are a big challenge. But a bigger one is cultural differences. Words and gestures that are innocent in your own country can be offensive in others. For example, the symbolic color of death in Western societies is black; in Eastern cultures, it's white. In some countries, a presenter is expected to give gifts to dignitaries; in other countries, that's considered bribery. Another big problem occurs with cultural imperialism — assuming that every culture does things the way yours does. They don't. A simple technique for countering this audience irritant is to quote some famous people from the audience's culture during your presentation. Quoting one of their writers, artists, or political leaders will show you've taken the time to learn about them. (To find out more on international presentations, travel ahead to Chapter 22.)

Another type of business presentation involves training (check out Chapter 19). New employees must learn company procedures. Customers must learn how to use your products. Vendors must learn your invoice system. You may be called upon to show a group of people how to do something in many situations — even if you're not a professional trainer. This gets into the psychology of adult education and how people learn. But don't worry. Just applying a few basic principles should ensure that your training goals are accomplished successfully. First, recognize that people learn in different ways. Some people emphasize the visual, others the auditory, and still others the *kinesthetic* (the sense of touch, balance, and body movement). That means you have to make your training appeal to all three types of learners in your audience. Second, adult learners have a lot of ego. You have to create a psychologically safe environment for them to participate. That means taking the risk out of giving wrong answers. Third, make sure your audience understands the relevance of what you're telling them. They like it to be directly connected to improving their performance at work.

Chapter 19 also covers informational briefings. These are a common type of presentation in the business world. Any time you give a status report, you're giving a briefing. The key to a successful briefing is getting reliable information, organizing it into short segments, and showing your audience members how the information affects them.

One last special situation covered in Part V is the virtual presentation. Remember when meetings were always held face to face — a bunch of people squeezed into a room? That's going the way of the dinosaur and disco dancing. Many meetings are now held in cyberspace and other virtual locations. Web conferences. Teleconferences. Videoconferences. These new types of meetings have new rules of engagement. You've got to present to people who are located in numerous time zones around the world. You've got to make sure that your audience understands you when you can't see them. You've got to hope that the technology works properly. And each type of virtual presentation comes with its own advantages and problems. For instance, appearance is important if you're participating in a videoconference. You've got to wear solid colors and avoid patterned clothes. But if you're using the phone or e-mail, appearance isn't an issue. How do you decide what virtual technology is best for you? It depends on your presentation's goals — and budget. (For more on virtual presentations, check out Chapter 21.)

# Chapter 2

# The Four Ws: Who, What, Where, and Why

*G*etting started is always the toughest part of any activity, particularly when you're preparing to make a presentation — and especially if you don't want to give one in the first place! But don't worry. Presentations don't have to be torture. They can even be fun. (Well, let me put it this way — more fun than getting poked in the eye with a sharp object.)

This chapter shows you several simple techniques for getting started on your presentation. (And it's okay to enjoy them, too.)

## Determining What Your Presentation Needs to Do

I know of three types of presenters: those who make things happen, those who watch things happen, and those who wonder what happened. If you don't want to wonder what happened, you'd better know what you want to make happen. This section tells you how to do that.

## Informing, persuading, entertaining

The traditional functions of a presentation are to inform, persuade, or entertain. Here's the uncommon knowledge: A more useful analysis can be made in terms of motivation — your motivation for making the presentation and the audience's motivation for listening. Have you been asked to present? Have you been ordered to present? Do you want to make a presentation? Does the audience want to hear you? Has it been forced to hear you? Will it listen to you?

However you slice the analysis, the purpose remains the same: You want to know why you're giving this presentation and what you hope the result will be. And you want to build your presentation around that purpose.

## Setting specific goals

What do you want to accomplish? Your answer to that question is central to every decision you make about your presentation. Yet most people answer it in the vaguest terms:

> I want to be a hit.
>
> I want to impress my boss.
>
> I want to get it over with.

To remedy this, management communication counselor Jim Lukaszewski suggests creating a set of specific message goals. "Do you want to build your credibility?" he asks. "Do you want to get the audience members to agree with your position on an issue? Do you want them to learn something? Do you want to make them laugh? What do you want them to do?"

Write down your goals, and refer to them as you develop your presentation. This helps you make decisions about what to include. Anything that doesn't further a goal should be rejected.

## Asking for essential information (occasion, setting, and stuff like that)

No matter what type of presentation you've been invited to deliver, certain information is basic and essential to shaping your talk. You must first know the name of your contact person. Armed with that knowledge, you can ask your contact to provide the rest of the information that you need. Even if you're presenting within your own company, you may not be familiar with the department or division where you're scheduled to talk. The person who arranged your presentation should help prepare you. The following lists go over some of the questions you want answered.

Ask these questions about the event:

✔ What's the purpose of the meeting?

✔ Is it a regularly scheduled meeting or a special event?

✔ Is it a formal or an informal event?

✔ What's the atmosphere — very serious or light?

✔ Is my presentation the main attraction?

Ask these questions about the format:

✔ What's the agenda for the day?

✔ What's the format for my presentation? (A general session? A breakout session? A panel discussion? Before, during, or after a meal?)

✔ What time do I begin presenting?

✔ How long am I expected to present?

✔ Will there be other presenters?

✔ When will they be presenting?

✔ What will their presentations be about?

✔ Will any of their presentations be competitive with mine?

✔ What occurs before my presentation?

✔ What occurs after my presentation?

Ask these questions about the location:

✔ Where will I present? (In my own office building? At another company's headquarters? In an out-of-town convention center?)

✔ What type of room will I present in? (A meeting room? An auditorium?)

✔ How will the room be set up?

✔ What equipment is available to me?

# Analyzing Your Audience

How do you relate to an audience? You start by discovering as much about the people in the audience as possible. Who are they? What do they believe in? Why are they listening to you? This process is known as *audience analysis*.

The more information you possess, the more you can target your remarks to reflect an audience's interests. By targeting your audience's interests, you increase the likelihood that members of the audience are listening to you. Audience analysis also helps you shape your message. What types of arguments should you make? What will be the most effective examples? How complex can you make your explanations? What authorities should you quote? The answers to these and similar questions should determine much of the structure and content of your presentation.

In the next few sections, I give you a lot of questions to answer about your audience. How do you find the answers to them? First, if you're presenting at a particular company or organization, read its Web site, which should provide a lot of information about the people who work at the organization. Second, talk to the people who arranged your presentation. Ask them to give you information about your audience and to provide other sources of information.

## What's the demographic information? Age, sex, and stuff like that

The first thing I always want to know about an audience is its size. Will it be 10 people, 100 people, or 1,000 people? The size of the audience determines many aspects of the presentation. For example, a large audience eliminates the use of certain types of visual aids and requires the use of a microphone. A smaller audience is often less formal. Certain gimmicks that work with a large group will seem silly with a small one. ("Turn around and shake hands with the person behind you" just doesn't cut it when the entire audience is seated in one row.)

The second thing I want to know is the general nature of the audience. What's the relationship of the audience members to one another? Do they all come from the same organization? Do they share a common interest? I use this information to shape my message at a very basic level.

The next thing I want to find out is specific demographic data about audience members. What's their age range? What kind of schooling have they had? Here's a list of standard demographic items:

- ✔ Age
- ✔ Sex
- ✔ Education level
- ✔ Economic status
- ✔ Religion
- ✔ Occupation
- ✔ Racial/ethnic makeup
- ✔ Politics
- ✔ Cultural influences

The common knowledge is that you should gather as much demographic information about your audience as possible. Here's the uncommon knowledge: You can collect a lot more of this stuff than you'll ever use. Yes, theoretically you may want to tailor your presentation to reflect every last characteristic of your audience, but in reality, you may not have the time or inclination to do that. In fact, being adept at picking out only the most important demographics may give you a more successful presentation.

For example, suppose that you work for a drug company. You've been asked to present an overview of the company to a group of prospective investors. Is their age, sex, or religion going to affect what you say? Certainly, you could think of ways to take advantage of your knowledge of these characteristics, but the shape of your presentation will probably be a lot more heavily influenced by your knowledge of the audience's occupations and educational backgrounds. Are some of the prospective investors doctors? (They may know more about drugs than you do.) Are they professional investment advisors? Or are they wealthy individuals without a clue about corporate finance? (How sophisticated should you make your analysis of the "numbers"?) You get the idea. Instead of wasting a lot of time impersonating a census taker, zero in on the audience characteristics that make a real difference to your presentation.

## What are their attitudes, values, and beliefs?

Although presenters tend to focus on audience census data, they tend to overlook audience beliefs, attitudes, and values. The reason is simple. It's difficult to develop this information. You can easily find out how many audience members are male or female, but you have a much tougher time if you want to know what they're thinking. Yet their beliefs, attitudes, and values color their interpretation of every aspect of your presentation.

What exactly do you need to know? In essence, you want to compose a psychological profile of your audience. You want to know "where they're coming from." Here are some of the questions you want to answer:

- What is the audience's attitude about the subject of my presentation?
- What is the audience's attitude toward me as the presenter?
- What stereotypes will the audience apply to me?
- Will anyone have a hidden agenda?
- What values does the audience find important?
- Does the audience share a common value system?
- How strongly held are its beliefs and attitudes?
- What companies and departments within an organization do audience members work for?
- Will the audience include any of my rivals within the organization?
- Will the audience include anyone who can reward or punish me? (My boss, top management, stockholders?)

The answers to these questions help determine your approach to the subject.

## What do they know, and when did they know it?

Legendary football coach Vince Lombardi was giving his team a lecture on the basics. "We're going to start from the beginning," he said. "This is a football." That's when one of his players responded, "Hold on, coach; you're going too fast."

Want to start at the beginning with your audience? Then you'd better find out how much it already knows. Two of the biggest mistakes presenters make are talking over the heads of their audiences and talking at a level that's too elementary.

Ponder these questions before you make your presentation:

- How sophisticated are the audience members about the material I'm presenting?
- Will any experts on the topic be in the audience?

✔ Have the audience members heard other presentations about my idea?

✔ Why are they interested? Am I presenting something that will change the way they work or change their corporate relationships?

✔ If different departments are included, will they understand the background and the jargon related to my topic?

✔ Do they already know the basic concepts of my topic?

✔ Do they think they know a lot about my topic?

✔ How did they get the information that they already have about my topic?

✔ Are they familiar with my approach and attitude toward the topic?

Once again, the answers to these questions play a major role in how you construct your presentation. What your audience already knows determines how much background you need to provide, the sophistication of the language you can use, and the examples you include.

# What do they expect?

"I saw a world-famous economist speak to a group of 3,000 people, and he made time go backward," says high-tech executive Neil Baron. "He used arcane language from the semiconductor industry, but no one was from the semiconductor industry. And no one cared about it. After the first hour, people started breaking out magazines. And because it was a dark room, they used cigarette lighters and flashlights to read. It looked like a candlelight vigil in memory of the guy's speech."

Why would anyone talk about semiconductors to people who had no interest in them? What did the presenter think the audience expected? Sometimes, you've just got to wonder.

But you shouldn't wonder about what *your* audience members expect. Find out why they're attending your presentation:

✔ Are they interested in my topic?

✔ Were they ordered to attend?

✔ What do they expect to learn or see or hear?

✔ What do they expect me to say or do?

✔ Are they open to surprises?

# Relating to Your Audience

The major goal when relating to your audience is to establish rapport with them — a feeling of mutual warmth and a sense that you're on the same wavelength. The following sections present a few ways to achieve that goal.

## Focusing on the audience's needs, not yours

Focus on what your audience needs to know in order to understand, vote upon, or implement the concepts that you're presenting; not just what interests you about the topic. You need to be clear about what you expect the audience to do with the information. "I see speaker after speaker violate this basic rule," Neil says. "If people have been sitting on their butts for 10 hours, they don't care that you prepared a 60-minute talk. Cut it down to 20 minutes, and they'll think you are a genius." How often do presenters condense their presentations for the sake of their audience? Not often enough — and that's Neil's point. Put the audience's needs ahead of your own. Respect their time and attentiveness. You don't have to ignore your own need to wax eloquent about a topic you've been working on for months, but your needs aren't served when no one's listening.

## Putting your audience in the picture

If you really want to relate to your audience members, you have to see the world from their point of view and let them know that you can see it their way. How do you do this? One of my favorite examples comes from management communication advisor Jim Lukaszewski. He was scheduled to make a presentation to the executives of a large waste-removal company. Prior to his presentation, he arranged to spend three days working on a garbage truck. So as soon as he got up to speak, he let them know that he'd just spent three days hauling garbage. His audience could relate to him, because he demonstrated an understanding of their experience.

Here are two more techniques for putting your audience in the picture.

### Localize and customize your remarks

Big-time politicians and big-time comedians have something in common (besides the fact that people laugh at them). Both use *advance men* to gather information about local news, business, and people at the places where they'll be performing. Why? So they can work local references into their presentations. Customizing your presentation to your audience is one of the most powerful and effective ways of relating to your audience when you're talking to partners, prospects, customers — anyone outside your own organization. It even works if you're talking to a different department or group within your own company. Customizing grabs the audience's attention and gets the audience involved in your presentation. It makes the presenter a bit of an insider and lets the audience know that the presenter went to the trouble of finding information about the audience.

Here's the really good news: A little — and I mean very little — customization goes a long, long way. I've given presentations in which I made five or six references geared specifically to a particular audience, and afterward, I was showered with praise for the research I did on the group.

What kind of information should you use for these specific references? The names of key members of the audience are always good — especially if you can use them in a way that reflects their personalities. For example, during a presentation about using humor in the workplace at an insurance company's management retreat, I suggested that the audience start every memo with a funny, relevant quote. "Everyone will pay attention to it," I said, "except Mr. Executive. Never send him anything in writing. Memos disappear on contact with his desk." The audience of managers who had been frustrated for years with Mr. Executive's lack of response to memos roared with laughter. (By the way, Mr. Executive isn't his real name. But you already knew that, right?)

How did I know about Mr. Executive? I worked closely with the company's communications director as I prepared my talk. He told me about the key players and what I could or couldn't say about them. Remember that point. You don't want to offend anyone. When I'm going to use a name, I always clear it with a high-ranking member of the group.

What else can you refer to? Local news events, if you're speaking out of town. Customs or rituals associated with the organization you're addressing. The organization's history. Use your imagination. If you were a member of the audience, what would impress _you_ if an outsider referred to it?

## Push the audience's hot buttons

You can use a specialized form of customizing your remarks that immediately establishes a connection with your audience: pushing their hot buttons. You purposely work in a reference to a buzz issue — some source of minor controversy with the audience. The key word is "minor." You want to get a rise out of them, not have them rise up against you.

One of my favorite examples is the time I suggested that an audience ease up on memo and report writing. "You're wasting too much Xerox paper," I explained. The room burst into laughter and applause. Why? The people in the audience, employees of a Fortune 500 company, had been ordered to reduce their use of copier paper as a cost-saving measure. They thought it was ridiculous.

When digging for buzz issues, you need to keep a couple of things in mind. First, you have to find an issue that will cut across the entire audience. (Very often, when I ask my contact for a buzz issue, I get something that would be hilarious to a handful of key players but that no one else would comprehend. Use your judgment. Make sure that the "issue" is an issue for everyone.) Second, you have to make sure that the issue isn't too controversial to mention. Again, you must make a judgment call.

One of the simplest ways to find a buzz issue is to ask your contact whether any recent or pending legislation could negatively affect the audience. When the answer is yes, you have your issue. Or if you're presenting to another department within your company, just ask what department policy bothers audience members. That's always a winner.

## Sharing something that helps the audience know you

Jim Lukaszewski believes that one of the quickest ways to bridge the gulf between presenter and audience members is to share something personal. Tell them something that lets them get to know you. What can you share?

- **An unusual experience:** Sharing an unusual experience helps the audience relate to you in a concrete way. "I talk about when I was 14 in Minneapolis and I was involved in a fire rescue program," Jim says. "Talking about it helps the audience see me as a real person, not just as an expert in management communications."

- **Your personal principles or beliefs:** When you share your personal beliefs, the audience can understand where you're coming from. They're better able to evaluate your remarks and put them in a context — two things that we routinely do with people we already know.

- **Your avocations and hobbies:** What are your interests outside of work? How you entertain yourself says a lot about you. Providing that information helps the audience feel like it knows you.

This sharing-something-personal technique is particularly effective in a business presentation, because it's so rarely used. Here's the problem: The content of many executive presentations is interchangeable — and boring. Any vice president of any company could give the same presentation. "We must work as a team." "We've got to improve productivity." "Our budget will be tighter this year." Yawn. But if you put in something personal and real that tells the audience about you, then your presentation stands out. Plus, no one else could give it! Of course, whatever personal material you use must support one of your points. You can't just throw it in haphazardly.

## Identifying and addressing audience subgroups

Keep in mind that an audience may be made up of numerous subgroups — each with special needs and agendas. You need to include something for each of them if you want to create rapport with your entire audience. (An example of this situation is the "all hands" company meeting attended by everyone in an organization. Members of various departments constitute different audience subgroups: accounting, legal, marketing, sales, engineering, and so on. They have divergent interests that you must address. And a large organization may even have subgroups within a single department.)

## Highlighting the benefits of your presentation

Make sure that the audience knows what your presentation has to offer. Identify and emphasize the benefits early in your talk, and issue frequent reminders.

Communications expert Allen Weiner says that all audience members subconsciously ask themselves a benefits question: Will they hear anything to help them save or make money; save time; or reduce stress, anxiety, ambiguity, and confusion? So a smart presenter addresses as many of these issues as possible.

"Using those key topics of saving money, saving time, and reducing stress is at the heart of audience analysis," Allen explains. "They should always be included in your introduction in some form or another. The secret to audience analysis is the perception that you've done an audience analysis."

## Controlling Your Topic

You have a lot more control over your topic than you may suspect. When you're asked to give a presentation about a certain subject, the discussion isn't over. The discussion has just begun.

Even after you consider your audience and the purpose and goals of your presentation, you still have a lot of leeway in how to proceed. Suppose that you're a computer guru, and you're asked to speak about the latest upgrade to some software package that everyone wants to use. Will you give a broad overview? Will you give a list of specific tips for using it most effectively? Will you give a history of how it was developed? *You can still essentially pick your topic even though it's been assigned.*

The amount of time you have to make your presentation also affects the scope of your topic. A 15-minute talk doesn't allow as much detailed discussion as a 60-minute talk. Take that into consideration when you plan how much to cover.

# Chapter 3

# Pumping Up Your Research

························································

························································

An executive posted a sign in his office that said, "Do It Now." The next day his top salesman quit, his secretary asked for a raise, and his partner made a deal for immunity with the IRS. Despite these risks, I'm going to advise you to "Do it now." If you have a presentation to make, get started on it. Open a quote book. Go to the library. Tap into the Internet. Do something. Do anything. Just get started.

In this chapter, I tell you about a couple of people who can actually help you research your presentation, give you the lowdown on primary and secondary sources, and help you get your feet wet in navigating the Web.

## Two People Who Can Get You Started

Yes, you really can get other people to do some of your research. No, you don't have to trick them, you don't have to beg them, and you don't have to know any secret passwords. Helping you is their job.

### Using reference librarians

The most valuable resource at any library isn't found in a collection of books or periodicals. This resource is found behind a desk answering questions and is known as the *reference librarian*. This person doesn't know everything, but a good one knows how to *find* anything.

Don't be shy. Tell the reference librarian what you're working on and what you're looking for. He can provide invaluable assistance in directing you to the appropriate resources and can save you a tremendous amount of time when you're beginning to prepare your presentation.

Two more tips: First, find out whether the reference librarian will answer your questions over the phone. Many libraries provide this service. It's a great convenience, so you should take advantage of it. And it's great for speaking with someone at an out-of-town library. All it costs is the price of a long-distance phone call. (Yes, it's obvious, but most people don't think of libraries outside their immediate vicinity.) Second, don't forget that all kinds of libraries employ reference librarians — everything from your neighborhood public library to college and university libraries to corporate and association libraries.

## Contacting government public information officers

Government agencies produce a steady stream of reports, brochures, newsletters, surveys, statistics, and other data that cover everything from agriculture to UFOs. Want to tap into this fountain of information? Contact any agency or department that seems like it may relate to your topic, and ask for the public information officer. Almost every governmental entity has one. And here's the best part: *This person's job is to give you information.* That's what she gets paid to do. If you're a taxpayer, these people are *your* employees. Ask them to obtain the facts and figures that you need for your presentation. Just remember to treat them politely and with respect. They're public servants — not public slaves.

The easiest way to locate (and contact) these local, state, or federal officials is to look on the Internet. Try www.whitepages.com or www.yellowpages.com. You can also do an Internet search at www.google.com to locate the agency's Web site.

## Gathering Primary Sources

A *primary source* provides firsthand information. It can include information ranging from eyewitness accounts to diaries to government records to photos and artifacts.

## Making yourself an eyewitness

Suppose that you have to give a presentation about trends in the economy, and you don't have any firsthand information about the topic. Get some. Are you going to mention new housing starts as a trend indicator? Drive around and count the number of housing developments you see under construction. Now you have a personal observation to fit to your data. "One of the most important indicators of our economic future is housing starts. As I drove to work the other day, I counted 15 houses under construction. Each one was swarming with workers sawing, hammering, and nailing. Dump trucks pulled in and out, hauling earth away. Architects studied plans. Little sandwich trucks stopped by to sell lunch to the construction workers. It's amazing how much economic activity building a house generates. So it's good news that housing starts nationally have increased *x* percent during the past year."

Is your presentation about television advertising? Watch some. Is your topic small business? Attend a chamber of commerce meeting. No matter what you discuss, you can always find an easy way to gather firsthand information.

## Interviewing people in other departments, companies, and industries

One of the best, and most neglected, sources of primary material is other people. They have stories. They have experiences. They have insights. You just have to interview people to get hold of this vast source of information. Writers and journalists do it. Police do it. Even game-show hosts do it. Businesspeople, however, tend to ignore interviews as a source of information, and that's a mistake, because you have tons of sources to interview: people in other departments, companies, and industries.

Arranging and conducting an interview is easier than you may think. People love to talk about their work. If your presentation is on car marketing, call some auto dealers. Tell them you'll be giving a presentation about car marketing, and ask if they could spend five minutes talking with you. Most people won't refuse. They're delighted to give you information. Whatever your topic is, interview a few people in that profession or industry.

Before interviewing someone, make sure you get her permission to use her quotes in your presentation.

The smart source sees your request for an interview as a networking opportunity. She, as well as the prospective speaker-turned-interviewer, is making a contact that may be beneficial in the future.

Now I want to talk about the interview. The common knowledge is that the last two questions should be "Is there anything you thought I should have asked that I didn't ask?" and "Do you want to add anything?"

Here's some uncommon knowledge from comedy coach John Cantu: The single best question you can ask is: *"What do you know now about (the topic) that you wish you knew when you were starting out?"* (It's especially useful in situations when you may have less than a minute to conduct the interview — talking to someone in an elevator, buttonholing someone at a business function, meeting an executive on a plane.) The information you'll get can be invaluable. If you can ask only one question, ask this one.

## Consulting with outside vendors

Outside vendors can provide you with information and ideas. And they're motivated to keep you happy. You're their customer! Whether an advertising agency, accounting firm, or insurance company, your vendors know a lot about their industries — and yours. They may also know a lot about your competitors. Don't overlook an opportunity to obtain statistics, examples, and anecdotes from them. All you have to do is ask.

---

### Making an anecdote checklist (and checking it twice)

Personal anecdotes are among your most valuable assets as a presenter. They gain a lot of attention because they're real and they come from a primary resource — you. Need some help recalling an anecdote based on a real-life experience? The following list may help jog your memory:

- Your most embarrassing experience at work
- The angriest you've ever been at work
- The most inappropriate business letter you've ever received
- The strangest habit of a friend, relative, or coworker
- The dumbest thing you've ever heard at work

- Your first day on the job
- The worst boss you ever had
- The saddest thing that ever happened at work
- The biggest mistake you ever made at work
- The weirdest thing that ever happened at a business meeting
- Business lunches: strange restaurants, waiters, food, poor service
- Your first job interview
- Something that seems funny now but didn't when it happened
- The strangest business gift you've ever received

## Calling trade journal writers and editors

Trade or professional journals, newsletters, or other specialized publications cover almost any topic you can think of. The people who work at these publications are a fantastic source of information. Are you going to give a presentation about environmental costs of atomic energy? Call up *Nuclear Waste News,* and ask to speak with the writer who covers the issue you're interested in. Depending on the publication's size, the writer (more than the editor) knows all about this subject area. Ask if she is on a deadline and whether she has the time to talk. She will probably be delighted to speak with you if you're polite and keep it short. Writers (or editors) can give you data and statistics — and direct you to other sources of information. Talking with them is one of the simplest and least expensive ways to do market research — or any other type of research.

How do you identify these publications? Look through *Bacon's Magazine Directory* (Bacon's Information, Inc.), *Newsletters in Print* (Gale Research, Inc.), and *Reader's Guide to Periodical Literature.* Many associations publish magazines or newsletters devoted to their areas of interest. You can locate them by looking in the *Encyclopedia of Associations* (Gale Research, Inc.). These directories should be available in the reference section of your local library. You can also ask your contact person what professional publications your audience reads.

# Checking Out Secondary Sources

The traditional definition of a *secondary source* is anything that's not a primary source. For example, the original copy of an ancient Egyptian scroll detailing trade disputes is a primary source. Books and articles about the scroll, as well as business pundits talking about it, are secondary sources. Although primary sources are preferred, they're often impossible to obtain. For example, unless you have access to that ancient Egyptian scroll, you have to settle for a book about one. How do you know which secondary sources are reliable? That's a judgment call based on your assessment of the credibility of the secondary source.

## Down to basics: Using basic reference tools

A trip to the local library gives you access to a cornucopia of research tools: almanacs, dictionaries, encyclopedias, and indexes.

Want some general information about your topic? Try these sources:

- ✔ *The New York Times Index*
- ✔ *Readers' Guide to Periodical Literature*

Want some quotes, facts, or statistics? Try these sources:

- ✔ *Familiar Quotations,* John Bartlett
- ✔ *Information Please Almanac*
- ✔ *Facts on File Weekly World News Digest*

Want some "offbeat" facts? Try these sources:

- ✔ *Guinness Book of World Records*
- ✔ *The Book of Lists,* David Wallechinsky, Irving Wallace, and Amy Wallace

Want to know who did what? Try these sources:

- ✔ *Biography Index*
- ✔ *Who's Who in America* (and other *Who's Who* publications)

## Utilizing industry resources

Trade and professional associations provide the quickest route to becoming an instant expert on virtually any business topic. Just talk to someone at the association, or read its publications. You can quickly become familiar with the problems facing a particular industry, their background, and their possible solutions. You also get a crash course in jargon and buzzwords. Then you can sound like an insider. Where can you find out about trade associations and trade journals? *The Encyclopedia of Associations* is a standard reference work that should be available in any library. It devotes a large section to trade associations, including their publications. You can also find information about free subscriptions to a wide variety of trade publications at www.tradepub.com.

## Reading The Wall Street Journal

Many businesspeople use *The Wall Street Journal* as a source of statistics, anecdotes, and examples. Look at the stories on the front page, which always start with a very specific anecdote and use it as a springboard to discuss a general theme. For example, the lead paragraph may give a detailed description of a car accident caused by brake failure. Then the rest of the article becomes a discussion of brake safety. So if you're making a presentation about the automobile industry, safety costs, insurance, product quality, or any other related topic, you can use that opening anecdote somewhere in your presentation. You'll probably find some relevant statistics elsewhere in the article.

# Perusing Chase's Calendar of Events

*Chase's Calendar of Events* is a book published annually that provides an easy way to write the opening to a presentation. Just look up the events from past years that occurred on the same date that you're presenting. Then pick one or more events, and use them to lead into your presentation. "Today is the Fourth of July — the birthday of the United States, but also the birthday of Abigail Van Buren, whom you know as Dear Abby. So in honor of the occasion, I'm going to spend our time together today by giving you some advice about employee retention." (The opening is only the most obvious place to refer to an event of the day. You can drop this type of reference into any section of a presentation. The line about advice could be used as a transition to a major point or to lead into the conclusion. For more on introductions, transitions, and conclusions, check out Chapter 9.)

In addition to the standard birthdays and events, *Chase's* includes many local and regional listings. And lots of bizarre ones. For example, the Big Whoppers Liar's Contest is held in New Harmony, Indiana, on September 19. (A great lead-in for a presentation about business ethics.) You get the idea.

# Reviewing Vital Speeches of the Day

*Vital Speeches of the Day* is a periodical that compiles speeches from business, government, and cultural leaders. It's published every two weeks, and it began publishing in 1934. So it offers a tremendous archive of presentations that you can review. It's an excellent source for information about a wide variety of topics, as well as presentation style and organization ideas. You can read exactly how prominent executives have constructed their presentations. It also provides a good source for quotes, statistics, and ideas for introductions and conclusions. *Vital Speeches of the Day* should be available in any good research library. You can find out more about it at www.votd.com.

To locate a specific speech, look in the annual index that lists speeches by topic and speaker. *Vital Speeches of the Day* is also catalogued (by subjects, along with other periodicals) in *Readers' Guide to Periodical Literature*.

# Ensnaring a Web of Resources

The Web is like the Wild West of knowledge and information — an untamed frontier that keeps expanding faster than anyone can rein it in. It's full of gold mines and oil wells, but you don't see a lot of street signs. So allow me point you to some useful Web sites, because the Web also has some traps. Just remember that you can't believe everything you read. This section can help weed out the bad guys.

## Now presenting . . . the three best Web sites

If I had to give a presentation on a desert island, and I could bring three Web sites with me, I'd bring the Virtual Reference Desk, the Online Speech Bank, and the Museum of Humor.com. (Yes, this is totally subjective. So what?)

### The Virtual Reference Desk

You have to see The Virtual Reference Desk to believe it. It contains links to anything that may conceivably pertain to any presentation you may write or deliver. (And just in case the site missed anything, it contains links to numerous search engines. For more on search engines, see "Search engines" later in this chapter.) You can find the Virtual Reference Desk at `www.refdesk.com`.

### The Online Speech Bank

Guess what's in the Online Speech Bank? That's right, transcripts of speeches. (How'd you know?) This site contains presentations from business leaders, government officials, and clergy from around the world. It's a fantastic resource for getting ideas, quoting other presenters, finding out about particular topics, and seeing how others organize their ideas. You can find it at `www.american rhetoric.com/speechbank.htm`.

### Museum of Humor.com

This site is a gold mine of humor for presenters — especially ones who can't tell a joke. It divides humor into categories — quotes, anecdotes, definitions, one-liners, and so on — and offers hundreds of links to each kind. So people who want to use humor but can't tell a joke, or those who can tell a good joke but just can never remember them, can find plenty of material. A large list of links to offbeat news items offers additional amusing material that applies to a wide variety of subjects.

The Museum of Humor.com also has indispensable writing tools such as rhyme generators, simile generators, cliché lists, phrase finders, "Today in History," *Guinness World Records,* and new-word generators. And if you have to use statistics in a presentation, check out "Calculated Humor" in the Exhibits section of the museum. It provides tools for making statistics less boring and more entertaining. (Just to see the *Penguin-o-matic Convertor* is worth the visit. It converts weights and distances into numbers of penguins.) You can find the museum at `www.museumofhumor.com`. (For more tips on using humor in presentations, check out Chapter 8.)

## Working with search tools

Because the Web has such a vast amount of information, getting lost or distracted is easy. Fortunately, some computer geeks recognized and addressed this. Search devices let you navigate the Web in an intelligent way. Use some of the following search tools to help you with your research.

### Search engines

Search engines allow you to find information by keying in a word or phrase related to your topic. The search engine then searches through the Web pages it has indexed and provides a list of relevant links. Because the number of Web pages is constantly expanding, no search engine is ever completely up to date. In fact, a recent study showed that most search engines had indexed less than half of all the pages on the Web. That's why using more than one search engine is a good idea. What turns up on one may not turn up on another. Some of the most popular search engines include

- Alta Vista at `www.altavista.digital.com`
- Excite at `www.excite.com`
- Google at `www.google.com`
- Hotbot at `www.hotbot.com`
- Infoseek at `www.infoseek.com`
- Lycos at `www.lycos.com`
- WebCrawler at `www.webcrawler.com`

For best results, make your search terms as specific as possible to help filter out thousands of useless links and increase the chances that you find what you want. For example, a search for "public speaking" is less effective than "eulogy" if you're looking for information about eulogies.

### Meta-search engines

A meta-search engine is just what the name suggests. (Okay, the name doesn't really suggest anything. So I need to explain it.) It's a search engine that looks through several search engines simultaneously. Popular meta-search engines include

- ✔ Ask Jeeves at `www.askjeeves.com`
- ✔ Dogpile at `www.dogpile.com`
- ✔ Inference Find at `www.infind.com`
- ✔ Mamma at `www.mamma.com`

You can find these and other meta-search engines conveniently listed on one page at `www.searchgateway.com/meta.htm`.

(And as Will Rogers might have said, "I never met a search engine I didn't like." Sorry, I couldn't resist.)

### Web rings

One of the best-kept secrets about conducting research on the Internet is the Web ring. A *Web ring* is a group of linked Web sites devoted to a similar topic. If you can find a Web ring related to your interests, you have an instant gold mine of relevant information. For example, say I'm a health benefits analyst giving a presentation about smoking and cancer. I type smoking and cancer into the search form at `www.webring.org`. It finds two Web rings. One is called Stop Smoking Ring, and it contains 57 Web sites — all of which are relevant to the topic of smoking and cancer.

### News archives

Many traditional sources of information — newspapers, magazines, television stations, radio stations, and so on — are represented on the Web. Even better, many of them have online archives that allow you to search through old editions. Use these sites to get started.

Popular business magazines with a Web presence include:

- ✔ Business 2.0: `www.business2.com/b2/`
- ✔ Business Week: `www.businessweek.com`
- ✔ The Economist: `www.economist.com` (archive content isn't free)
- ✔ Fast Company: `www.fastcompany.com`
- ✔ Forbes: `www.forbes.com` (archive content isn't free)
- ✔ Fortune: `www.fortune.com` (archive content isn't free)
- ✔ Inc.: `www.inc.com`
- ✔ Industry Week: `www.industryweek.com`

If you want more localized business information, check out the Web site for American City Business Journals at www.bizjournals.com. The company publishes weekly business periodicals in 42 cities throughout the United States. The Web site has links to each of the business journals.

## Finding government information

Government regulations, economic indicators, and labor policies affect the business environment at any given time. The following Web sites provide government information that's very useful for business presentations:

- ✔ **U.S. Congress Thomas Legislative Service:** We live in a nation of laws — and lawyers. So chances are that anything you talk about will eventually be the subject of congressional action (or inaction). Want to find out if there's any pending legislation that you should mention in your presentation? Point your browser to http://thomas.loc.gov. And here's the best part: It's searchable by keywords.

- ✔ **FedWorld:** FedWorld is the mother lode — a gold mine of information compiled by the federal government about . . . everything! Just go to www.fedworld.gov. The really valuable feature of this site is a list of subject categories ranging from administration and management to veterans' affairs.

- ✔ **State and local governments on the Net:** The federal government isn't the only agency that puts information on the Web. State government agencies, counties, and cities also provide a wealth of resources. You can find them at www.statelocalgov.net. This site also contains links to government-related associations.

## Getting aid for visual aids

Need a picture for a slide, overhead, or PowerPoint presentation? The Web has almost anything you may want. I list three good places to start. (For more information on visual aids, see Chapter 10. For the scoop on PowerPoint, check out Chapters 14, 15, and 16.)

### ImageFinder

A large collection of images (and the rules for using them) is available at the Berkeley Digital Image SunSite ImageFinder at http://sunsite.berkeley.edu/ImageFinder. It provides search forms for 11 databases of specialized images, including photographs and images from the Library of Congress, Smithsonian Institution, and the National Library of Australia.

### Clipart.com

This site includes easy-to-search databases of more than 2.6 million images. The bad news is you have to pay for access. The good news is you don't have to pay much. A one-week subscription is less than $10. You can find it at `www.clipart.com`.

### PowerPoint templates

Thousands of professionally designed PowerPoint templates are available on the Web. And they're free! How do you find them? Just type **free PowerPoint templates** into any search engine. Here are a few sites to get you started:

- `www.soniacoleman.com/templates.htm`
- `www.websiteestates.com/ppoint.html`
- `www.presentersuniversity.com/downloads.php`

  This site requires you to register, but registration is free.

Remember to get any required permissions before you use material from the Web or anywhere else. It's not that you're likely to be sued for copyright infringement (although that's possible). It's that an audience member may yell, "Did you get permission to use that?" And that can be embarrassing.

See Chapter 14 for more on using templates in PowerPoint presentations.

## Accessing help for your writing

The Web is loaded with resources that can help you write a presentation. These range from online versions of printed reference works to special tools that take full advantage of computing's unique power. No, the computer won't write the presentation for you — yet. But it makes writing one a lot easier than it used to be.

The most common reference works used for writing a presentation, or almost anything else, are the dictionary and the thesaurus. Both are readily available online.

### Web of Online Dictionaries

An excellent site for finding dictionaries is the Web of Online Dictionaries at `www.facstaff.bucknell.edu/rbeard/diction.html`. At the top of its home page, you find a form for searching the tenth edition of *Merriam-Webster's Collegiate Dictionary*. But that's only the beginning. A quick scroll down reveals links to dictionaries in 169 languages — from Afrikaans to Yiddish. (There's even a Vulcan dictionary for you *Star Trek* fans.) Type in a word in English, and you get the word in the other language. It's great if you want to accent your presentation with a foreign phrase or two.

Are you too lazy to look in one dictionary at a time? Click on "Multilingual Dictionaries." You can find dozens of dictionaries that translate words among several languages simultaneously.

The best part: You've still only scratched the surface of this site. Click on "Specialized English Dictionaries," and you find a table of 64 categories, everything from agriculture and law to slang, sports, and travel.

The site claims to be linked to more than 800 dictionaries in 160 different languages, and I have no reason to doubt it.

### Roget's Thesaurus

Do you have a word that comes up repeatedly in your speech? Boring. You need to find some synonyms. That means using a thesaurus. You can find the traditional *Roget's Thesaurus* at `http://humanities.uchicago.edu/forms_unrest/ROGET.html`.

### Deadwood Phrases

Deadwood Phrases is a collection of commonly used verbosities that can be replaced with simpler language. For example, instead of saying "due to the fact that," you can say "because." Instead of "in the neighborhood of," you can say "near" or "about." Weeding out deadwood phrases makes a speech tighter, crisper, and more concise. You can find Deadwood Phrases at `www.pnl.gov/ag/usage/deadwood.html`.

### Common Errors in English

After you get rid of the deadwood, make sure that the remaining words and phrases are used properly. How? Check out Common Errors in English at `http://www.wsu.edu:8080/~brians/errors/errors.html`. You find a list of commonly misused words and phrases, how they're misused, and the correct way to use them.

### The Semantic Rhyming Dictionary

Some of the best writing tools on the Web make life simpler by automating routine tasks. What do I mean by automating routine tasks? A good example is The Semantic Rhyming Dictionary at `www.rhymezone.com`. You type a word into its search engine, and it produces a list of rhyming words.

### Phrase Finder

Another cool tool is the Phrase Finder at `phrases.shu.ac.uk/search`. Type in a word, and it produces a list of phrases including, or relating to, your word. It's a great device for brainstorming aspects of your speech. It gives you ideas for different directions you can go with a particular theme.

Then you can get creative with your introduction. "We picked him up for a song, but he made us face the music." "Now I'd like to introduce one of our company's most original thinkers. Or to put it another way, he's definitely not the same old song." You get the idea.

### Cliché Finder

Want to expand your list of phrases? Check out the Cliché Finder at `http://www.westegg.com/cliche`. Just don't overdo it with the clichés. You want your speech to be fresh and interesting, not trite and boring.

### Lexical Freenet: Connected Thesaurus

One of my favorite cool tools is Lexical Freenet: Connected Thesaurus at `http://bobo.link.cs.cmu.edu/lexfn`. Unlike a traditional thesaurus, the Lexical Freenet *isn't* limited to finding synonyms. It generates a list of concepts related to a word. It also lets you search for a variety of relationships between two words.

## Picking up performing tips

The Web is also a great resource for discovering how to *deliver* a presentation. How? By watching and listening to presentations available all over the Web.

The two most popular formats for receiving audio and video over the Web are Windows Media Player and RealPlayer. If you run Windows on your PC, you've already got Windows Media Player. Want RealPlayer too? You can download it at `www.real.com`. (Free of charge!) It allows you to hear or see material available in the RealAudio or RealVideo format.

What does that mean for you? It means that after you have Windows Media Player or RealPlayer, you have access to thousands of hours of presentations. You can review what works and what doesn't. You can listen to timing and pacing. And in many cases, you can hear the audience response.

A good place to start is the National Press Club Online at `www.connectlive.com/npc`. You'll find streaming video of presentations delivered by many prominent business, government, and cultural leaders.

# Chapter 4

# Organizing Your Message

*H*ere's the standard advice for organizing a presentation: Tell the audience what you're going to say, then tell them, and tell them what you've told them. I've heard many consultants offer this bromide and then wait to be hailed as geniuses. (They look meaningfully into their clients' eyes like they've just delivered some great insight.) But here's the problem with the tell, tell, tell formula — it doesn't really tell you anything. (How's that for irony?) It's like informing someone that you build a ship by assembling a bunch of material so that it will float while you're in it. Okay, great. But how do you do that?

This chapter provides a detailed look at how to organize a presentation. I cover everything from how to decide what to tell your business audience, to how to arrange your material, to how much information to give out. It's a tell-all chapter. (Hey, at least it's not a kiss-and-tell.)

## Picking Material That Makes Your Point

Before you can organize your presentation, you must choose your material. Your real task is deciding what *not* to use, because no matter what your topic, you can always find more material than you have time to discuss. (Your job is to find a lot more than you need so you can pick out the best stuff to use and have some in reserve.) And, more important, audiences have a limit to how much material they can absorb. Keep these guidelines in mind when choosing material:

✔ **Select a variety of material.** A variety of material makes your presentation more interesting. It also increases the chance that each member of your business audience will find something appealing in your presentation. Use anecdotes, statistics, examples, quotes, and so on.

✔ **Keep your audience in mind.** Choose material that your audience will understand and find interesting. The question you need to ask in order to make your presentation a success isn't what *you* know about the topic: Instead, ask yourself what your business audience needs to know. (For more on analyzing your audience, check out Chapter 2.)

✔ **Keep some material in reserve.** You never know when you'll need an extra example, statistic, or anecdote. They come in handy when someone doesn't understand or believe a point that you've made. You can also find them useful when answering questions after your presentation.

Want more information on having control over your topic? Check out Chapter 2. For details on researching your topic, see Chapter 3.

# Picking a Pattern of Organization

Imagine that someone hands you a piece of paper that says "m," "d," "u," "y," "m." It doesn't seem to mean much. (Unless it's supposed to be an eye test.) Now assume that the person hands you the paper with the letters arranged as "d," "u," "m," "m," "y." Is your reaction a little different? Congratulations, you've recognized a pattern.

Patterns play a critical role in how people assign meaning and how they interpret messages. You could read a lot of perceptual-psychology theory to figure out this stuff, but I give you a break and skip it. Suffice it to say that human beings have a natural tendency to organize phenomena into patterns. The way people shape those patterns determines much of the outcome of their communications with each other — especially how easily people understand each other.

## Reviewing commonly used patterns

Although patterns are infinite in variety, certain ones appear over and over again. Take a look at a few of the most common patterns you can use to give shape to presentations:

✔ **Problem/solution:** State a problem, and offer a solution. What you emphasize depends on what the audience members already know. Do you need to make them aware of the problem, or do they already know about it? Are there competing solutions? And so on.

✔ **Chronological:** Will you be making a presentation about a series of events? (The increasingly important role of product development at your company over the last five years.) Organizing your presentation in a past/present/future pattern makes it easy to follow.

✔ **Physical location:** You may want to use this one if you're talking about things that occur at various locations. Are you giving the company orientation presentation to new employees? You can divide the talk by floors (first floor, second floor, third floor), buildings (Building A, B, and C), or other physical areas (North American operations, European operations, Asian operations).

✔ **Cause/effect:** Scientific discussions are a logical place to use this pattern, but it also works well for assigning blame. "The southern region decided to listen to some management guru this quarter. So it instituted new procedures, bought new expense-reporting software, and made a commitment to innovative sales methods. As a result, its gross sales declined by 50 percent, and its margins shrank 10 percent." (But the guru had record profits.)

✔ **Divide a quote:** "In 'The Art of War,' Sun Tzu states that 'All warfare is based on deception.' What does this really mean? Let's start with warfare. Is it limited to physical altercations? Or can it apply to a modern marketing campaign?"

✔ **Divide a word:** "Today, I'm going to talk about 'SUCCESS.' *S* stands for sales. Sales are critical to our success because . . ."

✔ **Catch phrase:** "What you see is what you get. What I see today is a research and development department that's overworked, underbudgeted, and less innovative than it used to be. Let's take a look at these problems."

✔ **Theory/practice:** You can use this one for talking about something that didn't turn out as planned. (The big gap between theory and practice.) "Last year, our company announced a bold new corporate ethics program. It sounded good in theory. But last week, our CEO was arrested for financial irregularities."

✔ **Topic pattern:** This is a free-form pattern. You divide your topic into logical segments based on your own instinct, judgment, and common sense. (I often use this pattern in my talks about humor. The segments are: why humor is a powerful business tool, how to make a business point with humor, and simple types of nonjoke humor any executive can use. It's an easy-to-follow pattern that makes sense for the material.)

## *Packaging as a powerful pattern*

According to management communication advisor Jim Lukaszewski, *one of the most powerful ways to organize information is in the form of a numerical list.* You can say, "I have some good ideas." Or you can say, "I have four good ideas." The number makes the statement much stronger. "When you make the answers numerical, you grab people's brains," Jim explains. "They'll count them. Mention that you have four good ideas, and just talk about three. Sooner or later, someone will ask about the fourth idea."

You can use this technique to organize your entire presentation ("Ten Ways To Improve Profits"). Or you can use it for individual segments. ("We've talked about the importance of advertising and public relations. Now let's talk about six simple ways to get a higher response rate from direct mail.") "When you package and bundle the elements of your talk, the audience members know exactly where you're going," Jim says. "It helps them follow and understand your message."

But don't go overboard. If you make the list too long, you can actually lose the audience. "A politician running for higher office designed a program of 101 reasons to vote for him," Jim recalls. "The opening line of his speech was always 'First . . .' But by the time he got to 'Fifteen . . .' the audience realized that he was going to discuss every one of those 101 reasons. Have you ever seen facial expressions of panic mixed with boredom?"

So use your common sense. "It's like the press conference that Moses held after receiving the Ten Commandments," Jim says. "That night on the TV news, this is how the story was reported: 'Today, Moses went up Mount Sinai and received the Ten Commandments. The top two are . . .' " Keep the lists short.

# *Outlining to Stay on Track*

An outline is a blueprint for your presentation. It lets you see what points you're making, how they're related to one another, and whether they're arranged in proper order. A good outline shows you how to construct a good presentation. And like a blueprint for a building, an outline for a talk can take many shapes and forms.

Most people associate outlines with the traditional method emphasized in high school — the Roman-numeral outline. (Each Roman numeral represents a major point. Each uppercase letter represents a subpoint, and each Arabic numeral represents a support for the subpoints.) But look at some uncommon knowledge: You can create outlines in many different ways. The key is to choose a method that works for you. As long as your method lets you break the talk into parts and see the relationship among the parts, you're fine.

# Outlining before or after you write your presentation

You have two basic choices regarding when to make an outline: Make the outline before you've written your presentation or after you've written it. The experts disagree on which way is best. (But I can resolve that issue. The best way is the one that works for you.) The following subsections cover the good points of each method.

## Before you write the presentation

With this approach, you focus on your purpose and identify the ideas that can help you achieve that purpose. Then you turn the ideas into major and minor points and fit them into an outline structure. Only then, when you can see exactly what you're going to say, do you begin to flesh it out. This is an absolutely logical way to proceed. If the outline makes sense, it helps ensure that the presentation makes sense. (In fact, I was taught in law school to answer exam questions this way — always outline first.)

## After you write the presentation

Alternatively, you may just plunge right into developing the presentation word for word. "What would you tell a close friend about the topic?" asks Allatia Harris, district director, faculty development and core curriculum, Dallas County Community College District. "You'll do a better job just talking it through off the cuff to a friend than starting with an outline." She advises that you think about the order in which you'd tell it to your friend, as well as what examples you'd use. "If you care about the person you're talking to and you care about the topic, everything else falls into place," she says. Write the outline after the presentation is written, which enables you to discover any flaws in the structure so that you can rewrite where appropriate.

# Choosing the right number of points

The number of points in an outline should reflect the number of points in your presentation. So the real question is: How many points should you have in your presentation? A few guidelines follow:

- **Decide what the audience needs to know.** What points are absolutely essential for you to include in your message? (And I mean *absolutely* essential. If one of these points were omitted, your presentation couldn't succeed.)

- **Don't put in too much information.** Many people try to pack too much information into a single presentation. This is a mistake because there are limits to how much an audience can absorb and process during your talk. If you provide a constant stream of information, your audience won't "get" all of it. You need to break up the information with stories, quotes, and other devices.

✔ **Don't include more than seven main points.** Experts disagree over the maximum number of points that you can safely include in a presentation, but the highest number I've come across is seven. Fewer is usually better. (Some experts believe that an audience can't recall more than five main points. Or, as Allatia says, "When you have to count them on more than one hand, they get tough to remember.") The amount of time you have is also a critical factor. Many experts suggest three major points for a half-hour presentation.

✔ **Reorganize to reduce the number of points.** You've gone through your material and found 15 main points that are absolutely essential. Don't even think about doing your presentation that way. First, try your hardest to lose a few of them. Second, reorganize and combine the points so that they're included under fewer headings. Think of 5 to 7 major points under which your 15 subpoints can be subcategorized.

# Using Index Cards and Scripts

After you organize your ideas, you need to organize your presentation notes. Two of the most common formats are index cards and word-for-word scripts. This section gives you the lowdown on each method.

## Putting your presentation on cards

Index cards are probably the most popular format for organizing presentation notes. Index cards are easy to handle and easy to carry in your pocket, and they make it easy for you to restructure a presentation in a hurry. (You just shuffle the deck.) What do you put on the cards? Take a look at a few ideas:

✔ **Roman-numeral outlines:** If you use a traditional Roman-numeral outline to develop your talk, just put the outline on cards. Even if you develop your presentation using other methods, you can still take the finished talk and reduce it to a Roman-numeral outline.

✔ **Key words:** Some presenters just write a series of key words on their cards. This allows you to glance at your notes and minimize the time spent looking away from the audience. But if you forget what ideas the key words represent, you're in trouble.

✔ **Key sentences:** Some presenters write out key sentences. This practice overcomes the problem of forgetting what a key word represents. Its disadvantage is that it encourages reading from the cards like a script.

The following are some do's and don'ts for putting your notes on cards:

- ✔ **Do use only one side of the card.** The exception is if you can fit all your notes for an entire presentation on both sides of a single card.

- ✔ **Do number each card.** If you drop them, you'll be able to put them back in order.

- ✔ **Do code your cards for cutting.** Mark your cards so that you can easily shorten your presentation if you need to. You can mark certain cards or sections of cards as nonessential. For example, anything written in black is important, but anything written in blue can be cut.

- ✔ **Do format each card for easy reading.** Leave lots of white space, and make sure that your writing is large enough to read under actual presentation conditions. That means that your cards should be readable if you have too little light (a common problem).

- ✔ **Don't go berserk with highlighting.** Some people highlight their notes to indicate different parts of their talk: main points, subpoints, quotes, and so on. If you use a color system to highlight your notes, don't go wild. If you use too many colors, you may forget what they mean.

- ✔ **Don't use abbreviations that you may forget.** In the desire to reduce the number of cards you're using, you can easily get carried away devising key words and abbreviations. Don't take chances. Use abbreviations with which you're familiar. Use a key phrase rather than a key word if you think that you may forget what the word represents.

For more tips on reading notes when giving your presentation, check out Chapter 5, which covers rehearsals, and Chapter 11, which focuses on keeping eye contact.

## Working from a script

Most presentations are more effective without a script. Why? Well, unless you're a professional actor, when you read a script word for word, it sounds like — you're reading a script word for word. You want to sound like you're having a conversation with your audience. So avoid working from a script.

Of course, exceptions abound. Are you presenting at a trade show or convention where the text of your presentation is released in advance? Are you giving detailed technical information to scientists or engineers? Have you been directed to read a prepared statement to the press? These types of situations require scripts.

If you do require a script, make sure that it's easy to read. Use a large font size, double- or triple-space the text, leave a lot of white space in the page layout, use only one side of the paper, and number each page.

# Timing for Maximum Impact

Most people associate timing with how to tell a joke. That's not how I'm using the term here. By *timing,* I mean how much time it takes to deliver a presentation and how to make the presentation fit the time you've been given. This section presents some thoughts on the subject.

## Making your presentation time out just right

So how long should a presentation be? Abraham Lincoln's response was, "Like a man's pants — long enough to cover the subject." Take a look at a few additional guidelines:

- ✔ **Don't feel obligated to fill your entire time slot.** Just because you've been given 30 minutes doesn't mean you have to present for 30 minutes. Give your presentation in 20 or 25 minutes if you can. (But use your common sense. I recently spoke at a conference where another presenter, who was slotted for a one-hour talk, finished in ten minutes. The conference organizers were less than thrilled.)

- ✔ **Being a little too short is better than a little too long.** If you conclude five minutes early, people in the audience are thrilled. If you conclude five minutes late, they're impatient and possibly angry. Your audience members are busy. They have people to see and places to go. They expect you to be done on time. Don't disappoint them.

- ✔ **Twenty minutes is a good length.** If you can choose the length of your presentation, pick 20 minutes. It's long enough to cover a lot of information thoroughly, let the audience get to know you, and make a good impression. And it's short enough to do all that before the audience's attention span reaches its outer limit.

## Filling time or trimming back

Einstein's theory of relativity may say that time and distance are identical, but many presenters apparently disagree. They just can't go the distance in the time they've been allotted. Want to avoid that problem in your next presentation? The following sections give a few tips and tricks to ensure that you and your audience finish at the same time.

### Estimate the time from the length of the script

Here's an accurate script-to-speech ratio: One double-spaced page of 10-point type equals two minutes of speaking time. So preparing a standard 20-minute presentation is like writing a 10-page essay. (Keep that in mind when the person inviting you to give a presentation says it will be easy to do.)

### Convert practice time into a realistic estimate

Many people practice their presentation aloud to get an idea of how long it will take to deliver. But when you practice alone, your presentation will be shorter than when you present in front of people. Why? They laugh and applaud. Plus, you slow down to wait for their reactions. If you're talking to a large audience (several hundred people or more), the length of your presentation may increase by up to 50 percent. As a rule of thumb, figure that your presentation will lengthen about 30 percent when you do it in front of an audience.

### Make an adjustment for humor

If you use humor in your talk and it's effective, part of your presentation time will be consumed by audience laughter and applause. Don't forget to account for that time, especially for audiences of more than 300 people. "Large groups laugh in three waves," observed the late John Cantu. "The first group gets the joke right away. The second group gets it a little later. And the third group laughs after they hear everyone else laughing." His rule of thumb: 10 to 15 seconds per wave of laughter in a large crowd. "So figure 45 seconds per joke," he said.

### Be prepared to cut . . .

You were told that you'd have 30 minutes to make a presentation. But the meeting doesn't go as planned, and the organizer says you have only 15 minutes. What do you do? Talking faster won't work (although that's what many people try). Big mistake. The presenter comes across as hyperactive, and the audience comes away with nothing — except a bad impression of the presenter.

### . . . But don't cut the conclusion

When you need to cut part of your presentation, don't cut the conclusion. Your presentation is like the flight of a plane, and the passengers are your audience. When you forgo the conclusion, you're attempting a crash landing. If you've been told in advance that your time will be shortened, cut from the body of your talk. Eliminate some examples or even a main point if necessary. What if you need to cut while you're giving a presentation and you're rapidly running out of time? Find a logical place to stop, and sum up what you've already said. Even better, have a conclusion that you can go into from any point in your talk.

### Communicate your awareness of time

Audiences have been burned over and over again by presenters. You can ease their fears by making occasional references to indicate that you know how much time has passed (and how much more time will pass until you're done). It's as simple as saying things like: "I can't teach you everything there is to know about outsourcing in 20 minutes, but in our time together today . . .", "For the next five minutes, I'd like to discuss . . .", "Now we've arrived at the second half of my presentation, and I'd like to shift gears to . . .", or "And in conclusion, I'd like to spend the next three minutes summarizing what we've just discussed. . . ."

# Organizing Your Presentation with PowerPoint

What if you don't have time to develop the perfect organization? Don't worry. If you have to put together a presentation quickly, and you want to be sure it's reasonably well organized, you're in luck. PowerPoint will do the work for you. Just click the PowerPoint AutoContent Wizard, and follow its onscreen instructions. It provides a wide variety of content templates for common business presentations. These include ready-made outlines for the following situations.

✔ Presenting a business plan

✔ Conducting an employee orientation

✔ Presenting a technical report

✔ Recommending a strategy

✔ Giving a project overview

✔ Selling a product or service

✔ Giving a status report

✔ Presenting financial data

Although the PowerPoint outlines may not be the most original ways to organize your presentation, they do provide a solid organization if you stick to them. (For more cool PowerPoint tricks, see Chapter 15.)

# Chapter 5

# Me, Worry? Controlling Anxiety

. . . . . . . . . . . . . . . . . . . . . . . . . . . . . . . . . . . . . . . . . . .

. . . . . . . . . . . . . . . . . . . . . . . . . . . . . . . . . . . . . . . . . . .

*O*ne day in ancient Rome, a Christian was thrown to a lion. The crowd in the Coliseum cheered as the lion ran up to the Christian, bent over him, and prepared to eat him. Just when the end seemed imminent, the Christian whispered something, and the lion bolted away in fear. The emperor, clearly impressed, asked the Christian how he performed this miracle. The Christian said, "It was easy. I told the lion that after dinner, he'd be expected to say a few words."

Stage fright. The words themselves make me nervous. (They even make lions nervous!) Maybe that's why social scientists have abandoned the term. First, they changed it to *communication anxiety.* Now they talk about *communication apprehension.* (If you've ever heard a social scientist speak at an academic conference, you know why these people are apprehensive.) But whatever you want to call this condition, the symptoms are universally recognized. Your heart pounds. Your hands shake. Your forehead sweats. Your mouth goes dry. Your stomach feels like a blender on high speed. And that's just when your boss tells you that you have to give a presentation next month. You feel *really* bad when the time comes to give the presentation.

Well, congratulations. You're in the majority. According to a frequently cited survey, most people consider public speaking more frightening than death. (How would they feel delivering a eulogy?) If misery loves company, you've got plenty of it. Celebrities alleged to suffer from this affliction include Abraham Lincoln, Mark Twain, Carol Burnett, Johnny Carson, Erma Bombeck, and Laurence Olivier.

Stage fright is like an incurable disease. You have to accept that you may always have it. You have to figure out how to control it and even use it to your advantage.

# Is It Stage Fright If There's No Stage?

The term *stage fright* actually covers a wide range of reactions. It can run the gamut from a slight unease before speaking to a paralyzing fear of standing in front of an audience. Perhaps the most common description is feeling like you have butterflies in your stomach. The most useful way to understand stage fright is to think of it in terms of stress.

Much of today's knowledge of stress originated with Dr. Hans Selye. He defined stress as "the nonspecific response of the body to any demand made upon it." (I have no idea what that means either.) So I asked prominent psychiatrist and stress management expert Dr. Steven Resnick to explain it in English. (He's in private practice in Princeton, New Jersey, so he definitely knows about stress.)

"There are three key points," Steven explains. "First, stress is your body's response to something *you* perceive as stressful. It's totally subjective. Second, what you perceive as stressful can be good or bad. Winning a million dollars can be just as stressful as losing a million dollars. Third, you'll get the same type of stress response — muscle tension, mental preoccupation, general body stimulation — no matter what's causing your stress."

So what does this have to do with stage fright? Plenty. "When you encounter a stressful situation, your body goes into a stress reaction," Steven says. "Your adrenaline starts flowing. You sweat. Your blood pressure and heart rate increase. Your muscles get tense." Sounds like the symptoms of stage fright to me! Giving a presentation is a stressful situation for most people and is often even more stressful when you're giving a business presentation.

The first step in reducing stage fright is specifically identifying the factors that cause your anxiety. The following sections cover anxiety issues in different business presentation settings.

## Anxiety issues when presenting to your colleagues, your boss, or your boss's boss

Giving a presentation to your boss can produce anxiety even if you like making presentations. Why? First, ponder the practical considerations: Your performance can affect raises, promotions, or even continued employment. Second, think about the psychological factors of responding to someone in power. According to Steven, people tend to respond to authority figures when they're adults the same way individuals responded to their parents when they were children — often irrationally. That's where some of the fear comes from. "Even presenting to colleagues may cause anxiety," he says, "because they can talk with higher-ups later on. So it's just as if you were presenting to your boss."

## Anxiety issues when presenting to an unknown group

A different sort of anxiety may occur when you present to an audience that is unfamiliar to you — new prospects, trade-show attendees, members of a professional association, or any other people you've never met. In this case, you're nervous because you *don't* know much about your audience. This information vacuum is filled by fear — the infamous fear of the unknown.

## Anxiety issues when presenting to a potential corporate partner

A potential partner has qualities of both an authority figure and an unknown audience, notes Dr. Steven Resnick. "There are also concerns about commitment, can we work together, and are we compatible," he observes. "That's why corporate partnerships are often compared to marriage." No wonder this is frightening.

# Changing Your Perceptions to Reduce Anxiety

Teacher to pupil: "Think positive." Pupil to teacher: "I am. I'm positive I'm going to fail." This old joke highlights an important point — stress is a mental phenomenon. However, if stress can be caused mentally, it can be cured mentally. It's all in the way you look at things. I cover methods of reducing mental anxiety in the following sections.

## Realizing what your audience expects

Stage fright is a very egocentric affliction. *I'm* scared. *I'm* nervous. *I'm* going to pass out. Me. Me. Me. You can easily lose sight of your audience's interests, but the audience has as much at stake as you. In fact, your audience may be more scared than you. It may suffer from *seat fright* — the fear of wasting time listening to a bad presentation. You need to know the following four things about your audience.

### The audience wants you to succeed

By showing up, your audience members give you a tremendous vote of confidence. They don't want to spend their precious time listening to you fail. Even if they've been ordered to attend, they want your presentation to be a success. Again, no one wants to listen to a bad presentation. Life is too short.

Furthermore, your audience members can probably relate to you. They've been in your shoes before, and they generally don't want to see you experience a hurt they would also find painful.

### You have knowledge that the audience wants

You were asked to present for a reason, probably because you have information that the audience desires. You're the expert. You have the data that audience members clamor for. Even on the rare occasion when the audience knows more than you about your topic, you can still provide new information. Only *you* can provide your own unique insights. No one else knows *your* view and interpretation of the material. Think of yourself as sharing valuable knowledge and ideas with your audience.

### The audience doesn't know that you're afraid

Social science research shows that the presenter and the audience have very different perceptions about stage fright. Often, an audience can't even detect anxiety in a presenter who claims to be extremely nervous. This situation is like the acne lotion commercial you see on TV. A teenager gets a pimple on his nose. He imagines that the pimple is as big as a watermelon and that people are staring at it wherever he goes. Of course, no one even notices it. Stage fright works the same way. You can think of it as a mental pimple that seems a lot worse to you than to your audience.

### You can answer the audience's question

Dr. Allen Weiner says that his clients tell him all the time that "they love to answer questions, but they hate to give speeches." As president of Communication Development Associates, Allen gets paid to advise these people. (And his clients include senior executives of Fortune 500 companies.) Take his advice free of charge: View your presentation as the answer to an *implied* question. In other words, what question does your presentation answer? Instead of *making a presentation,* make believe you're just *answering a question.* Presentations are far less frightening when you think of them this way.

## Visualizing success like the pros

The concept of visualization is simple and straightforward. You just imagine yourself performing a task successfully. A number of athletes use this training technique. They imagine themselves hitting home runs, scoring touchdowns, or signing autographs for $100 apiece. They imagine these activities in vivid detail, try to remember past successes, and build them into the image.

Apply visualization techniques to *your* presentation. Imagine yourself giving your talk. Your voice fills the room with wisdom. People in the audience hang on your every word. (If they lean any farther forward, they may fall out of their chairs.) They give you a standing ovation and rush the stage to carry you out on their shoulders. (You get the idea.)

## Talking yourself into a great presentation

Your audience has to hear you only once. You have to hear yourself all the time, so the messages you send yourself are very important. I'm talking about your *internal dialogue* — the things you say to yourself in your head. When you repeat them over and over, you start to believe them. So you have to be careful what you say. If you keep telling yourself that you're going to flub your presentation at a critical moment, you probably will. Remember that your mind experiences the negative talk as real and reacts accordingly.

Talking to yourself positively can be another way of visualizing success — instead of talking yourself into failure. But it's more than that. Successful visualization techniques apply to a specific task — like giving a presentation. Your internal dialogue has a much broader focus. It applies to *everything* you do.

So how can you keep the self-chatter positive? Follow these techniques from prominent stress expert Dr. Steven Resnick:

- ✔ **Dispute irrational thoughts.** Say that you have the irrational thought "If I stand in front of an audience, I'll forget everything I know about the topic." Think of an opposite thought that can dispute this fear. A disputing thought could be "I'll have no reason to remember all that stuff if I *don't* tell it to an audience."

- ✔ **Use personal affirmations.** "I'm the greatest presenter in the world.", "My subject is fascinating, and the audience will love it.", or "I'm an expert." Yes, affirmations are corny, but they build confidence. The more you talk yourself into believing them, the less stress you encounter when you give (or think about) your presentation.

> ✔ **Imagine the worst-case scenario.** Face your fear directly. Think about the worst possible thing that could happen, and realize that it's not that awful. If you make a mistake while you're presenting, you can correct it and continue. If the audience doesn't give you a standing ovation, it may still applaud. Even if the presentation is a total disaster, your world won't come to an end. No one will shoot you. And besides, you now have a great personal anecdote about "bombing" that you can use the next time you present.

# Managing Physical Symptoms of Anxiety

A man went to the doctor for a physical. He said, "I look in the mirror, and I'm a mess. My jowls are sagging. I have blotches all over my face. My hair is falling out. What is it?" The doctor said, "I don't know, but your eyesight is perfect."

Unfortunately, a lot of other people have perfect eyesight, too — especially when it involves examining your physical symptoms of stage fright. But here's the good news: Eliminating or disguising the sweating and shaking isn't that hard.

## Doing stress-busting exercises

You understand mentally that stress is all in your head — that if you don't view a presentation as stressful, it isn't. But darn it, you just can't seem to accept this belief emotionally. You've tried all the mental tricks — thinking positive, visualizing success, focusing away from yourself — and they didn't work. Your heart is still pounding, you're still sweating profusely, and you still feel nauseous. Now what can you do?

Don't sweat it (so to speak). Even though stress is technically all in your head, its effects can be quite physical. So if you can't treat your mental state, treat your physical symptoms. Following are some recommendations from Dr. Steven Resnick.

### Breathing

Take a deep breath. Hold it. Hold it. Now let it out slowly. Good. Do it again. Breathe deeply and slowly. Keep it up. Don't you feel better already? Steven says that breathing exercises are one of the world's oldest techniques for relieving stress. "We release carbon dioxide every time we exhale," he explains. "That decreases the acidity of our blood." It also increases the oxygen in your brain. (And gives a whole new meaning to the term "airhead.")

### Stretching

Stretching is a great way to relieve muscle tension quickly, and it doesn't take long to do. Stretching for as little as 10 or 15 seconds can be beneficial. Now, you can't just do yoga in the middle of a banquet when you're the after-dinner presenter, but you can excuse yourself and do a few quick stretches in the restroom just before you speak. Use the following exercises to get you down the home stretch:

- ✔ **Head rolls:** Slowly turn your head from side to side. You're warmed up. Now move your head clockwise in a circle (look up, right, down, and left). Do this three times and then reverse the direction. You'll feel the tension flowing out of your neck.

- ✔ **Arm lifts:** Stretch your right arm up into the air as far as it will go. Hold it a few seconds. Bring it back to your side. Now stretch your left arm up as far as it will go. Keep repeating the process. In high school, your gym teacher made you do this exercise as a form of torture. Now you're going to do it for relief. It helps stretch out your back.

- ✔ **Jawbreakers:** Open your mouth as wide as possible (as if you're going to scream). Then close your mouth. Keep opening and closing your mouth. This exercise helps relieve tension in the jaw. You can also use your fingers to massage the muscle that joins the jaw and the rest of the head.

### Moving around

Some presenters like to take a quick walk or jog in place to get rid of nervous energy. Are there stairs in the building where you're presenting? A few trips up and down some flights of stairs may be helpful, but don't overdo it. You don't want to be sweaty and tired by the time you go on!

## Internalizing the real secret: Don't look nervous

The common knowledge is that a little nervousness is good and a lot of nervousness is bad. So you're supposed to control your nervousness, keeping it at an acceptable level. You do that by following all the standard techniques described in this chapter.

It doesn't really matter how nervous you are — *as long as you appear calm.* As Dr. Allen Weiner puts it, "You have to *look like* you're under control, not *be* under control. As long as the audience thinks you're confident — that's what counts." Use Allen's tips and tricks for disguising some of the common signs of stage fright:

✔ **Fidgeting:** Fidgeting is an announcement that you're anxious. Touching your face with your index finger or rubbing it under your nose or scratching above your lip are all signs of nervousness. The solution: Keep your hands in front of you in the *steeple position*. (See Chapter 11 for a description of this position.) If you're using a lectern, place your hands on it as if you're playing the piano.

✔ **Pacing:** Pacing is another indicator of anxiety. The solution: Move closer to the audience and then stop for a moment. Then move somewhere else and stop.

✔ **Sweating:** How you handle the sweating is what counts. If you take a handkerchief, open it up, and swipe at the sweat, you look like a nervous wreck. The solution: Never open the handkerchief. Keep it folded in a square. *Dab* at the sweat and then replace the handkerchief in your pocket.

✔ **Hands shaking:** If your hands are shaking like leaves, people can tell you have stage fright. The solution: Use cards rather than sheets of paper for your notes. (Paper, which is larger and weighs less than cards, makes your shakiness more apparent.) Also, don't hold props or other items that show that your hands are shaking. You can also try placing them on the lectern as if you're playing the piano, or use the steeple position.

# Tapping Into Tricks That Target Stage Fright

Are you worried about getting stage fright? Don't be. Just keep the next several tricks in mind, and you'll be ready for anything. (Unless you get so nervous that you forget the tricks.)

## Write out your intro and conclusion

The student was 6 feet, 2 inches tall. He was standing in front of the class, preparing to start his speech. You could tell he was nervous by the way he gripped the podium; the color had drained from his hands. He started to speak. He got out a few words, and then he fainted. As he fell to the ground, the podium went down with him. He never let go.

The student was in a class taught by speech expert Allatia Harris. She says that the incident is a perfect example of why she advises speakers to write out the introductions to their presentations. "Nervousness is most intense just before you start talking," she says. "You see all those people looking at you, and words start coming out of your mouth, but your mouth's not connected to your brain. You may not even be aware of what you're saying." Give special attention to the introduction. You need to have it down cold so you don't fall down cold.

Similar preparation should be given to the conclusion — the second most anxiety-producing part of a presentation. (See Chapter 9 for tips on introductions and conclusions.)

## Double-check the order of your visuals

You can't check your visual aids too many times. Much of the anxiety associated with presenting comes from the fear that the visuals will screw up. The more you check them, the more confident you are. (For more tips on visual aids, check out Chapter 10.)

## Double-check your equipment

Many people worry about their computer, projector, and other equipment. Take the extra few minutes to check them to make sure they work properly. Then you can stop worrying.

## Anticipate problems, and have solutions ready

Anticipate any problem that may arise, and have a plan ready to deal with it. For example, whenever you stumble over a tongue-twisting name or phrase, you can have an all-purpose recovery line ready. "Let me try that again — in English."

What if you forget what point you were going to cover next? You can buy time by asking the audience a survey question that requires a show of hands. Or you can review what you've already covered. Or you can skip ahead to a different point.

What if you have an equipment failure? Bring spare supplies — an extra light bulb for the projector, an extra marker for the flip chart, an extra battery for the laptop. You get the idea.

# Get to the site early, when possible

Fear of the unknown probably produces more anxiety than any other cause. Until you get to the site where you're presenting, you face a lot of unknowns. Is the room set up correctly? Did they remember to give you an overhead projector? Is an audience actually going to show up? Plenty of little questions can add up to big sources of stress if you don't have answers for them.

You can get the answers simply by going to the room, so do it early — at least an hour before you present. That extra time allows you to correct any mistakes and calm down. You also get a chance to meet members of the audience who arrive early, which can reduce stress by making the audience more familiar to you. (Check out Chapter 26 for more on getting a room ready.)

# Divide and conquer

Many presenters who suffer from stage fright claim that only a large audience triggers their fear. A few people? No problem. A big group? Forget it. Try this: Look at one face in the audience at a time — especially faces that appear interested in what you're saying. Keep coming back to them. (No, normally you shouldn't stare at only a few people. That's a basic rule of eye contact that I discuss in Chapter 11. But stage fright creates an exception. If the only way you can prevent yourself from passing out is to look at only a few people, then do it. Just don't stare at only one person for the entire time.)

# Don't apologize for nervousness

Many presenters feel compelled to apologize for being nervous. Don't apologize for making a mistake, flub, or goof-up. Just let it go. You don't want to draw additional attention to your nervousness. As Allatia Harris says, "Never apologize to the audience unless you've injured someone."

# Watch what you eat

Everyone's heard that you are what you eat. Maybe and maybe not. But here's some food for thought — what you eat before you present *will* affect your anxiety level. So avoid drinking coffee, tea, and other caffeinated beverages before you go on. You'll be jittery enough without the added stimulation they supply. You also probably want to avoid carbonated beverages unless you're giving a presentation about burping.

## Have water handy

One consumable that you should have available is water. If anxiety dries out your mouth, take a sip of water. If you're overwhelmed by negative emotions, pause and take a sip of water. And if you're thirsty? You know what to do. Just make sure that you don't drink all your water within the first 30 seconds of your presentation. Remember, don't drink too much water, or you may have to make a mad dash to the restroom — not something you want to do during your presentation.

## Keep your breathing even

Feel like you're going to pass out? Pause and take a breath. And then a few more. This pause seems like a dramatic flourish to your audience. But it gives you a chance to get your emotions under control. (For more breathing tips, check out "Doing stress-busting exercises," earlier in this chapter.)

# Rehearsing Your Presentation

Some say that familiarity breeds contempt. But when it comes to public speaking, familiarity breeds confidence. Practicing your presentation can help reduce stage fright. Take a look at a few tips for rehearsing away your fears.

## Rehearse out loud

The only way that you can tell how your presentation will sound is by listening to it. *That means that you have to say it out loud.* Listening to the voice in your head doesn't count; that's not the voice that your audience hears.

Don't rehearse the life out of your presentation. Run through it enough times to become familiar with the material and lose any anxiety you may have. But don't memorize it word for word. And don't rehearse your gestures. You don't want to look like a robot. Your gestures should flow naturally as you talk.

## Simulate real conditions

The more closely you can simulate actual speaking conditions in your rehearsals, the more confident you will be for the actual event. Use the actual notes that you plan to use when you present. Use the actual clothes that you plan to wear. (At least wear them in your dress rehearsal. Ever wonder why dress rehearsals are called "dress" rehearsals?) Will you be using a handheld microphone for your presentation? Most people don't have a sound system at home for rehearsal purposes. Don't worry. Here's a tip from the late comedy coach John Cantu: When you practice at home, use a hairbrush to simulate the microphone. The average hairbrush is about the same length as the average handheld mike. And most important, rehearse using your visual aids — especially if you'll be using a laptop, projector, or other electronic equipment.

If you'll be presenting in a conference room where you work, try to reserve it for a rehearsal a few days before your presentation.

## Time it

Time your entire presentation. Do it while you're rehearsing in front of an audience. (Audience reactions can affect the length of your talk.) Recruit friends, family members, or colleagues — any live bodies who can sit and listen to you. (And ask for their feedback when you conclude. They may observe something that you have overlooked.) Timing your presentation is the only way to determine whether your talk will fit its assigned time slot. And having that knowledge can relieve a lot of anxiety. If you can't find a rehearsal audience, time your presentation by speaking it into a tape recorder. Then figure in that audience reaction will make it a few minutes longer. (For more on timing your presentation, see Chapter 4.)

## Rehearse questions and answers

If you're going to have a question-and-answer period after your presentation, preparing for it is essential for reducing anxiety. Anticipate questions that you may receive. Rehearse your answers. (For more information about this process, see Chapter 13.)

# Avoiding Popular "Cures" That Don't Fight Fright

Throughout history, human maladies have inspired remedies that claimed fantastic curative powers but actually proved worthless: snake oil for the common cold, bloodsucking leeches for fevers, earplugs for political speeches. Naturally, there have been a few "cures" for stage fright. I want to tell you about two famous ones that don't work.

## Imagining the audience naked

An alleged cure for stage fright that's probably as old as human speech itself is to imagine your audience naked. (I can just see this advice being dispensed by one caveman to another. Caveman #1: "Don't be nervous; just imagine that the audience is naked." Caveman #2: "But they *are* naked.")

As Allatia Harris observes, this "cure" doesn't work for a couple of reasons. "First, there are some folks in the audience I wouldn't want to see naked — especially if I'm trying *not* to be frightened. Second, there might be a few I'd *really* like to see naked." Either way, the effect isn't calming.

## Taking booze and pills

Another folk remedy often suggested for stage fright is to have a drink or take a tranquilizer, which is supposed to help you calm down. Here's the problem: The desired effects normally wear off just before you get in front of an audience — especially if you consume the drink or pill 30 to 60 minutes before you're scheduled to present. Then the fear returns with a vengeance, and it makes the speaking experience much worse instead of better. In addition, you're not at your best, because you're still a bit groggy. You also run the risk of being downright plastered and humiliating yourself.

# Using Your Nervousness As an Asset

I remember hearing in grad school that Cicero, or one of those other ancient orators, once said something to the effect that anyone who isn't nervous when they speak is an idiot. His point was that words are powerful. And presenters who recognize the potential power of their words will always be nervous.

So when you present, you have adrenaline coursing through your body. And that's not bad. Adrenaline is what gives athletes the strength to hit the ball out of the park during the big game. It also gives you an extra edge when you present.

Use your adrenaline rush to give a more animated and enthusiastic performance — broader gestures, more movement, excitement in your voice. Channel your nervous energy into your presentation. Believe me, your audience would rather hear and see an "energized" presenter than one who is falling asleep.

# Part II

# Creating a Presentation: The Basics

The 5th Wave   By Rich Tennant

"Well, I think this proposal meets all of your business needs. For the rest of your needs, I'd recommend a competent tailor, a low-fat diet and regular flossing."

## In this part . . .

**G**reat presentations don't happen by accident.
Careful preparation is the key. In this part, I show
you how to write an attention-grabbing introduction,
create a memorable conclusion, use exciting words, and
engage your audience with humor. I also show you how to
use statistics and quotations for maximum impact, as well
as how to develop stories, examples, and analogies. In this
part, you can also discover how to enhance your message
with stunning visual aids.

# Chapter 6

# Building the Body with Stories, Statistics, and Other Good Stuff

After you have a topic and an outline, you still have to figure out exactly what you're going to say. How can you support your ideas and arguments? How can you get the audience to understand what you mean and agree with you? That's what this chapter is all about. (For details on researching your presentation topic, check out Chapter 3. See Chapter 4 for more on outlining and organization.)

*Support* refers to the items you use to prove and illustrate your points — the basic material that makes up your speech. Stories, statistics, quotations, definitions, analogies, and examples are all forms of support, and I cover each one in this chapter.

But before you get started, check out these three basic rules regarding supports:

- ✔ **Make sure that your supports really support something.** Don't throw in quotes, statistics, and stories just to show off. Use them only to prove, clarify, or illustrate a point.

- ✔ **Use a variety of supports.** Why? Different people respond to different types of information. Some people like statistics. Others like quotes and stories.

- ✔ **Less is more.** One dramatic statistic is better than three boring statistics. One great example is better than two so-so examples.

# Using Stories to Make Your Point

As communications expert Jim Lukaszewski says, "A picture may be worth a thousand words, but a good story is worth 10,000 pictures." Well, maybe only 9,999. But his point is well taken. In the world of business, the ability to tell "your story" is essential — whether your story is motivational, financial, technical, or the company story.

## The do's and don'ts of using stories

The following sections give you some guidelines for using stories effectively. Most of them come courtesy of Jim Lukaszewski. (He's founder of The Lukaszewski Group, Inc., a management communication consulting company based in White Plains, New York.)

### Tell stories for a purpose

A story should have a reason for being told. And the reason — a lesson, moral, objective — should be obvious to the audience. One of the fastest ways to turn off a business audience is by telling pointless stories.

### Tell stories about people

Face it, human beings are a narcissistic species — they like to hear stories about themselves. So if your story involves people, it gets attention. And if you can talk about people familiar to the audience, such as other industry members, even better. Here's the uncommon knowledge: If you can't talk about real individuals, talk about hypothetical people. Use names. Personify your stories. Jim guarantees that this gets your audience involved.

### Try out stories first

The first time to tell a story shouldn't be when you're standing at a podium addressing your audience. You need to know how the story works. Try stories on your friends, neighbors, colleagues, and anyone willing to listen. Theoretically, the story will get better every time. By the time you use the story in a presentation, you should have a polished gem.

Develop a repertoire of stories. Every story won't work with every audience, so having a selection of stories from which to choose is nice. Develop several stories that you feel comfortable telling; then you can fit them to your topic and your audience.

For example, one of my favorite stories involves advice I received for a job interview. I was told to look at the pictures on the interviewer's walls, which would reveal the interviewer's interests. Then I could talk about those things to connect with the interviewer. Well, a friend of mine used this technique very successfully. He went to an interview, and there were pictures of fish all over the walls. So he talked about fishing. And he got the job. I figured, this is pretty good. So I got an interview. When I got there, there was nothing on the walls. They were bare, white walls. So I talked about snow. I didn't get the job. But the technique would have worked if I hadn't guessed wrong. Turns out the interviewer was a big fan of the Beatles' White Album.

Job seekers can use that story in a presentation about interviewing techniques. Or you can use it to make a point to salespeople about being ready for the unexpected. The only limit to its use is your imagination.

### Collect stories

Most people are exposed to good stories every day. You see them in the newspaper. You hear them on radio and TV. People tell them to you. Write down the stories you like. Collect them. Start a file. Then you have them at your fingertips when you need them.

## Checking out different types of stories

You can use many different types of stories to liven up your presentation. Here are a few of the more common ones.

### Success story

A success story documents the triumph of people, actions, or ideas. Think of the stories that you liked as a child. Most of them ended with the words "happily ever after." Those words are the sign of a success story. People like to hear stories about how an idea or action worked out successfully — especially in the business world. They're popular in any type of business presentation.

### Personal story

Any time you add a personal story, you get people's attention. People are much more interested in personal stories than they are in just plain facts. By *personal story,* I mean a story about something that happened to you, the presenter, with your friends, colleagues, or relatives — anything that really occurred. These are the stories that you can't make up. The time your friends dared you to jump into a pond with your clothes on when you were 8 years old. The time you flipped a coin to answer true-false questions and aced a test. The time you got bumped from a flight and met someone who ended up being your biggest customer. You can use all these types of personal stories to make points in a business presentation.

What if you don't have many personal stories? Interview other people, and tell *their* stories. Getting stories from other people — coworkers, clients, vendors — is so simple to do, yet so few presenters do it. Other people's stories are a great source of material that you shouldn't overlook. (Just make sure you don't mislead your audience and claim the story as your own. And ask for permission to use this story. If the person you're telling the story about is in your audience, make sure she doesn't have any objections to you using it.)

### Humorous story

A humorous story amuses your audience while making a point. It can be a funny story about your work or anything else. Humorous stories provide a great way to create rapport and get attention — as long as they don't embarrass anyone in your audience. They're particularly useful in sales presentations. (For more information on using humor, see Chapter 8.)

### Parable

A parable is a story with a simple moral or lesson — and you don't need to be a preacher to tell one. Parables have become popular with presenters who talk about business ethics. They can also be very useful for sales and marketing presentations. (The moral of the story is that the company that didn't buy my product went bankrupt.)

# Doing It by the Numbers: Statistics and Other Numerical Data

Statistics can provide some of the most influential support in your entire presentation, but they commonly lose their impact, because presenters use them incorrectly. Statistics enable you to slice up reality in a way that suits your perspective — no matter what type of presentation you're giving. The following sections cover some suggestions for getting your numbers to register on your audience's bottom line.

## Don't spew numbers

Most people can't process numbers as rapidly as they can process other types of information, so don't drown your audience in numerical data. Give your listeners time to digest each statistic. If you don't space statistics out, the audience will — space out, that is. (An exception to this rule involves *startling* statistics. A discussion of this exception appears in "Use startling statistics," later in this chapter.)

# Round off numbers

If exact numbers aren't critical to your subject matter or audience, give everyone a break — round them off. Your listeners don't need to know that your new product has captured 59.8 percent of the market. Just say 60 percent.

# Use a credible source

A statistic is only as impressive as its source. Did you get your numbers from *The Wall Street Journal* or *The Smallville Gazette?* There's a big difference.

Don't jump to the conclusion that *The Wall Street Journal* is the more credible source. Credibility all depends on your audience. You may be presenting to people who read *The Smallville Gazette* religiously and distrust *The Wall Street Journal* as a tool of the rich. Only your audience can bestow credibility upon a source. Keep that point in mind when you select your statistics.

# Repeat key numbers

If you want people to hear and remember an important statistic, say it more than once. "We are going to lay off only 5 percent of the sales force in the London office. Let me say that again. Only 5 percent of the London sales force will be laid off."

# Put statistics into familiar terms

Numbers are abstract concepts. Want them to have an impact? Explain them in terms that have meaning for your audience. Here's how Richard Stegemeier, former chairman, president, and CEO of Unocal Corporation, did it in a presentation about global competitiveness:

> Economist Thomas Hopkins estimates that federal regulations are costing American consumers $400 billion every year.
>
> How much is $400 billion?
>
> It's about ten times the size of our trade deficit with Japan.
>
> It's about double the annual cost of public education in America, from kindergarten through the 12th grade.
>
> It's about 33 percent larger than our entire defense budget.
>
> It's enough to give every household in America $4,000 every year.

# Create a picture out of numbers

One of the best ways to put statistics into familiar terms is to transform your numbers into a concrete image. Paint a picture for them. For example, in a presentation to employees about office remodeling, you could say that the new carpet will be about 98 feet long. But that's boring. Instead, you can say the new carpet will be 98 feet long — that's as long as 26 emperor penguins lying end to end.

Want an easy way to create a picture with numbers? Compare your abstract statistics to easy-to-visualize images. Here's an example from former president of the American Medical Association, Dr. Lonnie Bristow:

> Right now it requires four workers to pay for each Medicare beneficiary. But in a few years, as the whole population gets older and older, there'll be only two workers available to pick up the tab. And all the while that bill keeps swelling up just like a balloon. That means by the time most of the Baby Boomers are ready for Medicare, the balloon may have burst.

# Use startling statistics

An exception to the rule that statistics are boring is the *startling* statistic. This term refers to numerical data that's so surprising that it just grabs your attention. Here's an example Jeff Davidson, executive director of the Breathing Space Institute, used in a presentation about overpopulation:

> The Lennon sisters, who appeared on *The Lawrence Welk Show*, had 11 children in their family. If each family member had 11 children for 11 generations, they would exceed the current population of earth — and that's just one family!

# Consider using visual aids

If you have a great deal of numerical data in your presentation, consider putting it into a visual format — slides or overheads of charts or graphs. If your audience members can see the data, they can digest it much more easily. (See Chapter 10 for an extended discussion of this topic.)

# Gathering More Support: Quotations, Definitions, Analogies, and Examples

Humans don't live by bread alone. And presenters don't support their ideas with stories and statistics alone. In this section, I discuss four types of support that enhance a presenter's ideas: quotations, definitions, analogies, and examples.

## Using quotations for maximum impact

Quotes get immediate attention — especially when they're attached to a famous name. In today's sound-bite society, quotes provide a great way to gain "mindshare" with your audience. The following sections give you a few guidelines for using quotes effectively.

### Relate the quote to a point

You want to use a quote to make a point. Otherwise, the quote is irrelevant — no matter how funny or insightful it is. Sometimes, you may find a great quote that just doesn't fit, and you can't make it fit without reworking a great deal of your presentation. Just accept the fact that the quote doesn't fit. Save the quote for your next presentation.

### Don't drop names

If you use quotes only to drop the names of the people you're quoting, you may come off as a jerk. "As Albert Einstein once said . . ." "According to Socrates . . ." "I believe it was James Joyce who observed . . ." The giveaway is that the quotes have nothing to do with what you're talking about. They're forced into your presentation so that you can drop the famous name. Including such quotes is a dumb way to seem smart, and it doesn't work.

### Use a variety of sources

Unless you're doing a tribute to a particular celebrity, no one wants to hear endless quotes from a single source. That type of repetition gets boring fast. If you're only going to quote Yogi Berra, then why didn't you just get Yogi to give your presentation? Mix it up a bit.

### Keep it brief

You don't want to lose the conversational quality of your presentation, and a long quote starts to sound like you're reading it, even if you're not. Shorten lengthy quotes, and tell the audience that you're paraphrasing.

### Don't say "quote . . . unquote"

It sounds stupid unless you're doing a dramatic reading from a trial transcript. Just say Mr. or Ms. So-And-So once said — and give the quote. Or give the quote and then say who said it.

### Do use surprising quotes

One of the most effective uses of quotes is citing a surprise source. A Republican speaker supports his position by quoting a Democrat. A union leader advances her cause by quoting management. Tipper Gore quotes Snoop Dogg. This contrast always gets attention because it's so unexpected.

## Mark Twain said what?

One of the biggest media brouhahas during Dan Quayle's tenure as vice president involved his misspelling of the word *potato*. While visiting a school in New Jersey, Mr. Quayle told a sixth grader that the word was spelled "potatoe." He made the mistake because he read from a flash card that had the word misspelled that way. Two days later, the national press was still hounding Quayle about the incident. He responded: "I should have caught the mistake on that spelling bee card. But as Mark Twain once said, 'You should never trust a man who has only one way to spell a word.'"

That should have been the end of the incident. But a new controversy ignited when reporters checked the quote with Twain scholars around the country. The scholars claimed that Twain had never said it. And then the whole thing hit home — Mr. Quayle's staffers defended him by saying the quote came right out of a book that I had written.

It was true. I had written a book called *The Light Touch: How to Use Humor for Business Success* (Simon & Schuster), and in it, I had advised using the Twain line to defend yourself if you were ever accused of making a spelling mistake. The vice president used it perfectly. The defense should have worked. (And it would have worked for anyone else. The fact that reporters bothered to call Twain scholars around the country to check the quote shows how much they had it in for Quayle.)

But this is a cautionary tale, and I bring it up now to show you the dangers involved in quote attribution. My source for the Twain quote was a book called *The Dictionary of Humorous Quotations,* published by Doubleday in 1949. No, it wasn't *Bartlett's Familiar Quotations,* but it was a reference book from a major publisher. And it was written by Evan Esar, one of the major American humor scholars for the first half of the 20th century. If you can't rely on that type of source, what can you rely on? And that's my point: Be ready to defend your attributions, because if you look in several quote books, you'll often find the same line attributed to several different people. You can quote me on that.

### Be careful about attribution

If you're not sure who said the line that you're quoting, cover yourself. Say, "I believe it was Mr. Famous Name who once said . . ." Another hedge is to say, "As an old philosopher once said . . ." After all, everyone is a philosopher of one sort or another. So if you find out that the line came from Donald Duck, you can still argue that he was being philosophical.

# Spelling it out with definitions

A famous legal case involving a contract worth thousands of dollars turned on the definition of the word *chicken.* One side said that *chicken* referred to a fryer. The other side said that the same word referred to a roaster. If you don't want to be fried or roasted by *your* audience, make sure that you're all speaking the same language — especially when you're giving a technical, financial, or international presentation. The following section shows you a few ways to use definitions in a presentation.

### Use the dictionary definition

Here's an example from a speech about ethics given by Dexter Baker, retired chairman, executive committee, board of directors, Air Products and Chemicals, Inc.:

> *Webster* says ethics is about dealing with good and bad, with moral duty and obligation. A system of moral values. Principles of conduct that help mold our judgments and guide our decisions.

### Use your personal definition

Here's an example from a speech given by Brent Baker as rear admiral, United States Navy, chief of information:

> How do I define *quality* in a news report or analysis? My measure is summed up in three words: *accuracy, objectivity,* and *responsibility.*

### Explain your definition if the word is emotionally charged

When a word is emotionally charged, some members of your audience may misinterpret your remarks unless you clearly explain *your* use of the term. The following is an example from a speech that George Marotta, a research fellow at Stanford's Hoover Institution, gave to a local chapter of the National Association of Retired Federal Employees:

Thank you for inviting me to speak to you today about two subjects, which I believe are very much positively correlated: bureaucracy and the national debt.

Bureaucracy is a pejorative term used to refer to organizations which are large and hierarchically structured. Today I am using it to refer to the bureaucracy of the federal government. In all of this, please understand that we all were federal bureaucrats and were proud to serve our government.

### Use the derivation of a word to define it

Explaining the history of a word's meaning reinforces its definition with your audience. (Doing so also makes you sound smart.) Here's an example from a speech about the crisis in solid waste management given by William Ruckelshaus when he was chairman and CEO of Browning-Ferris Industries:

> Many of you have seen the famous old painting of a Victorian doctor at the bedside of a sick child. The doctor is sitting with his head bowed, not performing any medical miracles, just waiting. The title of this painting is *The Crisis,* and it refers to the period in an illness when all that can be done has been done; the patient will either get better, or she will die.
>
> This was the original meaning; but a word like "crisis," so exciting and laden with emotion, could not long be confined to medicine alone. It became our general term for any situation in which disaster is somewhere in the offing, however remote. We don't have squabbles, or problems, or difficulties; in everything from international affairs, to government budgets, to education we have crises.
>
> And naturally, we have a crisis in solid waste disposal, too. I mentioned the original derivation of this term, and its true meaning, because I think it's important in understanding where we really are regarding solid waste in this country . . .
>
> . . . In the past few years we've been able to diagnose the "disease," as it were, and we've been able to apply some basic cures. Is the crisis over?

## Amazing by analogies

An analogy is a comparison that highlights similarities (and differences) between two objects or concepts. Analogies allow individuals to explain the unknown in terms of the known and are one of the fundamental ways that people gain new knowledge. Here are two examples of interesting analogies that speakers have used in their presentations:

Under these [civil discovery] rules, litigants can force their opponents to open a staggering number of their files to inspection. Like a medieval king's demand that his knight ride out and find the Holy Grail, it's a task that's easy to request and hard to fulfill.

— Stephen Middlebrook, former senior vice president and executive counsel, Aetna Life & Casualty

MBAs are like sea turtles. MBAs, like sea turtles, are hatched by the multitudes from business schools around the world only to perish moments later. As they flop frantically from the beaches to the relative safety of the sea, many are gobbled up and picked off by predators and competitors. The few that survive seem to live long, endless lives.

— Karen Stephonson, anthropologist

## Edifying with examples

Two of the most frequently used words in the world are *for example*. Many people use these words to illustrate what they're talking about, and that's why examples are probably the most common devices for supporting ideas and assertions. You can use them in any type of presentation.

In this section, I go over three different types of examples. A real example is based on fact. A hypothetical example is based on imagination — it's made up. But you can also think of examples in terms of positive and negative. I cover each kind in the following sections.

### Are you for real?

The strength of a real example is that it's real. Sounds obvious, right? But making up an example to support an argument is easier than finding a real one. And that's the bad news: You have to do some research to come up with real examples.

A good illustration of a real example comes from a presentation about the need to take risks in developing technology given by Lockheed Martin chairman and CEO Vance Coffman. He uses the Hubble Space Telescope to support his thesis that there can be no progress if we're unwilling to tolerate risk.

And yet, we all remember that Hubble had problems when it was first placed in orbit. An error of less than the width of a human hair in grinding the primary mirror made photographs taken by the spacecraft blurry. You'll recall that critics had a field day, citing the "trouble with Hubble." But three years later, a courageous team of Astronauts fixed the flaw — and to date, Hubble has sent back more than 270,000 images, giving humankind the ability to see back in time, virtually to the beginning of the universe.

### Hypothetically speaking

The strength of a hypothetical example is that you can tailor it to make your exact point. The weakness is that it can be attacked as "made up." Here's a hypothetical example from a presentation by Jim Albaugh, president and CEO of Boeing Integrated Defense Systems. He's discussing how technology may help preempt terrorism:

> Here's a hypothetical: Suppose a suspected terrorist booked a flight from Paris to L.A. The integrated system might correlate address information with two other individuals living on the West Coast of the United States. It might show that one had a hazardous material–trucking license and the other was employed at Long Beach harbor. In connecting the dots, the system could trigger and alert to authorities to gather more information to determine if there was a threat.

### Don't ignore positive examples

Too often, presenters tell you what you shouldn't do, but they never say what you should do. That's a pet peeve of Jim Lukaszewski, and I agree with him. So here's some uncommon knowledge from Jim: Use wrong-way, right-way examples, and make sure that you're prepared to show the right way. "You can take a specific situation and talk about how it might have been handled differently," Jim says. "But if you're going to give just one side, talk about the right behavior and allude to the wrong one — not the other way around. You don't want to leave the audience hanging."

# Chapter 7

# Setting a Style: Choosing Your Words Carefully

. . . . . . . . . . . . . . . . . . . . . . . . . . . . . . . . . . . . . . . . .

*In This Chapter*

▶ Choosing words that create a powerful message

▶ Coming up with a catch phrase

▶ Employing classic rhetorical tricks

▶ Checking out painless editing techniques

. . . . . . . . . . . . . . . . . . . . . . . . . . . . . . . . . . . . . . . . .

**S**everal people have told me that there are more than 10,000 useless words in the English language. Many of them come in handy for political speeches. Some of them may come in handy for *your* business presentations. It all depends on what you want to accomplish. Whatever your goal, making successful presentations requires choosing your words carefully.

# Honing Your Tone and Style

A politician gave a speech denouncing the welfare nature of big government. His booming voice thundered across the room: "From federal payments for prenatal care to Social Security death benefits, the government is taking care of people from womb to tomb." The rhyming words "womb" and "tomb" gave the line a nice ring and always got applause. But the politician got bored with the line, so he introduced a new version during a luncheon speech to a women's political club. Instead of "womb to tomb," he said he was sick of the government taking care of people from "sperm to worm." The audience silence was deafening.

What can we learn from this? Three things:

✔ Don't talk about sperm to a women's political club.

✔ Don't talk about worms while people are eating.

✔ Don't forget that tone and style are important — they have a major effect on how your ideas are received.

# All words aren't equal

Several years ago, I attended a seminar held by Ronald Carpenter, a professor in the English Department at the University of Florida at Gainesville. One of his major themes was that word choice is critical in the communication of ideas. To make the point, he posed a question. If a monument were built for John F. Kennedy, what Kennedy quote would be engraved on the monument? The seminar participants answered instantly and unanimously: "Ask not what your country can do for you; ask what you can do for your country."

President Kennedy delivered that line during his *Inaugural Address* on January 20, 1961. It's a powerful arrangement of words that is universally associated with Kennedy.

Carpenter believes that the choice of words and their order has made that line immortal. His proof? He contrasted the famous quote with a line delivered by Kennedy several months earlier. During a campaign appearance on September 6, 1960, Kennedy had said, "The New Frontier is not what I promise I am going to do for you; the New Frontier is what I am going to ask you to do for your country."

Would that line appear on a Kennedy monument? Not a chance. But substantively, this long-forgotten line says *exactly the same thing* as the famous line. Word choice and arrangement made the critical difference. (Need another example? Imagine the *Gettysburg Address* beginning with the words "Eighty-seven years ago . . .")

# Power words make powerful points

Management communication counselor Jim Lukaszewski also places a heavy emphasis on the power of words. As principal of the Lukaszewski Group, he performs corporate troubleshooting for large companies throughout the United States. Much of his advice to executives involves how they can use language more effectively.

He divides words into three categories: blah words, color words, and power words.

- **Blah words** are just what you'd expect — blah. They're colorless filler that take up space without getting noticed. An example is "nice."

- **Color words** exist at the other end of the spectrum. They're colorful, but they generate an emotional reaction. Examples include the following: defective, guilty, greedy, brainwashed, and aggravate. "Color words can get you in trouble," Jim explains. "Every person in the audience interprets them differently, and they often overshadow anything else you say in a talk."

✔ **Power words** grab attention without really saying anything. That's why Jim recommends using power words such as interesting, unusual, decisive, hot, exciting, new, critical, urgent, and compelling.

His proof? "If I say, 'This is an urgent matter' or 'This is really important,' I've said nothing to you, but I've got your attention," he observes. "That's what power words do. They grab attention without giving away what you want to talk about."

## Jargon is as jargon does

Real-mode device drivers are fine, as long as you hook them up to a hybrid 16/32-bit OS and retain control of the configuration of the SNMP agent and log-on domains. Yeah, right. The traditional thinking on jargon in presentations can be summed up in two words: Avoid it. Jargon is often incomprehensible. It creates a barrier between you and your audience.

Jargon can also create a bond. In order to explain why, I need to introduce an academic concept: the inclusionary and exclusionary functions of language. It sounds complicated, but it simply means that one of the ways that groups of people define themselves is through the use of language. It's like knowing a secret password. If you speak the language, you're in (or *included*). If you don't speak the language, you're out (or *excluded*). Jargon is the language that's unique to each group.

Jargon is so widespread because every group creates its own jargon as a way of defining membership. Each trade and profession has its own jargon. Many companies have their own jargon. Clubs and associations have their own jargon. Even individual families have their own jargon.

So what does this mean for presentations? Plenty. Are you an outsider in relation to the group you're addressing? You can create rapport with the audience by using some of its jargon in your talk. Using jargon is relatively easy to do, and it demonstrates that you made an effort to gather information about the audience. It also suggests that you understand something about the audience. Talking to managed health care executives? Find out what *accrete* means, and refer to it in your presentation. Talking to real estate agents? Find out what *FSBO* means, and drop it into your talk.

What if you want to introduce jargon from *your* trade or profession that the audience doesn't know? Many presenters get themselves into trouble when they use their own jargon, and that's why the common knowledge says to avoid jargon. You really shouldn't have a problem with using your own jargon as long as you educate your audience. Tell the audience what it means. That's the secret. It's also the part that most presenters forget, which is why jargon has such a bad name.

Rather than using jargon, you may want to define it and use terms that your audience can understand. Like a cliché or euphemism, jargon tends to lack emotion. Instead of using jargon, draw a true picture with descriptive power words that grab and hold the audience's attention.

# Creating Catch Phrases

The *catch phrase* provides a tried-and-true method for drawing attention to a key point and helping audiences remember it. Want some examples? Turn on your radio or television set. The advertisements are full of them.

The phrases in advertisements "catch" in your memory, and that's what they're designed to do. Every time you think about one of them, you automatically think about a product and its key sales point. Constant repetition of the phrase by advertisers augments this effect.

Be careful about co-opting catch phrases directly from advertisers. These phrases may already be trite and therefore turn off your audience.

The catch-phrase technique isn't limited to advertising. Anyone, including business leaders, can use it in any type of presentation. Howard Nations, one of the country's leading trial lawyers, advises attorneys to create catch phrases that will stick in a juror's mind. And, of course, the most famous catch phrase from recent legal history comes from the O.J. Simpson trial: "If it doesn't fit, you must acquit."

Business leaders are also fond of this technique. In a speech about the future of telecommunications, when he was chairman of United Telecom/U.S. Sprint, William Esrey coined a phrase to describe the marriage of the telephone and the computer. He called it *infonics.* After defining his catch phrase, he repeated it more than 20 times throughout the rest of his speech.

You can apply this technique to emphasize points in your presentation too. Just pick an important point, build a catch phrase around it, and repeat it endlessly. "I'm tired of our company being run by arrogant midlevel bureaucrats. They're manajerks. You know what I mean. Someone who thinks their memo is critical to the future of the company — that's a manajerk. Someone who puts down your ideas and then includes them in their memo that will save the company — that's a manajerk. Someone who kisses the CEO's butt more than they kiss their spouse — that's a manajerk."

# Using Classic Rhetorical Tricks

There was good news and bad news if you had a dispute in ancient Greece. The good news: There were no lawyers. The bad news: You had to argue your own case. That's why the ancient Greeks developed all sorts of rhetorical devices to improve their presentations. They wanted to win.

This section presents a few of the classic devices. And don't worry; they still work today. (Your lawyer probably uses them.)

## Alliteration

*Alliteration* refers to a phrase in which the words begin with the same sound. A classic example is former Vice President Spiro Agnew's description of the media as "nattering nabobs of negativism."

You can also use alliteration to make the title of your talk more memorable. When I was in high school, an English teacher talked about a paper written by one of her college classmates. It was titled "Freshman Father of Four." She said that the alliteration had made the title stick in her mind for years. I can vouch for that, because it's stuck in my mind since high school.

## Allusion

An *allusion* is a reference to a person, object, or event from the Bible, mythology, or literature. Here's an example from a speech about balancing work and family given by John Adams, as chairman and CEO of the Texas Commerce Bank:

> Opponents of work and family programs say that employers should not involve themselves more deeply in workers' lives, that to do so opens a Pandora's box of raised expectations, employer liability, invasion of privacy, and even accusations of unfairness in providing work-family programs.

Allusions provide an easy way to explain your position in terms of something already familiar to your audience. "Some investors say that our start-up can't compete against Fortune 500 companies. Yes, we may be a David amid a bunch of Goliaths. But we'll see who prevails." If you include allusions, make sure your audience understands them without much, if any, explanation.

# Antithesis

*Antithesis* refers to putting two opposites near each other in a sentence. John F. Kennedy used them all the time: "If a free society cannot help the many who are poor, it cannot save the few who are rich." Antitheses are catchy, and they make the presenter sound eloquent. Just listen to this:

> We find ourselves rich in goods, but ragged in spirit; reaching with magnificent precision for the moon, but falling into raucous discord on earth.

> We are caught in war, wanting peace. We're torn by division, wanting unity. We see around us empty lives, wanting fulfillment. We see tasks that need doing, waiting for hands to do them.

Sounds good, right? Want to know who said it? President Richard M. Nixon. And that's my point — Nixon was known for many things, but inspirational public speaking wasn't one of them. Yet this passage from his *Inaugural Address* sounds terrific. Why? Antithesis. It can make *anyone* sound great.

The stark contrast and parallel construction are what make antithesis an effective rhetorical trick.

Antithesis is one of the easiest rhetorical devices to use in a presentation. When I attended Ronald Carpenter's seminar, he even offered a step-by-step formula for writing one. Take a look:

1. Pick two opposites (words, phrases, or concepts).

2. Write a sentence with one of the opposites in each half of the sentence.

3. Make it sound balanced. (Put an equal number of words in each half of the sentence. Locate the opposites in approximately identical positions in their halves of the sentence.)

4. The closer together the opposites are placed, the more dramatic the antithesis sounds.

5. An antithesis generally works better if it's short and simple rather than long and cluttered. (Edmund Gwynn's famous line is a good example: "Dying is easy; comedy is hard.")

6. The antithesis will be more effective if it ends on a positive note. (The classic example is John F. Kennedy's "Ask not what your country can do for you; ask what you can do for your country." Let's reverse it. "Ask what you can do for your country; ask not what your country can do for you." It just doesn't have the same impact.)

You can use an antithesis in a garden-variety presentation. If you're speaking about the need to get past the planning stage on your corporate strategy, you may say, "We must stop talking and start acting." If you're presenting the quarterly results of your business operations, you could say, "Our profits are down, but our sales are up." If you're talking about the venture capital your company wasted, you may say, "Easy come, easy go."

# Hyperbole

*Hyperbole* is a fancy word for exaggeration. People use hyperbole instinctively in everyday conversation: "I was waiting a year for you to get off the phone." It's a wonderful device for emphasizing a point in a presentation. Here's an example from a speech that the late San Francisco comedy coach John Cantu gave about his roots in comedy:

> One of the first clubs I performed at was a small, dark place. It was so dark I could barely see the three people in the room — the two in the front row listening to me and the guy in the back row developing film.

# Metaphor

A *metaphor* is a short, implied comparison that transfers the properties of one item to another. A classic example comes from Martin Luther King's *I Have a Dream* speech:

> The manacles of segregation and the chains of discrimination.

Not every metaphor has to be a poetic gem. A garden-variety metaphor can do a good, solid job of conveying your point as long as it creates a strong image. The following is an example from a presentation about energy policy given by former Exxon Corporation chairman L.G. Rawls:

> Federal responsibility for energy rests in the hands of 51 committees and subcommittees of Congress, 6 Cabinet secretaries, 3 offices of the President, and 4 independent agencies. With so many cooks working on so many different recipes, it's not surprising that we face a smorgasbord of ill-conceived and inconsistent policies.

# Repetition

*Repetition* refers to repeating a group of words in an identical rhythm. This draws attention to the phrase and can even be used to pull a whole talk together. Martin Luther King's *I Have a Dream* speech is a classic example. Dr. King repeated the phrase "I have a dream" throughout the speech.

But repetition doesn't have to run throughout an entire presentation. It can be used to dramatize one section, or even one sentence, of your presentation.

## Mixed-up metaphors

Metaphors provide a colorful way of injecting some zest into a presentation — sometimes, too colorful. Inspired by the passion of the moment, speakers may stumble when reaching for that perfect image to galvanize their audience. Instead of finding one metaphor, they grab two off their mental shelf and combine them. That's what's known as a mixed metaphor. Here are some examples of what can happen when words collide:

We've got to seize the bull by the tail and look him in the eyes.

From now on, I'm watching everything you do with a fine-tooth comb.

That's the way the cookie bounces.

That's like the pot calling the kettle's bluff.

We'll burn that bridge when we come to it.

It'll be a dark day when you see a light at the end of the tunnel.

The big cheese smells a rat.

Don't put all the egg on your face in one basket.

He'd be spinning in his grave if he could see you now.

Here's how former Coastal Corporation President and CEO James Paul used the device in a presentation about the oil and gas industry:

It's a system with inferior public services; at the same time there are more government employees in the country than manufacturing.

It's a system with intrusive government meddling increasing by the hour into every phase of your business and your private life.

It's a system with entitlement programs gobbling up 49 percent of the national budget.

So repetition is a dramatic way to create a rhythm. It's a dramatic way to make a point. It's a dramatic way to show your style. It's a dramatic way to be dramatic.

## Rhetorical question

A *rhetorical question* refers to a question that the presenter asks without expecting the audience to answer. Rhetorical questions are designed to focus attention on the subject of the question. They're often used as introductions, conclusions, or transitions.

Here's an example used by the late Benjamin H. Alexander, president of Drew-Dawn Enterprises, Inc.:

> Are we free when we cannot leave our homes at night without fear of being assaulted, beaten, or robbed? Are we free when, as the richest nation in the world, we permit poverty, beggars, and homeless people everywhere amongst us?
>
> Are we brave or courageous when we are afraid to bring back the "Whipping Post" for hoodlums — one of whom, three months ago, in Washington, D.C., casually walked to a swimming pool crowded with youngsters; and for no reason began to shoot at children?

## The rule of three

The *rule of three* refers to the technique of grouping together three words, phrases, or sentences. For some reason, a grouping of three items makes a powerful impression on the human mind. (The number 3 is the first number that denotes a pattern, and the importance assigned to "3" is consistent across cultures.)

Some of the most famous passages from the world's greatest oratory have used this technique.

> *I came, I saw, I conquered.*
>
> — Julius Caesar

> *Government of the people, by the people, for the people . . .*
>
> — Abraham Lincoln

Business presenters frequently use this technique. Here's an interesting example used by Stephen Middlebrook when he was senior vice president and executive counsel at Aetna Life & Casualty:

> Voltaire once said of the Holy Roman Empire that it was neither holy, nor Roman, nor an empire. The same might also be said of the civil justice system in the United States: that it is neither civil, nor just, nor a system.

The beauty of the rule of three is that it can work its magic on any topic — no matter how commonplace. Just take a few minutes to think about your subject. You can always come up with three items to group together. Are you talking about a new accounting procedure that must be followed by all employees? It affects managers, hourly staff, and temps. Is your subject quality management? It starts with awareness, training, and commitment.

## Simile

A *simile* is like a metaphor except that it's a directly stated comparison of one thing to another. (It usually uses the words "like" or "as" to make the comparison.)

Here's an example from a speech given by former United Telecom/US Sprint chairman and CEO William Esrey:

> The flow of information has since swelled far over the traditional banks, flooding the social landscape such that today, countries . . . companies . . . even individuals . . . are like islands in a sea of information.

His simile conveys a strong image and gives his point more impact. Want a great source of similes? Find *The Book of Similes* (Routledge & Kegan Paul).

# Editing Yourself Painlessly

W. Somerset Maugham once said, "There are three rules for writing a novel. Unfortunately, no one knows what they are." Fortunately, the rules for *editing* are better known. This section contains a few that apply to presentations.

## Be conversational

One of the most common mistakes presenters make is the failure to distinguish between oral and written language. They write a presentation as though it's a memo or a report, which is a big mistake, because a talk must be read orally, not visually. It must be designed for the ear, not the eye.

Try a little experiment. Take a standard written document — a report, memo, or white paper — and read it aloud. How does it sound? Do the words "awkward," "boring," or "stilted" come to mind? Here's why: People's reading and writing vocabularies are much larger and more complex than their speaking vocabularies. When you write a presentation, some of your writing vocabulary creeps in. When you edit the presentation, you must find those instances and eliminate them. Keep your language conversational.

You can make a few edits to give your talk more of a conversational tone. Adding contractions, using second person ("you" instead of "they" or "we"), and eliminating uncommon vocabulary words can take you a long way.

## Practice out loud

If you write for the ear, you need to hear what you're writing. The only way to do that is to read your presentation out loud. How does it sound? Does it have a good rhythm? Can you communicate each idea without running out of breath? Have you cut out all the tongue twisters? Have you eliminated phrases that appear harmless on paper but are embarrassing when spoken? (Here's a classic example: "One smart fellow; he felt smart. Two smart fellows; they both felt smart. Three smart fellows; they all felt smart." Say it aloud quickly a few times. You'll find out why it's cherished by little kids throughout the English-speaking world.) For more information on rehearsing your presentation, check out Chapter 5.

## Use simple language

Many presenters feel that they have to throw in a lot of big words to show how smart they are. Wrong. Smart presenters do just the opposite. Abraham Lincoln is a good example. Smart guy, right? Well, check out his *Gettysburg Address.* Most of the words aren't more than five letters long. Or how about Franklin D. Roosevelt? Legend has it that one of his speechwriters wrote, "We're endeavoring to create a more inclusive society." Roosevelt changed it to: "We're going to make a country in which no one is left out." Which one sounds smarter to you?

## Keep sentences short

Brevity is the soul of understanding. No, that's *not* a mistake. I know the expression is really "Brevity is the soul of wit," but I want *you* to know that brevity also has a big impact on comprehension. The more words a sentence contains, the more difficult it is to understand. Look through your presentation. If you find a lot of sentences with more than 20 words, your audience had better consist of PhDs. If you're talking to anyone else, start rewriting (and shorten those sentences).

## Speak boldly in active voice

*Active voice* involves something doing the action, while *passive voice* involves something being acted upon. The active voice makes your sentences more powerful. The passive voice makes them sound wimpy. But you be the judge. Here's an example of the passive voice: "There's a bonus given by the boss once a year." Here's the same idea rewritten in the active voice: "The boss gives a bonus once a year." The passive voice is like a weed that creeps into your writing. You must keep digging it out by the roots.

## Be specific

Writing instructors have an old saying that also applies to presentations: "Specific is terrific," which means that concrete words and examples are more effective than vague words and descriptions. Contrast "I went to work" with "I went to a cubicle with my name on it on the fourth floor of a sky-scraper in downtown Chicago." The additional words form a picture that's more specific than "work." It creates a stronger image. Or say you're talking about a customer reaction to a product demonstration. You could say, "The prospect loved it." You could also say, "The prospect's eyes got wide when he saw the last screen. You could almost see the wheels spinning in his head as he was calculating how much money the software could add to his bottom line in just the first year. He was breathing so hard, I thought he was going to faint with excitement." By being specific, you can hold your audience's attention and give them a clearer picture.

## Use verbs with verve

Verbs are where the action is. So make them exciting. Let them help create a picture for your listeners. Say you're telling some war story from work: "I asked Smith to give me the file." Asked? Why not begged, pleaded, or implored? A good thesaurus can do wonders. (Most word-processing programs have a the-saurus built right in to help you.)

## Cancel clichés

People are our most important resource. We partner with our customers. Synergy. Re-engineering. Excellence. Strategic. Enough, already. Give everyone a break. Instead of parroting the latest corporate clichés, come up with some-thing fresh. It's not that difficult. Just take a few moments to think about what you're really saying. Clichés don't work because they're worn-out, overused phrases.

## Vary your pace

If all your sentences are the same length, your audience will fall asleep. So vary the pace. Use short sentences and long sentences. Use simple, compound, and complex sentences. Throw in a rhetorical question. Don't let the rhythm become monotonous. Also remember that pausing in appropriate places can add drama to a presentation.

# Chapter 8

# Using Humor Effectively

## In This Chapter

▶ Making humor work even if you're not "naturally funny"

▶ Putting simple types of humor to work

▶ Joking about yourself to create rapport

*H*umor is a powerful communication tool, even in business presentations. It can gain attention, create rapport, and make a presentation more memorable. It can also relieve tension, motivate an audience, and enhance your reputation when used appropriately. However, when humor isn't used appropriately, it can sink a presentation faster than a politician can make an excuse. In this chapter, I show you what humor can do for you as a presenter and how to avoid its major pitfalls.

## The Secret of Not "Bombing"

Have you ever heard someone start a presentation with a joke that had nothing to do with anything? I'm talking about an absolutely pointless, no connection to anything, completely irrelevant joke. What was your reaction? If the joke was funny, maybe you laughed. But even if you did, the joke was still just a distraction, because it didn't make any point. It just wasted your time.

And if you didn't laugh? Well, that's called *bombing*. Everyone knew the presenter was trying to be funny, but no one laughed. So the presenter was left facing that deafening silence emanating from the audience, and the audience began to feel uncomfortable, because the presenter seemed uncomfortable. (Perhaps the audience noticed the torrents of perspiration pouring forth from the presenter's brow.) The presenter was trapped in that peculiar twilight zone known as bombing and had no way out.

*If you use humor to make a point, then you won't bomb.* Now let me be perfectly clear. I'm not saying that your audience will always laugh at your joke. I *am* saying that you won't bomb. Here's why: When you tell a joke that makes a point, people recognize that fact. So even if they don't find the joke funny, they still realize that you're making a point. If they don't laugh, it doesn't matter. The joke still serves a purpose and moves the presentation forward. After the joke, you just go on to your next point. When you tell a pointless joke, people realize that, too. If no one laughs, then the joke serves no purpose whatsoever, and you're stuck with no place to go.

How do you relate the joke to a point? Just analogize it. An analogy allows you to compare two different objects and show how they're related. (For more on analogies, check out Chapter 6.) Establishing this relationship is at the heart of the creative process, and it's quite useful for ensuring that your humor is relevant.

To see the analogy method in action, check out the following example from a speech made by Robert Clarke, former Comptroller of the Currency. Speaking to the National Council of Savings Institutions, he discussed how regulatory tools could be used to promote a sound banking system.

> A friend of mine, an honors graduate of Texas Agricultural and Mechanical University (an *Aggie*), spent the first half of the 1980s lusting for a car phone. Finally, he convinced himself that it was a necessity, not a luxury, so he bought one. The day he bought it, he called me from his car to tell me the news. And I didn't hear from him again for about a month. Finally I saw him on the street and he seemed really down in the dumps. I asked him what was wrong and he said it was the car phone. "What do you mean?" I asked. "You wanted that phone more than anything you ever did." And he said: "Yeah, but it's wearing me down having to run to the garage every time it rings."
>
> Regulations — like telephones — are instruments. They can be used effectively. They can be used adequately. Or they can be misused.

The story is effective because it illustrates a key point — that regulations are merely tools. You should notice three other things:

- ✔ First, this story would never be listed under "regulations" in any joke book. The presenter used analogical thinking to relate the joke to his point about regulations.
- ✔ Second, the story can illustrate other ideas. You could use it to make effective points about office automation, productivity, and training. In fact, you can use the story to illustrate any point to which you can analogize it. The process is limited only by your imagination.
- ✔ Third, the story isn't offensive. It's not off-color, sexist, racist, homophobic, or otherwise inappropriate.

# Simple Types of Nonjoke Humor That Anyone Can Use

"So these three guys walked into a bar, and the bartender had a parrot on his shoulder. No, wait, I mean one of the guys had a parrot on his shoulder. And the bartender wanted to know why the parrot was on his shoulder. And the guy said . . . no, wait, I mean the parrot said . . . umm, one second, it will come to me in a moment. Oh, yeah, I forgot to say that the parrot was wearing a little hat and singing the national anthem."

Can't tell a joke? Don't worry. You have lots of other options for incorporating humor into your presentation.

And you don't have to use jokes only in your introduction. You can use humor throughout a presentation as long as it makes a point. Of course, some presentations call for more humor than others — motivational, training, and sales presentations, for example. What type of humor should you use? That's up to you. Any type works if you find it amusing and it makes a point. Here are a few choices to get you started.

## Abbreviations and acronyms

An abbreviation is formed by combining the first letters of a series of words. Two familiar (but boring) examples are IRS (Internal Revenue Service) and the accounting principle known as LIFO (Last In First Out). Funny abbreviations are much more entertaining. This type of humor is particularly useful for breaking up dry technical presentations that are already chock-full of acronyms.

You can make abbreviations funny in a variety of ways. The simplest way is to change the meaning of the underlying words. For example, PBS usually refers to Public Broadcasting System, but Daniel Brenner, former director of the Communications Law Program at the UCLA School of Law, used it differently in a presentation about the information revolution:

> I've just come from a meeting of the Corporation for Public Broadcasting in Washington. Public broadcasting has its own problems. Most people think PBS stands for Plenty of British Shows.

You can also use acronyms (abbreviations that form a word) in a humorous way. You can make up funny ones by abbreviating a funny phrase. Here's an example from a presentation about corporate ethics given by William Dimma when he was deputy chairman of Royal Lepage Limited:

> Ten or 15 years ago, corporate ethics was a MEGO topic . . . My Eyes Glaze Over . . . but not today and not likely ever again.

Another way to add humor is to redefine a negative word by making it an acronym for something positive. I recently heard an engineer use this technique after his department was referred to as a bunch of nerds. He said that NERDS stood for Nouveau Engineering Research and Development Stars.

## Analogies

An analogy is a comparison between two objects or concepts. A funny analogy makes the comparison in an entertaining way. And analogies don't require comic delivery, because they're so short.

Following is an example from a presentation about regulatory reform given by Eugene Ludwig, former Comptroller of the Currency of the United States:

> Being a regulator these days is a lot like being the nearest fire hydrant to the dog pound. You know they'll have to turn to you in an emergency, but it's sure tough dealing with those daily indignities.

Now I admit that funny analogies are difficult to think up yourself, but you can use other people's analogies in your own presentations by switching some of the facts. The analogy about the regulator and the fire hydrant is a perfect example. It could apply to a secretary, a manager, or anyone who feels that his or her work is important but disrespected. So any time you come across a funny analogy, write it down and file it away. You can never have too many analogies at your fingertips. (See Chapter 6 for more on analogies.)

## Bumper stickers

One of the great breakthroughs in the history of presentations occurred with the invention of the car. It provided a fantastic new source of material: bumper stickers.

---

### A few amusing analogies

Need an amusing analogy for your next presentation? I include a few you may be able to use. See if you can tie one into a point you'll be making.

✔ I feel like Elizabeth Taylor's seventh husband. I think I know what to do, but I don't know if I can make it interesting.

✔ It's like a Pia Zadora movie. Everybody's heard of it, but nobody's seen one.

✔ Trying to analyze leadership is like studying the Abominable Snowman. You see footprints . . . but never the thing itself.

From stickers concerning driving (Forget world peace — visualize using your turn signal.) to stickers offering self-insight (I just got lost in thought. It was unfamiliar territory.) and general advice (Be nice to your kids. They'll choose your nursing home.), wisdom previously limited to great minds became available to the masses. Now anyone can add a pithy comment to a business presentation just by looking at the rear of a car. It gives a whole new meaning to "keep your eyes on the road."

Here's an example from a presentation about public education given by Bob Chase, president of the National Education Association:

> Everyone is for change in the abstract. But when you challenge people to change in real, substantive, concrete ways, it's a different story. Then people avoid change. They stall it. They fight it. I love the bumper sticker that says: "Change is good. You go first."

## Cartoons

Even people who insist that they can't tell a joke admit that they can describe a cartoon that appeared in a newspaper or magazine. I see people do this all the time. Someone joins a gathering of coworkers taking a coffee break. The conversation turns to some business topic, and the person describes a cartoon from *The Wall Street Journal* that relates to the discussion. The coworkers laugh, and the conversation continues. If you can do this (and I know you can), you can use cartoons to make points in a presentation.

One of my favorite cartoons is a picture of two shipwrecked survivors standing on a tiny island. One of the survivors is holding a bottle that floated onto the shore. He looks at the note that was in it and says to his companion, "It's from your alumni association." I can use this cartoon to make points about relentlessly pursuing an objective, finding what you're looking for, and how you can run but you can't hide.

You can even describe an entire comic strip in your presentation — if it makes a point. The next quote shows how Martin Coyne, executive vice president of the Eastman Kodak Company Photography Group used a *Cathy* comic strip in a presentation called *The Future of Photography.* He was making a point about the gap between the sophisticated photographer and the mass-market consumer. Attached to his e-mail was this comic strip. *Cathy* is syndicated in 1,500 newspapers worldwide.

> The cartoon shows a woman reading a book called *The Digital Decision.* Its subtitle says it will destroy her sanity.
>
> Her family is about to buy a digital camera. But first they have to spend time visiting retailers and reviewing buyer's guides.

---

# Bumper-sticker wisdom

Haven't been on the road lately? Don't worry. Take a look at some bumper-sticker wisdom that I've already gathered for you. And don't forget — honk if you love this stuff.

- Take everything in stride. Trample anyone who gets in your way.

- I get enough exercise just pushing my luck.

- Everyone has a photographic memory. Some don't have film.

- Artificial intelligence is no match for natural stupidity.

- If at first you don't succeed, destroy all evidence that you tried.

- Ever stop to think and forget to start again?

- You can't be late until you show up.

- Confidence is the feeling you have before you understand the situation.

- It's not an optical illusion; it just looks like one.

---

Then they need to "study the megapixel situation," explore battery choices, understand optical versus digital zoom lens options, and so on.

And then they need to — quote — "find a ten minute window when the technology isn't changing, buy our camera, and then spend two weeks studying the instruction manual and upgrading our computer."

## Definitions

Funny definitions are extremely easy to use. Just pick a word or phrase from your presentation and define it in an amusing way. Take a look at this example from a presentation to the Ag Bankers Association given by Dale Miller when he was president and CEO of the Sandoz Crop Protection Corporation:

> A cynic once defined a farm as an irregular patch of nettles bounded by short-term notes.

Here's another example from a presentation by Norman Augustine, former president and CEO of Lockheed Martin:

> I bring you greetings from my hometown, "America's Most Confused City," Washington, D.C., which I have occasionally referred to as "a diamond-shaped city surrounded on all four sides by reality."

Want a formula for inserting funny definitions into your presentation? Try the old "dictionary bit." You pick out a word or phrase that you look up in the dictionary and then state the meaning. Here's an example from a presentation about biotechnology given by Richard Mahoney, former chairman of the Monsanto Company:

For those six weeks I spent splicing genes in the lab, the scientists presented me with a certificate, designating me an official "journeyman in gene splicing." I was quite pleased, until I looked up "journeyman" in the dictionary: "An experienced, reliable worker, especially as distinguished from one who is brilliant."

Where do you find funny definitions? Most treasury-of-funny-stuff-for-presentations-type books contain them. Just look in your local library or bookstore. Trade journals and professional magazines are also good sources. These types of publications often have a humor page that includes amusing definitions related to their readers' occupations. (Check out Chapter 6 for more on definitions.)

## Laws

People live in a world of laws — civil laws, criminal laws, scientific laws. But no matter where they live, everyone answers to a higher law — Murphy's. That's the famous law that states that anything that can go wrong, will go wrong. This "mother of all laws" has spawned quite a brood. You can find entire books of Murphy-style laws, which is good because it means you can probably find a law that fits your subject matter. Why bother? Because funny laws provide a simple way to add humor to a presentation.

Here's an example from Norman Augustine, former president and CEO of Lockheed Martin:

> I have recently branched out from the rather narrow confines of laws governing aerospace management to promulgating the more general laws of nature. My latest endeavor in this arena has been the law, derived from a considerable base of empirical evidence that "Tornadoes are caused by trailer parks."

Where can you find funny laws? One of the best sources is *The Official Rules* by Paul Dickson (Dell Publishing). But don't rely solely on books. Make up your own laws specifically related to your topic and audience. (Like Kushner's Law of Advice: It is better to give than receive.)

## Letters

The funny letter is a wonderful device to use in a presentation. It doesn't require comic delivery. It gives you a prop to hold. And you don't have to worry about forgetting what you'll say; you just read the letter.

Here's an example from a speech about wasteful federal spending given by the late J. Peter Grace when he was chairman and CEO of W.R. Grace & Co.:

This letter was sent to me by one of our supporters as a glaring example of waste, and it's addressed to the Secretary of Agriculture. It reads as follows:

"Dear Sir:

"My friend, Ed Peterson, over at Wells, Iowa, received a check for $1,000 from the government for not raising hogs. So I want to go into the 'not raising hogs' business next year. . . .

"As I see it, the hardest part of the program will be in keeping an accurate inventory of how many hogs I haven't raised.

"My friend, Peterson, is very joyful about the future of the business. He has been raising hogs for 20 years or so, and the best he ever made on them was $422 in 1968, until this year, when he got your check for $1,000 for not raising hogs.

"If I get $1,000 for not raising 50 hogs, will I get $2,000 for not raising 100 hogs? I plan to operate on a small scale at first, holding myself down to about 4,000 hogs not raised, which will mean about $80,000 the first year.

"Now another thing, these hogs I will not raise will not eat 100,000 bushels of corn. I understand that you also pay farmers for not raising corn or wheat. Will I qualify for payments for not raising wheat and corn not to feed the 4,000 hogs I am not going to raise?

"Also, I am considering the 'not milking cows' business, so please send me any information on that, too.

"In view of these circumstances, you understand that I will be totally unemployed and therefore plan to file for unemployment and food stamps.

"Be assured you will have my vote in the next election. Patriotically yours, /s/ John Partridge"

Now some of you may think this letter is apocryphal, and maybe it is; but it gives you a good idea of what we're looking for.

How do you obtain funny letters? Start with a trip to a library or used-book store (many of these books are out of print), and look in the humor section for books that collect amusing letters. One of my favorites is *Dear Sir: Drop Dead!* It bills itself as "the first-ever collection of hate mail." (It's edited by Donald Carroll and was published in 1979.) Do an author search for the name Juliett Lowell. In the 1950s and '60s, she wrote a series of books collecting funny letters by various themes. (It was called the "Dear" series. Titles included *Dear Doctor, Dear Candidate, Dear Hollywood, Dear Justice, Dear Man of Affairs,* and so on.) Bill Adler is another name to find. (His books include *Love Letters to the Beatles, Love Letters to the Mets, Letters from Camp, More Letters from Camp,* and *Kids' Letters to President Kennedy.*)

Some of the funniest letters can be found right in your own mailbox. I'm talking about the "personal" letters you get from politicians, actors, and other celebrities asking you to support their causes. Quoting excerpts from these letters can provide great comic effect in a presentation.

## Lists

Any time your presentation includes a list, you have an opportunity to include some humor by adding an incongruous item to the end of the list. Your audience doesn't expect the item, so it'll be surprised and amused.

Take a look at this example from a presentation about technology given by Carly Fiorina, chairman and CEO of the Hewlett-Packard Company:

> We asked a group of high school students in California what classrooms would look like in the year 2025. One student imagined that classrooms in 2025 would have voice-activated chalkboards that write what you say so that your arm doesn't get tired along the way.
>
> Another imagined that each student would have a personal robot that would take notes, back up files, and even cut your lawn on a hot Saturday afternoon. Another student imagined that there would be virtual reality classes that would teach any subject. So if you needed help in Math, you'd press a button and presto! Einstein might appear as a personal tutor.
>
> And one of the best answers came from a student who suggested that the real question for the year 2025 wasn't what the future had in store for technology, but whether somebody would finally create a really good microwavable pizza.

Look for lists that occur naturally within your presentation — lists of budget items, product features, names of people, or rhetorical questions. (Remember, a list must be at least two items long, or it's not a list. The funny item that you add at the end must be at least the third item, but it can always be a higher number — fourth, fifth, or hundredth item — as long as it's the last.)

## Observations

The funny observation is a wry look at our everyday fortunes and foibles. These amusing lines don't require comic delivery and can fit almost anywhere in any type of presentation.

Take a look at this example from a presentation given by Walter Wriston, former chairman and CEO of Citicorp and Citibank, N.A.:

> We live in a world of people who make projections about the future. Most of these futurists use straight-line projections of today's data to paint a picture of tomorrow. My favorite illustration of this is the recent statement that if George Steinbrenner continues to behave as he has in the past, 70 percent of the male population of New York will have managed the Yankees by the year 2020.

Yet another example, from a presentation given by Cathleen Black, president of Hearst Magazines:

> The odds of finding success in a leadership manual are about the same as the Dixie Chicks singing the national anthem at the GOP convention.

## Personal anecdotes

A personal anecdote is a story based on a real experience — yours or someone else's. It's a story about something that happened with friends or relatives. It's a war story from work. It's an incident that occurred at school or home or anywhere. It's your life. These stories provide an absolute gold mine of humorous material for any presentation, including motivational, training, sales, and even financial talks. And their best feature? You've already been telling them for years, so you don't have to worry about delivery.

Instead of telling these stories for no particular reason while conversing with friends or acquaintances, use them for a purpose: Use them to make a point. What follows is a personal anecdote from Alexander Sanders, Jr., who was chief judge of the South Carolina Court of Appeals:

> I am reminded today of something that happened when Zoe was just a little girl. When she was three years old, I came home from work to find a crisis in my household. Zoe's pet turtle had died. And she was crying as if her heart would break. Her mother, having coped with the problems of the home all day, turned that one over to me to solve. At the time, I was practicing law and serving in the Legislature. Frankly, it was a problem a lawyer/politician was not up to solving.

> The mysteries of life and death are difficult, if not impossible, for the mature mind to fathom. The task of explaining them to a three-year-old was completely beyond either my confidence or experience. But I tried. First, I made the obvious argument that we would get another turtle to replace the one that died. We would go down to the pet store and buy another one just like the one who was gone.

I got nowhere with that argument. Even at three years old, Zoe was smart enough to know that there is a certain nontransferability about living things. A turtle is not a toy. There's really no such thing as getting another one just like the one who died. Zoe's tears continued.

Finally, in desperation, I said, "I tell you what, we'll have a funeral for the turtle." Well, being only three years old, she didn't know what a funeral was. So I quickly proceeded to expand on my theme. You see, I was employing the typical lawyer's tactic of diversion. If you can't win on the issue at hand, take off on something completely beside the point.

"A funeral," I explained, "is a great festival in honor of the turtle." Well, being only three years old, she didn't know what a festival was either. So, I quickly proceeded to explain further. And, as I did so, I began to depart from the lawyer's tactic of diversion and engage in the politician's prerogative of outright lying. "Actually," I said, "a funeral is like a birthday party. We'll have ice cream and cake and lemonade and balloons, and all the children in the neighborhood will come over to our house to play. All because the turtle has died."

Success at last! Zoe's tears began to dry, and she quickly returned to her happy, smiling self again. Now, happy. Now, joyous. At the prospect of all that was going to happen. All because the turtle had died.

Then an utterly unforeseen thing happened. We looked down, and lo and behold, the turtle began to move. He was not dead after all. In a matter of seconds, he was crawling away as lively as ever. For once, a lawyer/politician was struck dumb for words.

I just didn't know what to say. But Zoe appraised the situation perfectly. And although this happened more than 20 years ago, I remember what she said as though it was yesterday. With all the innocence of her tender years, she looked up at me and said, "Daddy," she said, "Daddy, let's kill it."

The judge used the story to make a point about the lengths to which parents will go to make their children happy. But it could also be used to make points about knowing your priorities, analyzing a situation for maximum advantage, figuring out that appearances can be deceiving, and any other number of common business messages.

Personal anecdotes are real. Audiences instinctively recognize this quality, and they hang on every word of these stories. Remember that your audience can't hear these stories anywhere else. They're *your* personal anecdotes. You're the only one in the world who has them. Talk about positioning! The more personal anecdotes you use, the more you differentiate yourself from other presenters. In the jargon of modern business babble, that means they give you a "strategic competitive advantage." (For more on personal stories, check out Chapter 6.)

# *Predictions*

K. William Kapp said, "Had there been a computer a hundred years ago, it would probably have predicted that by now there would be so many horse-drawn vehicles, it would be impossible to clean up all the manure." If a computer had made that prediction, it wouldn't have done much worse than many of its human counterparts. Throughout history, leading authorities in every field of endeavor have felt compelled to make predictions that were dramatic, bold, and wrong. Although these pronouncements haven't served as a useful guide to the future, they do provide great comic material for presentations. They're particularly good for illustrating points about making predictions, the future, expertise, analysis, and change.

The following is an example from a presentation about competition and education given by Joseph Gorman, chairman and CEO of TRW, Inc.:

> Unfortunately, many of those charged with addressing these critical issues are all too reminiscent of past well-known naysayers. I offer a few illustrative quotes:
>
> "Heavier-than-air flying machines are impossible." (Lord Kelvin, president, Royal Society, 1895)
>
> "Everything that can be invented, has been invented." (Charles Duell, director of U.S. Patent Office, 1899)
>
> "Sensible and responsible women do not want to vote." (Grover Cleveland, 1905)
>
> "There is no likelihood man can ever tap the power of the atom." (Robert Millikan, Nobel Prize in Physics, 1923)
>
> "Who the hell wants to hear actors talk?" (Harry M. Warner, Warner Brothers Pictures, 1927)
>
> And those of you who are baseball fans will love this one: "Babe Ruth made a big mistake when he gave up pitching." (Tris Speaker, 1921)
>
> Now plainly implicit in my talk is the notion of change — change of profound and revolutionary proportion.

Want to see more inane predictions? The best source is *The Experts Speak: The Definitive Compendium of Authoritative Misinformation* by Christopher Cerf and Benjamin Navasky (Pantheon).

# *Quotes*

Funny quotes provide an easy way to get attention. Call it the cult of celebrity. Call it a fascination with the quoteworthy. Whatever you want to call it, the phenomenon remains the same — as soon as an audience hears a famous name, it perks up. If the famous name is followed by a really funny quote, then you've got them. (At least for a few seconds. But in today's computer age, that's a long time.)

This funny quote was used by Richard Lidstad, retired vice president of human resources for 3M, in a presentation about success:

> Second, you need to know that I don't consider myself an intellectual. I don't know everything. That's not all bad, however, since President Dwight Eisenhower once said, "An intellectual is a man who takes more words than necessary to tell more than he knows."

And here's an example from Mark Schannon when he was director of public relations at the Monsanto Company. He uses a quote from a comedian to make a point in a presentation about the ecology crisis:

> We have come a long way in 20 short years — our ability to continue to make progress will depend in large part on our willingness to acknowledge and address the complexity of the world around us.

> As Woody Allen once said, "More than at any time in history, mankind faces a crossroads. One path leads to despair and utter hopelessness, the other to total extinction. Let us pray we have the wisdom to choose correctly."

For more on quotations, check out Chapter 6.

---

# Fulfilling your quota of quotes

Want to display a touch of erudition in your next presentation? Quote a few quips from some modern-day sages. Here are a few pearls of wisdom to get you started:

"Life is what happens when you are making other plans."

—John Lennon

"Anywhere is walking distance if you've got the time."

—Steven Wright

"Power corrupts. Absolute power is kind of neat."

—John Lehman

"If you can keep your head while all about you are losing theirs, it's just possible you haven't grasped the situation."

—Jean Kerr

"Football incorporates the two worst elements of American society: violence punctuated by committee meetings."

—George Will

"I think of my boss as a father figure. That really irritates her."

—Mary Jo Crowley

## Signs

Have you ever seen a sign that made you laugh? They're all over the place these days. The "You Want It When?" sign posted in a secretary's cubicle. The "Mistakes Made While You Wait" sign hanging by a bank teller's window. The "Your Failure to Plan Does Not Constitute an Emergency on Our Part" sign taped to the wall of a printer's shop. All are potential material for a presentation. You just describe the sign and where you saw it. Then tie it to a point.

Take a look at an example from a presentation about health data given by James O. Mason when he was head of the U.S. Public Health Service:

> I was driving through a small town in Maryland the other day when I saw a sign on a home/office that said, "Veterinarian and Taxidermist." Underneath in very small letters it said, "Either way, you get your pet back." I thought if we collected data and analyzed it that way, we all would be successful. Everyone would have the data they needed to get the decision or policy done in a way that they wanted it done.

## Sitcoms

Need to establish common ground with your audience and get a chuckle? Just analogize your industry to a popular situation comedy. Take a look at an example from a presentation given by William Esrey, chairman of Sprint Corporation:

> I want to spend my time today discussing where telecommunications is headed and how some of the most exciting developments in telecom also have a direct impact on community planning, development, and the real estate industry. As background for that discussion, it is important to understand a little about the current state of the telecom industry.
>
> The most concise description I can give you actually came from the television comedy *Cheers,* which took place in a Boston bar.
>
> In one episode, Woody, the bartender, greeted Norm Peterson, a regular, by asking, "How's it going, Mr. Peterson?"
>
> And Norm replied: "It's a dog-eat-dog world Woody, and I'm wearing Milk Bone underwear."
>
> That's pretty much how it feels to be in the telecom industry just now. You can't pick up a newspaper or turn on a cable business channel without seeing the industry splashed across it.

Make sure you pick a sitcom that the audience is familiar with. References to *Cheers, Friends,* and *Seinfeld* are much more effective than references to *My Mother the Car.*

# Poking Fun at Yourself

In a world teeming with big egos, posturing, and pompousness, poking a little fun at yourself makes you stand out. It reflects confidence and security. Audiences love self-effacing humor. (They're usually astounded, because so few presenters display it. That's why it's so effective.) You just have to go about it in the right way.

Management communication consultant Jim Lukaszewski gives a lot of presentations. Like many presenters, he asks the person introducing him to read an introduction about how great he is. But unlike other presenters, he begins by poking fun at his credentials.

Here's what he says when he steps up to the podium: "Thanks for reading that material that I provided. But the fact of the matter is, my mother still has no idea what I do." Then he shows an overhead transparency of a man standing next to a roadway with a sign that says, "Will consult for food." People laugh and settle back. What message have they received? They've discovered that Jim is an expert in management communications (as described in the introduction), but that he's not a pompous, self-important, stuffed shirt (as reflected by his opening comments).

Now let me issue a word of caution. Don't go overboard with self-effacing humor. If you use it too often or make it too personal, you appear neurotic. Poking a little fun at yourself doesn't mean maligning or degrading yourself. I've seen seriously overweight presenters launch into ten-minute routines that make fun of their rotund physiques. Unless you're a comedian, you shouldn't bombard yourself with disparaging remarks. Rather than creating rapport, it creates embarrassment. No one wants to hear you barrage yourself with put-downs about your weight or other physical traits. Your quips should be designed to put people at ease, not to make them uncomfortable.

So what can you poke fun at? The following subsections start you out with a few ideas.

## Your status as a presenter

If you've been chosen to present at a special business event, such as a conference or a luncheon, the fact that you've been asked to speak gives you a certain inflated status. Many speakers take themselves down a peg by making fun of their role as presenters.

Check out this example from a speech given by Lee Hoskins, president of the Federal Reserve Bank of Cleveland:

> As a closing speaker at a multiday session, I am always a little anxious about the attendance, especially in such a beautiful resort as the Greenbrier. So I was relieved and, to be honest, feeling a little smug when I saw the size of today's turnout; that is, until I learned about the wonderful drawing for prizes and the condition that you must be present to win.

Here's an example from Stanley Gold, CEO of Merrill Lynch when he was the luncheon speaker at an investor conference:

> I'd like to thank Ruchi for giving me the lunch spot. Of course, with analysts, when you're invited for lunch, you're never sure if you'll be the guest of honor . . . or the main course.

## The length of your presentation

The long-winded presenter is a stereotype long associated with public speaking. (If the first phrase coined by our cave-dwelling ancestors was "Say a few words," the second phrase was "Get to the point.") This fear of a lengthy presentation has been passed down to modern-day audiences and is always a fit subject for self-effacing humor. Take a look at an example from a commencement address given by Philip Burgess:

> When I asked President Horton what I should talk about today, he said, with tight lips and a fierce gaze, "Talk about 15 minutes."

> I am the last lecturer you will have to endure. I promise to be brief.

## Your profession or occupation

If you occupy a position of high status by virtue of your job or profession or you're presenting to people outside of your own company and industry, your audience may expect you to be pompous or arrogant. (Certain occupations generate this expectation due to commonly accepted stereotypes. Lawyers, surgeons, venture capitalists, and investment bankers come to mind immediately.) Poking fun at your big-shot status is one way to shatter the stereotype and let the audience know that you're really an okay person.

The following is an example from a speech that Karl Otto Poehl delivered to the Economic Club of New York when he was president of the Deutsche Bundesbank:

Montesquieu, the eighteenth-century French writer and philosopher, said about economists and bankers: "For a country everything will be lost when the jobs of an economist and a banker become highly respected professions." I am not sure whether the Board of the Economic Club was aware of this judgment when they decided to invite John Reed and myself as guest speakers for tonight.

## Your public image

If you (or your occupation) are strongly identified with a particular trait, especially a negative trait, make fun of it. Sometimes, that's the best way to improve your image. A good example comes from John Qua, SVP Merrill Lynch, head of the Global Banking Group.

I'm proud to call myself a banker. I know some see negative connotations. I hear lots of jokes about bankers not having a sense of humor. Fortunately, I don't get any of them.

## Your less-than-lofty experiences

Have you ever had to change a diaper, unplug a toilet, or clean up after a puking pet? Any experience of this nature can become great material for self-effacing humor. It shows that you're not too high and mighty to perform a menial task; an endearing trait. The following is an example from a speech about saving the environment given by Fred Krupp, executive director, Environmental Defense Fund:

Thank you for that kind introduction. I'm a little surprised that you left out my most important qualifying credential. I have three small sons — ages 7, 4, and 14 months. So I do know a great deal about cleaning up after environmental disasters.

Although your audience likes to hear about your personal experiences, they don't want you to get too personal. The line about three small sons and environmental disasters is a good example. The line as told is funny, makes a point, and tells the audience about the presenter. But it would have lost its charm if the presenter had gone into the specific details of changing diapers.

## Your memberships and associations

Have you made poor choices when it comes to associating yourself with various organizations? Are you a member of the wrong club? A fan of the wrong team? Acknowledge that fact, and laugh at it. Take a look at an example from a speech given by Reed Hundt, former chairman of the Federal Communications Commission, to a group of radio broadcasters:

> I love radio. I grew up on AM, listening to the Washington Senators losing to everybody, the Washington Redskins losing to everybody, the Baltimore Bullets losing to everybody. So with all this experience in losing, I was well prepared to be a lifelong Democrat.

# Chapter 9

# Tying It All Together: Introductions, Transitions, and Conclusions

*In This Chapter*

▶ Crafting an outstanding introduction

▶ Moving smoothly with transitions

▶ Writing a powerful conclusion

M y model of making a presentation is the flight of an airplane. In this model, the introduction is equivalent to the plane's takeoff. The passengers want a smooth takeoff, and they want to know where they're going. They want to eat peanuts, drink sodas, read magazines, and get where they're going. They don't want to sit on the runway forever, gain altitude too fast, have the plane career wildly through the sky, or use the barf bag.

After the plane is off the ground, passengers want a smooth flight from one point to another, and they want to know where they're going, which is equivalent to using smooth transitions in a presentation.

Finally, an airplane must make a good landing. That corresponds to the conclusion of a presentation. The passengers — your audience — don't want the landing to be sudden, bumpy, or late. They don't want to land in the wrong place. And most important, they *do* want you to land.

## Starting Out with Style

The introduction is the most important part of your presentation — *it sets the audience's expectations*. It determines how the audience interprets and reacts to everything else you say. And it's your best chance to shape the audience's reaction in your favor.

Yes, the introduction has to gain attention, lead into the rest of your presentation, and perform all those other traditional functions you always hear about. That's the common knowledge. But all of those functions are encompassed in setting expectations.

Basic psychology says that the way people often perceive things is highly affected by what they've been led to expect. The classic example is Tom Sawyer and the fence from Mark Twain's novel *Tom Sawyer*. When Tom asks his friends to help him paint the fence, they turn him down flat. Why should they do his work for him? When Tom makes like painting the fence is a big deal — it has to be done just right, and not just anyone can do it — they beg him for an opportunity. By the end of that scene, Tom's friends are paying him for the privilege of painting the fence. It was all in the setup — how the fence painting was introduced.

Your goal is to set the audience's expectations and *surpass* them. That guarantees your presentation will be a success.

## *Looking at the introduction's functions*

Want your introduction to grab your audience and let them know a great presentation is coming? Then make sure it addresses the following items:

- ✔ **Gain attention.** The introduction must gain attention. This is a no-brainer. If no one is paying attention, it doesn't matter what you say — no one hears it. That's the common knowledge, but it must be qualified a little. You can gain attention in many different ways. (Think of the class clown from high school.) What you want is *positive* attention. Keep this in mind when you're planning that cheesy attention-getting opening involving a whoopee cushion and seltzer bottle. A classic example of a business presentation introduction that gets attention is "Our company is going to do some layoffs. I'm here to explain how those decisions will be made."

- ✔ **Create rapport.** The introduction must also create rapport between you and your audience. Research suggests that people form opinions about others within several seconds of meeting them. First impressions are everything, so you want to make a good one. You want the audience members to think highly of you. At a minimum, you want them to recognize that you've worked hard on their behalf to prepare your presentation.

- ✔ **Show your credentials.** Who are you? Why are you giving this presentation? What's so special about *you?* Inquiring minds want to know — especially the enquiring minds in your audience. Strictly speaking, providing this information does *not* have to be a function of the introduction you deliver; the person introducing you can handle it. And it's better that way — then it doesn't sound like you're tooting your own horn. But if the person introducing you doesn't provide your credentials, or no one is introducing you, then you have to handle it.

✔ **Provide reasons for listening.** What's in it for me? That's the overriding question that the audience members want answered — fast. Why should they listen to your presentation? The introduction has to give them motivating reasons to keep listening. "The new information system will be implemented over the weekend. I'm going to cover five things you need to do today for it to be successful. If you don't do all five things, you won't have access to your computer on Monday."

✔ **Describe what you'll talk about.** The introduction must give the audience some idea of what your presentation is about. This function can range from a general idea of the topic and your approach to a preview of your specific points. For the most effective fulfillment of this function, you should also give the audience an organizational pattern for your presentation. In other words, the introduction should tell the audience how to process the information that will follow. You can simply say that you're going to discuss a problem and a solution. First, you'll show the three historical causes of the problem. Then you'll show how the problem affects everyone here today. Then you'll discuss possible solutions. The point is that the introduction should give the audience members a conceptual framework that helps them easily understand your presentation. (For more on organizational patterns, check out Chapter 4.)

✔ **Include necessary background.** Do the audience members need certain information in order to understand your presentation? Give it to them in the introduction. If your presentation won't make sense unless audience members know the definition of a certain industry term, define it for them. Also, you may need to provide background about why you *won't* be covering a particular subject — especially if the audience expects you to address it.

The bottom line is that all the traditional functions of the introduction affect audience expectations and are affected by the audience's expectations. For example, how many reasons for listening do you need to give? It depends. If you know the audience expects to be bored, you better give a lot of reasons for it to listen. How big a deal should you make of gaining attention? It depends. If the audience already expects to be fascinated by you or your topic, then gaining attention isn't a problem — you automatically have it. How much does the audience know about you? What do you expect it to think about your message? Will it disagree with you? Will it be friendly? Do audience members care? You have to start with what the audience expects. Then you use the introduction to shape those expectations.

No matter how you conceptualize it, every presenter wants the introduction to accomplish the same thing: Have the audience say, "Wow. I've got to hear the rest of this talk."

## Creating a great introduction

There are as many ways to begin a presentation as there are presentations. (This must be true. I read it in a fortune cookie.) Your opening can be as simple as stating your topic: "Today, I will speak about our dismal performance in the fourth quarter." Or it can be as dramatic as this: "In a few minutes, I'll announce the layoffs, but first, I want to talk about . . ."

No matter how the introduction begins, the effect that every presenter desires is identical — you want the audience to sit anxiously waiting for more.

In planning your introduction, it never hurts to recall the show-biz formula: strong opening, strong close, and weak stuff in the middle. Your introduction is the strong opening. Your conclusion is the strong close. Those are the two parts of your presentation that have the most impact on how the audience remembers your performance. So make sure your introduction is strong.

### Looking at introduction options

So how do you become the center of an audience's attention? Well, I can't offer you a magic formula, but take a look at a few devices you can use:

- ✔ **Definition:** Pick a word or phrase central to the ideas you'll be discussing. Start by defining the word or phrase as a way of leading in to your discussion.

- ✔ **Joke:** The idea that you must open your presentation with a joke is simply a myth. But if you can tell a joke and you know one that's related to your topic, you've got a good opening.

    Any joke that's off-color, racist, sexist, homophobic, or insulting to an ethnic group is never appropriate in the workplace — even if it's related to your topic.

- ✔ **Quotation:** You can easily find a quote related to just about any topic. Whether funny or dramatic, a well-chosen quote gets immediate audience attention. (For more on quotations, check out Chapter 6.)

- ✔ **Rhetorical question:** Start by asking yourself a question. Then spend the rest of your presentation answering it. This type of opening has been popular for centuries.

- ✔ **Statistic:** A startling statistic makes a good opening because it gets attention — it startles the audience. Just make sure the statistic is easy to understand — and truly startling. (See Chapter 6 for details on statistics.)

- ✔ **Story:** The story you choose can be personal, amusing, historic, or emotional. In fact, just about any type of story can work as an introduction — as long as you tie it into your topic. (For the story on using stories, see Chapter 6.)

> ✔ **Today:** Is it a holiday, someone's birthday, or the anniversary of some historic event? You can begin by talking about something that happened on the day that you're presenting and then tie it into your topic.

## Choosing the opening that's right for you

You have all these ways to open. How do you choose one? Allatia Harris, district director, faculty development and core curriculum, Dallas County Community College District, offers a general approach to making your selection: Make believe you're going to talk to a friend about your topic. How would you grab his attention?

Allen Weiner, president of Communication Development Associates, has a specific recommendation: Go with an anecdote. He says his company's research and testing show that anecdotes make the most effective openings, followed by quotations and statistics.

Allen advises clients to make their first four words "About a year ago," "About a month ago," "About a week ago," or any other time frame. Why? "Because these are the adult equivalent to 'Once upon a time,'" he explains. "Anecdotes start back in time and move forward. They get and hold audience attention."

So what opening should you use? Here are some factors to consider:

> ✔ **Your style:** Can't tell a joke? Then don't even try. Something about giving a presentation makes people feel obligated to tell jokes. You're not obligated.
>
> ✔ **Your time limits:** Don't use a time-consuming opening — long story, complex magic trick, extended example — if you don't have a lot of time.
>
> ✔ **Your relation to the audience:** Do they know you? Do they know of you? Are you a complete stranger? Will they like or dislike your message? How much rapport do you need to establish?
>
> ✔ **Your rhetorical constraints:** The occasion and circumstances of your presentation may narrow your choice of openings. Is the event somber or festive? Is it formal or informal? Are certain topics off limits?

All right, bottom line, what opening should you use? The one that works best for *you*.

## Writing it out and writing it last

Write out your entire introduction word for word. Don't worry that you're just supposed to use key words or sentence fragments in writing your presentation, and don't worry that a fully scripted presentation may sound strained. The introduction is an exception. Here's why:

✔ First, if you write out your intro, you can edit it into its best form. If you just make a note that you're going to tell a certain story in the introduction, you don't practice the story. You figure you already know it. Then when you tell it, you end up rambling, you don't economize words, and the story doesn't achieve its maximum impact.

✔ Second, the introduction is the most anxiety-producing section of your presentation in terms of delivery. Stage fright is at its peak. If you get really nervous and your introduction is just a few key words, you may not even remember what they represent. Writing out the introduction word for word helps ensure that you'll carry it off successfully even if you suffer from a case of the jitters. (For more tips on dealing with anxiety, see Chapter 5.)

The introduction is the first part of your presentation, but you should write it last. Why? You need to know what you're introducing. After you write the body of your presentation and your conclusion, you've got something to introduce. That's when you write the introduction.

### Avoiding common pitfalls

Sometimes, what you don't say in your introduction is even more important than what you do say. You don't want to get started on the wrong foot — especially if it's in your mouth. Here are some common mistakes to avoid:

✔ **Don't say "Before I begin . . . "** This is a patently absurd phrase. It's like airline personnel who ask if anyone needs to preboard the plane. You *can't* preboard. As soon as you start going on the plane, you *are* boarding. And as soon as you say, "Before I begin," you've begun.

✔ **Don't get the names wrong.** If you're acknowledging people, professional or industry organizations, or geographic entities, such as towns or cities, make sure that you know their names and pronounce them correctly. No one likes to be called by the wrong name. Messing up names makes you look very unprepared, lowers your credibility, and makes the audience wonder what else you're going to goof up.

✔ **Don't admit that you're not prepared.** It makes you look very unprofessional. And it's insulting. If you're not prepared, why are you presenting? No one wants to waste time listening to someone who isn't prepared. Nonetheless, a lot of presenters make this mistake. Why? They're really making excuses in advance. They know they're not prepared. They know their presentations will stink, and they want the audience to know that they're really not terrible speakers — they're just not prepared. The logic seems to be that if you alert the audience in advance that you know your presentation is lousy, somehow that improves your image. Wrong. You just seem like a jerk for being unprepared. If you're not prepared and you're going to present anyway, just do it.

- ✔ **Don't admit that you've given the identical presentation a million times for other audiences.** Even if your audience knows it, don't rub their faces in it. Every group likes to feel unique. Let your audience operate under the illusion that you prepared the presentation especially for them. And throw in a couple of customized references to promote this illusion.

- ✔ **Don't use offensive humor.** A lot of presenters still labor under the myth that you've got to open with a joke. You don't. But if you do, it better not be a racist, ethnic, sexist, homophobic, or off-color joke. There's no faster way to turn off an audience, especially a business audience. And it makes you look very unprofessional.

- ✔ **Don't announce you had a ghostwriter.** It's like a magician showing how the tricks are done. Your audience likes to think it's hearing from you. Let it think so. Remember, a ghostwriter is supposed to be invisible — you know, like a ghost.

- ✔ **Don't ask about the time.** Maybe it's just a pet peeve, but I get irritated when presenters start by asking how much time they have. Don't they know? It seems a little late to be asking. Are they now going to completely change their presentations based on the answer? Asking this question also distracts the audience. Everyone starts thinking about what time it is and when she has to be somewhere else and how much work she still has to get done. It's not exactly the attention mode you want the audience in when you're presenting.

- ✔ **Don't make it too long:** The introduction should usually be about 10 to 15 percent of your presentation. Don't take forever.

- ✔ **Don't begin with endless greetings and acknowledgments:** Many presenters begin with endless greetings and acknowledgments. Boring. No one wants to hear you list the names of every key executive in the room. All right, sometimes you have to name names, but you don't have to do it as your opening line. If you have to acknowledge a bunch of people, do it as the second item in your introduction — not the first. That's what I do when I speak at meetings where a lot of VIPs must be recognized. I open by poking fun at myself for being an attorney, and then I survey the audience for its attitudes about humor and communication. At that point, the audience is laughing and has bonded with me. Then I can pause, go into what an honor it is to be addressing the group, and acknowledge some of its important members.

## Handling special situations with class

Certain situations put an extra burden on your introduction. Not only must the introduction motivate the audience to listen, but it must also address the unexpected circumstances of the situation. Here are some special situations and ideas for handling them:

✔ **The title of your presentation is in the program, but you've changed your topic.** Try this opening: "Don't believe everything you read — like your program."

✔ **You expect a large crowd but get a small one.** Whatever you do, don't proceed like you got the big crowd you expected. You look like an idiot if you make expansive gestures and speak at the top of your lungs to a handful of people, and they wonder if you're a bit out of touch.

So what can you do? Take a cue from high-tech executive Joe DiNucci. He expected 50 people at a sales presentation. Four showed up, and two of them didn't speak English. "I started by taking my jacket off to make it more casual," he told me. "Then I thanked them for coming and emphasized that we could take advantage of the small size of the audience. The presentation could now be more interactive. They could interrupt with questions. They would actually benefit from the low turnout." His goal was to make them feel rewarded, not punished, for coming.

✔ **Your audience has more technical expertise in the subject than you.** Change the focus of the presentation away from the technical details, and concentrate on the big picture. Michael O'Hare, professor of management at UC Berkeley, used this technique to talk about waste disposal to a group of people who use radioactive isotopes in their businesses:

> I've got some notes here about the importance and the central place of radioactive waste disposal in the economy of an industrial society. I'm going to save us all a lot of time. You just talk to the people across the table about that. There's nothing I can tell this audience that you don't already know more about in the context of your own businesses than I do.

> But I would like to make three major points about waste disposal. They generally go toward raising this issue to a higher and more important level.

✔ **You're the last presenter at an all-day conference.** The audience members are burned out. You know they're burned out. They know that you know they're burned out. So acknowledge it. That's what Neil Baron, a high-tech executive, did when he was the eighth speaker at an all-day technical conference. His topic was the three commandments for product sales.

> I was talking to my wife and she asked, "Why don't you have ten commandments? Shouldn't there always be ten?" And I said, "It's 4:30. Who the heck wants to stick around and listen to ten commandments? And second, Moses didn't have to follow seven other speakers."

Or you can try this line used by Chuck Lamar, a vice president of U.S. West Communications:

Thanks for sticking around for our closing session. I certainly hope we've saved the best for last.

# The Top Five Introductions to Avoid

Introductions are like strangers in trench coats. Some expose you to a world of wonderful new ideas. Others just expose themselves. Avoid the following introductions.

## The apology

Unless you accidentally activated the emergency sprinkler system, shut off the power for the room, or knocked the podium off the stage, *never begin by apologizing*. Here's why. First, it sets a horrible tone for the audience expectations. When you start by apologizing, something bad seems bound to follow. Why else would you be apologizing?

Second, an apology draws attention to something the audience may not otherwise notice. That's why you should never apologize in advance. If you don't start by apologizing for your presentation, the audience may actually think the speech is good. You can always apologize later.

## The bait and switch

This introduction gives a great build up to a speech that isn't given. The intro excites the audience. Everyone is tingling with anticipation. And then the presentation goes in a different direction. That's why it's called bait and switch — the speaker promises one thing in the intro and delivers another in the presentation.

## The cliché

You've heard the cliché introduction a million times — literally. That's why it's a cliché. "A funny thing happened to me on the way over here today." "We are at a crossroads." So what's wrong with these intros? Well, they're not horrible, but they don't exactly grab your attention. It's kind of like my grandfather used to say: "You can do better." (How's that for a guilt trip?)

## The nerd

You come to hear a presentation that is presumably in your language. But right from the start, you realize that something is wrong. The presenter is using phrases like "published API," "callable mechanisms," "Posix compliant," and "C++." You have no idea that C++ is a type of computer programming code. You think it's the grade that the speaker ought to receive for this presentation.

The rise of high tech has caused an increase in this type of introduction. Attending one of these talks is like watching an outtake from *Attack of the Killer Pocket Protectors*. But it's not just engineers who do this. It's anyone caught up in the jargon of his trade or profession. Using jargon is okay, but just don't open with such a heavy dose of it that you lose the audience. And when you use it, make sure that everyone understands it.

## The propmaster

The presenter is introduced. The audience gives a warm, welcoming round of applause. The presenter ascends the stage and walks to the podium. The presenter deposits a stack of notes on the podium. The presenter shuffles the notes until they're arranged in the desired order. The presenter looks at the

---

## Cool opening lines

Need some inspiration to create an introduction for your next presentation? Here are some cool opening lines used by executives:

✔ As you just heard, I'm president of the Chemicals Group at Eastman. This is a new title for me. Just a couple of months ago I was president of our Polymers Group. And at the end of this year, I'll get yet another title: CEO of Eastman Company. So if you ask for a business card, I hope you'll ignore all the whiteout I've used.

— Brian Ferguson, president, Chemicals Business Group, Eastman Chemical Company

✔ In honor of the 50th anniversary of the Sloan School of Management, I've managed to do something here this morning that I rarely did when I was a student: I made an 8 a.m. lecture.

— Carly Fiorina, chairman and CEO, Hewlett-Packard Company

✔ I'm always delighted to come back to Colorado Springs, the city that inspired "America the Beautiful." By way of comparison, I work in a suburb of Washington, D.C., the city that inspired America's 120,000-page federal tax code.

— Vance Coffman, chairman and CEO, Lockheed Martin Corporation

✔ Thank you for that kind introduction. You read it precisely the way my wife wrote it.

— Don Winkler, group vice president, Ford Motor Company

microphone. The presenter plays with the microphone until it's adjusted properly. The presenter puts on a pair of reading glasses. The presenter pours a glass of water. The presenter drinks the water. The presenter looks for the switch that turns on the podium light.

The audience is bored out of its mind. If the presenter is Marcel Marceau — fine. No one expects to hear anything. If the presenter is anyone else, get the props arranged ahead of time.

# Making Smooth Transitions

Although transitions are often overlooked, they're one of the most important parts of any presentation. Why? They're the glue that holds the whole thing together.

## The missions of transitions

Transitions have a lot of work to do. The following subsections go over three important transition tasks.

### Lead from one idea to another

The primary role of the transition is to lead your listeners from one idea to another.

Perhaps the most important transition in this regard is the one between the introduction and the body of your presentation. In my airplane model, this is when the plane pulls out of the takeoff pattern and settles into cruising mode. Turbulence here can make the passengers very nervous. They want to know that the plane is heading in the right direction.

Also very important are the transitions between major points. Some presenters screw this up. You know what I'm talking about. You're sitting in the audience listening to a presentation. The presenter is talking about the monetary policy of Bolivia. But the next thing you know, he's discussing a labor shortage in Eastern Europe. How did we get from Bolivia to Eastern Europe? Probably without a transition.

Fortunately, I have a simple way for you to handle the transition between introduction and body, as well as the transitions between main points. Here's the secret: Organize your presentation around a number of points, and state that number in your introduction. Then the transitions are a breeze. "Today, I will be talking about the three reasons for the coming worldwide depression. First is the monetary policy of Bolivia. . . . The second reason we are headed for a worldwide depression is the labor shortage in Eastern Europe. . . . Third . . ." It's transitions by the numbers. But you know what? The method is easy, and it works.

By the way, you can also use this numbering technique to make transitions to and between subpoints. "First is the monetary policy of Bolivia. Two aspects to Bolivian policy that are troubling . . ."

Even if you don't use numbers, you can still choose a simple organization and announce it in your introduction. "Today, I'll report on the profitability of our sales force for the first quarter. Let's start with the western region . . . In the north . . . In the eastern region . . ." Again, with this technique, the transitions write themselves.

I have one more important transition to discuss. It comes between the body of your presentation and the conclusion. And it's very easy to handle. Sometimes, you can just say, "In conclusion," and it works. You can also use conclusions such as "What can we learn from all this?", "Let me leave you with one final thought.", or "Now, in my three remaining minutes, let me remind you of what we've discussed." It has to sound like you're going to wind down and wrap up.

### Summarize internally

The second traditional function of transitions is to provide internal summaries — short announcements that let the audience know where it is, where it's been, and where it's going. The need for these summaries is frequently dismissed by inexperienced presenters who feel that they're too repetitive — that they're just filler. Well, yes and no. Internal summaries *are* repetitive, but they're *not* filler.

Here's why: When it comes to understanding a presentation, presenters have a distinct advantage over the audience — they know what they're trying to say. (All right, so maybe you can think of a few exceptions. They're in Congress, right?) Presenters know exactly what their message is, how it's structured, and all its points and subpoints. In creating the presentation, presenters have an opportunity to read their message many times. Audiences don't have that luxury. They only hear the presentation once — as it's given. They can't put it in reverse, play it again, and freeze-frame the parts they didn't catch.

That's why internal summaries are a necessity. And that's why you need a lot of them. They keep reminding the audience of how the presentation is organized and where you are in the presentation.

Here are a few tips about using internal summaries:

- ✔ An internal summary should succinctly state what you just covered and announce where you are in the presentation. "Now that we've talked about manufacturing, sales, and product development, I want to move on to human resources."

- ✔ Use an internal summary every time you move from one major point in your presentation to another major point.

- ✔ You can also use internal summaries when moving from subpoint to subpoint.

- ✔ The longer your presentation, the more internal summaries you need.

### Get attention

You can also use transitions to gain attention. Under the traditional view, transitions can serve as internal summaries telling your audience where it's been, where it is, and where it's going. It's this last part — *where it's going* — that raises interesting possibilities for gaining attention.

When you tell your audience where it's going, why not make it exciting? Instead of just restating the structure of your presentation in a straightforward, matter-of-fact manner, employ a little pizzazz. Use a teaser. A *teaser* is the short blurb you hear on radio and television programs just before the commercial. "Coming up in the next half of our show: A man abducted by a UFO reveals recipes he learned on board." or "A politician who *kept* a promise — right after these announcements." The teaser is designed specifically to get your attention and keep you from changing the channel.

You can use the teaser technique to make your internal summaries excite the audience members about what lies ahead in your presentation. How do you do that? Think about why the audience should even listen to your presentation. What's in it for them? As you write your transitions about what's coming up, frame them in terms of audience benefits. "We've talked about the new ads. In a few minutes, I'll tell you how they may translate into a bonus for each of you this year. But first, I'm going to discuss the advertising budget."

## Common mistakes with transitions (and how to avoid them)

Transitions are the glue that holds a presentation together. Unfortunately, many presenters become unglued trying to insert transitions properly. Avoid the following mistakes.

### Too few

The biggest mistake you can make in regard to transitions is not having enough of them. It never hurts to have more, because you can never make your presentation too clear to your audience. You've been living with your presentation for quite a while. You're intimately familiar with it; your audience isn't. The more guidance you can give the audience about how your presentation is structured and where it's going, the better. Not sure if you need a particular transition? When in doubt, *don't* leave it out.

### Too brief

If the transition is too brief, your audience can easily miss it. That's equivalent to having no transition at all. The most common, and overused, brief transition is "and." A close runner-up is "in addition." I've heard presentations that used "and" almost exclusively as a transition. The effect is almost comical. The presentation sounds like it's just a bunch of disjointed ideas tacked together — the tack is the "and." And . . . And . . . And . . .

### Too similar

Variety is the spice of life. It also works wonders with transitions. Don't use the same couple of transitional phrases over and over again. It gets boring. Use an assortment of transitions. Here are a few to get you started:

> Now let's take a look at . . .
>
> Let's change direction for a moment . . .
>
> The next point is . . .
>
> Turning to . . .
>
> Another area for consideration is . . .

The possibilities are endless.

# That's It, Everybody: Concluding Your Presentation

When I was a kid in New York, a popular battle cry on the playground was "Don't start what you can't finish." This advice was inevitably directed at a bespectacled young scholar who, after receiving an endless dose of harassment, had finally mustered enough courage to mumble a negative remark to the source of his ill fortune — the school bully. But the advice always arrived too late. Even as it was shouted, the bully was preparing to thrash him into tomorrow. Although my young colleagues' advice referred to the fisticuffs of the moment, they could have been talking about presentations. Too many people who start presentations don't know how to finish them.

The conclusion is one of the most important parts of your presentation. If the introduction is your first impression, the conclusion is your last one — *and your last chance to make one*. It plays a key role in determining how your audience will remember you and your message.

## Checking out the conclusion's main jobs

A cynic may say the conclusion's job is to let the audience know when to wake up. Whatever. For noncynics, the conclusion must accomplish each of the following three major functions in order to be successful:

- ✔ **Summarize your presentation.** The conclusion must provide a summary of your major points. This quick review should also remind the audience of your attitudes toward the ideas you've expressed. And the conclusion should show how the points relate to one another and your topic.

- ✔ **Provide closure.** The conclusion must give the audience a feeling that your presentation is complete. People have a psychological need for closure. They want a presentation to have a beginning, a middle, and an end — especially an end. They don't want to be left hanging. Your conclusion must address this need.

- ✔ **Give an opportunity for questions.** Always make yourself available for questions, even if you're talking to a large group and even if you don't have time for a formal question-and-answer session. Announce in your conclusion that you'll be staying around to answer any questions. If you don't make this offer, people may have unanswered questions and think you don't care about them. Making the offer always makes you look good.

## Creating the perfect conclusion

Remember the ending to every fairy tale you've ever heard? "And then they lived happily ever after." Your presentation may not have much in common with a fairy tale, but you can create a similarly perfect ending for it. The following sections give you the simple rules.

### Wrapping it up in style: Conclusion options

Someone once said that a presentation is like a love affair: Anyone can start one, but it takes a lot of skill to end one well. This section contains some ways to end *your* presentation that will keep the audience loving you:

- ✔ **Use a quotation.** You can never go wrong ending with an inspirational quotation related to your message. Just make sure it's inspired and related. Here's an example from a speech about the future of telecommunications given by Randall Tobias when he was AT&T vice chairman:

And I hope you would agree with the philosopher John Dewey who said, "The future is *not* ominous but a promise; it surrounds the present like a halo."

For more on quotations, see Chapter 6.

✔ **Recite a poem.** It should be short. It can be inspirational or funny, and it must tie into your presentation. Just make sure your audience easily understands your poetic reference. Here's a verse used to conclude a speech by Albert Casey, former president and CEO of the Resolution Trust Corporation (and it ties into *any* presentation):

> I should like to close with the immortal words of Richard Goodwin:
>
> I love a finished speaker. I really truly do. I don't mean one who's polished. I just mean one who's through.
>
> Thank you.

✔ **Tell them what to do.** This type of ending is very specific. The audience is told *exactly* what to do. Here's what the late J. Peter Grace, chairman of W. R. Grace & Co, told his audience to do as he concluded a speech on government waste.

> Get behind Citizens Against Government Waste and join the 535,000 Americans who care about the future of their country and are willing to stand up and be counted. Call 1-800-BE-ANGRY and find out how you can get involved.

✔ **Ask for help.** Just ask for help. People really do respond. My favorite example of this technique comes from a presentation that I gave to my local Rotary Club, describing an experimental humor program that I was organizing in our local high school. As an incentive for students to participate, I wanted to establish a prize fund, so I needed prizes. The entire conclusion to my presentation was a plea for help. They helped.

### Making your last few words memorable

President Ronald Reagan once gave a speech in an unusual time slot — *before* a luncheon. Here are the last two lines of his conclusion:

> Thank you and God bless you. And now the words you've been waiting to hear from me: "Let's eat."

The last few lines of your conclusion are the most important. So make them memorable. Go for an emotional connection with the audience members. Make them laugh. Make them think. Make them stand up and applaud.

Here's a simple formula for setting up your final line: Just say, "I have one final thought that I want to leave you with." (An alternative is "If you remember just one thing I've said today, remember this . . .") Then give them a heck of a thought. Word it strongly and make it relevant — to your presentation and your audience.

### *Watching out for conclusion problems*

Sometimes, what you don't say in your conclusion is even more important than what you do say. What follows are some common mistakes to avoid:

- ✔ **Don't go overtime.** Make the conclusion coincide with the end of your allotted time. If you want to be perceived as a genius, finish five minutes early, but don't go longer than expected. An old joke on the lecture circuit defines a "second wind" as what a presenter gets after he or she says, "In conclusion." Don't let that happen to you. It's not pretty. (The classic example is Bill Clinton's nominating speech at the 1988 Democratic convention. It clocked in at 32 minutes and became a source of national amusement.)

- ✔ **Don't change your delivery.** If you didn't begin with a sonorous oratorical style, there's no reason to end with one. Just keep doing what you were doing. (Unless the audience has fallen asleep.)

- ✔ **Don't ramble.** Reviewing the points you've already made should be done in a brief and orderly manner — preferably in the order you discussed them. Make the conclusion easy to follow. Stick to your plan.

- ✔ **Don't add new points at the end.** The conclusion is a time to review what you've already said — not make another presentation. Introducing new ideas in the conclusion means that you haven't properly fit them into the overall framework of your presentation, which in turn means that these ideas will have less impact. The audience will have to figure out where they belong. And you know what? The audience wants to go home.

- ✔ **Don't say you forgot to mention something.** It makes you look disorganized, and the audience worries that you'll make another presentation. Here's one solution: If the point is really important, boil it down to a very succinct statement. Then, after you've summarized the points you've already made, say you want to leave the audience members with one final thought. Then give them the point you forgot to mention. If you had already planned to leave them with a different final thought, don't worry. Just say you want to leave them with two final thoughts. First, give the point you forgot, and then give the final thought you had planned. (Yes, this is an exception to the rule against adding new points at the end.)

- ✔ **Don't be wishy-washy.** Sound like you believe in whatever it is you're talking about. Be decisive. Take a position. Let the audience know where you stand.

- ✔ **Don't thank the audience.** As presentation guru Allatia Harris likes to say, "Never thank the audience unless you're asking for money or votes." Not because you're ungrateful, but because it weakens your powerful ending. Do your conclusion, and let the audience applaud. Then thank it.

- ✔ **Make it the right length.** The conclusion should usually be about 5 to 10 percent of your talk. It can be too short, but a much more common mistake is making it too long. Don't go on forever. Sum up, and sit down.

### *Wrapping it up tight*

Have you ever done this? You're in the audience. You hear a presentation that you think is absolutely terrific. When it's finished, you go to talk with the presenter, and he or she gives you the brush-off. Bummer. First, you feel stupid. Then you get angry. And then you change your opinion of the presenter and the presentation, right? Now you think the presenter is a jerk, and the presentation wasn't so great after all.

So don't be a jerk. Be kind to your fans. And don't forget — the fact that you're finished presenting doesn't mean that you're done.

# The Top Five Conclusions to Avoid

Have you ever watched a Bugs Bunny cartoon? The conclusion is always the same — "That's all, folks." Although that closing works for a cartoon, it would never work for a presentation. (In presentation parlance, it's called a *nonexistent conclusion.*) The following sections tell you to avoid the nonexistent conclusion, as well as four other horrible yet common conclusions.

## The cloned conclusion

This one is especially frustrating for the audience. The audience listens to the speaker go into the close, listens to the speaker repeat the points, and everything builds toward a big finish. The audience is ready to applaud and head for the exits. But the speaker doesn't stop speaking. Suddenly, the speaker is doing another conclusion, and then another, and another. The conclusion is cloning itself. In my airplane model of public speaking, this is equivalent to the plane coming in for a landing, bouncing on the runway and heading back into the sky — repeatedly. Don't make this mistake. Bring your speech in for a landing — once. If the audience truly wants an encore, it'll let you know.

## The endless conclusion

You guessed it. This conclusion seems to go on forever. Is it really possible for a summary of the main points to take longer than the actual points? Not according to well-established laws of time and space. But the endless conclusion defies Newtonian physics. What goes up doesn't have to come down. It just keeps going, going, going . . . until the audience is gone.

# The nonexistent conclusion

A famous philosopher once said, "I think, therefore I am." Unfortunately, this philosophical principle doesn't apply to conclusions. Just because you think you have one doesn't mean you do. In fact, the nonexistent conclusion is an all-too-common mistake. The speaker comes to the last point and just stops. No review. No wrap-up. No conclusion. In my airplane-flight model of public speaking, this is equivalent to flying into the Bermuda Triangle. One moment, the plane is on the radar; the next, it's gone. In fact, the most common mistake with conclusions is not having one, and you can easily understand why. People run out of preparation time. So they never get around to writing a conclusion, and they figure they'll just wing it. (Famous last words — so to speak.)

# The run-out-of-gas conclusion

The speaker starts to review the various points made in the presentation. For the first point or two, this review sounds strong and confident. Then the speaker becomes more tentative and hesitant, as if he or she can't remember all the points. After struggling to complete the review, the speaker just sputters to a stop. It's as if the speaker had been cruising on fumes and then finally ran out of fuel.

# The tacky conclusion

This conclusion has no apparent connection with the presentation that precedes it. The speaker knows a conclusion is needed and just tacks one on. (Hence the name.) Don't *jump* to a conclusion. Build a bridge to it from the body of your talk, and help your audience across.

Visual aids don't automatically improve a presentation. You may have endured sessions where someone has written an endless number of points on slides or overheads and then read them to the audience, which is really very tiresome. In fact, visual aids are essential only when you're discussing highly complex material that wouldn't otherwise be clear to the audience. For example, a presentation about DNA testing would probably require a visual. But most topics can be handled successfully without one. (In fact, the highest-paid presenters on the lecture circuit, the ones who fetch between $20,000 and $50,000 per speech, rarely use visual aids.)

So the key question becomes: Does a particular visual aid improve your particular talk? What follows are some pros and cons for you to consider.

## *The cons*

"There are two things you need to remember about visual aids," says Allatia Harris, district director, faculty development and core curriculum evaluation, Dallas County Community College District. "Number one, they should be visible. Number two, they should aid."

Allatia's point reflects the two biggest mistakes presenters make with visual aids. They use aids that are so small and poorly done that no one can see them, and they allow visual aids to take over their presentation instead of just supporting it. This second mistake is a growing trend.

The following list shows you a few other pitfalls associated with visual aids:

- **A distracted audience:** Even if the visual aids don't overwhelm your presentation, they can still distract the audience from your message — particularly when the visual aid is inappropriate or poorly executed. Also, if other presenters have gone before you, make sure their visuals are out of sight before you start. They still distract your audience, even if they don't directly attack your message. (For more on this, see the sidebar "A coverup that's *not* a crime," later in this chapter.)

- **Talking to visual aids:** Many presenters fall into the trap of talking to their visual aids instead of talking to their audience. Even if your back is your best side, the audience still wants some eye contact. (However, this rule should be broken on some occasions. For more information, see the section "Talking to the visuals," later in this chapter.)

- **Equipment worries:** Using visual aids means worrying about equipment. Will the overhead projector be available as promised? Will it operate properly? Will the layout of the room accommodate slides and overheads? Even simple visual aids like flip charts can provoke equipment anxiety. (Will the marker dry out?) These extra pressures serve only as distractions from your main task: giving a great talk.

# Chapter 10

# Planning Powerful Visual Aids

**E**veryone's heard the old saying, "One picture is worth a thousand words." If that's true, then the average 20-minute presentation can be reduced to two slides or overheads. We can spend 40 seconds looking at them and go home. But it doesn't quite work that way, does it? It turns out that one picture is only worth a thousand words under certain circumstances. This chapter explores the nature of those circumstances. When do visual aids help? When do they hurt? What can they really do for you? (Get the picture?)

In this chapter, I cover some common visual aids, but this book also includes a whole section on working with PowerPoint. For the scoop on PowerPoint, check out Chapters 14, 15, and 16.

## Understanding the Power of Visuals

*Visual aids* encompass a wide range of items. The more common ones include slides, overheads, charts, flip charts, and props. Many have come to be almost required at the modern-day business presentation. (When was the last time you attended a training session that didn't include a flip chart? Or a sales presentation, strategic briefing, or financial talk that didn't include a PowerPoint presentation?)

## The pros

Visual aids can gain attention, help your audience remember key points, and help it better understand the flow of your presentation. (You figured there must be some reason visual aids are so popular, right?) They can also save a lot of time when it comes to descriptions. (In one of my talks, I discuss the layout of an intersection near my home — where the stop signs are located, where traffic bars might be painted, and so on. Showing an overhead with a picture of the intersection saves a lot of time.)

Two other benefits of visual aids are less well known. First, they can replace presentation notes. If your visual aids cover all the points of your presentation, they can function as an outline. Can't remember what you were going to say? Just talk from the visuals. (That's why I like to use them.) Second, and more important, visual aids help ensure that the entire audience receives your message in a uniform way. For example, say you talk about your annual customer conference. People in the audience have their own picture of the conference in their heads. If you show a photo of the conference, then everyone will see it the same way — your way.

# Checking Out Charts and Graphs

Charts and graphs are commonly used to depict numerical data. They're also useful for expressing such nonnumerical relationships as organizational structure, procedures, and lines of authority. Although they appear most often on slides and overheads, they've become increasingly popular in hard-copy versions that can be placed on an easel. Remember: The easel is low-tech. It seldom malfunctions, and even if it breaks or isn't there, you can always tape something to a wall. Businesspeople often get caught up in high-tech gadgets that aren't worth the hassle.

## Common types of charts and graphs

Take a look at some of the most common types of charts and graphs and how you may want to use them:

- **Bar graphs:** These graphs are handy for comparing all kinds of data: sales of widgets versus gadgets, defect totals under various quality management programs, drug reactions in infants versus adults.

- **Flow charts:** These charts are good for depicting any series of steps: company procedures, how raw materials are turned into products, the organization's chain of command.

✔ **Line graphs:** Line graphs are great for showing changes over a period of time. Any kind of trend data works well: stock market prices, shareholder voting patterns, productivity gains, that sort of thing. (See Figure 10-1 for an example.)

✔ **Organizational charts:** Who reports to whom? What's the exact relationship between the telecommunications department and the information services department? Is the European operation an independent unit or part of the main corporation? These types of questions can be answered with organizational charts. (See Figure 10-2.)

✔ **Pie charts:** Pies are good for showing percentages in relation to one another. (The western region generated 80 percent of the revenue, the east 10 percent, the south 7 percent, and the north 3 percent.)

✔ **Tables of numerical data:** This is your basic spreadsheet layout. It's a boring format, but sometimes, the numbers are so dramatic that the format doesn't matter. ("As you can see from the numbers in column three, half of you will be laid off next week.")

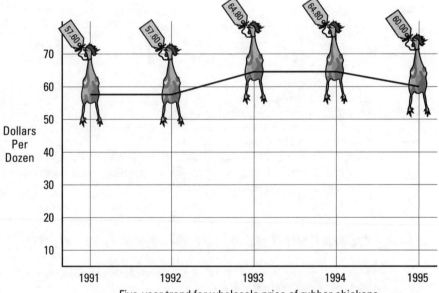

**Figure 10-1:**
A spiffy looking line graph with rubber chickens.

Five-year trend for wholesale price of rubber chickens.
(Based on data from Malcolm Kushner's annual Cost of Laughing Index)

Organizational Chart for Laughter Inc.

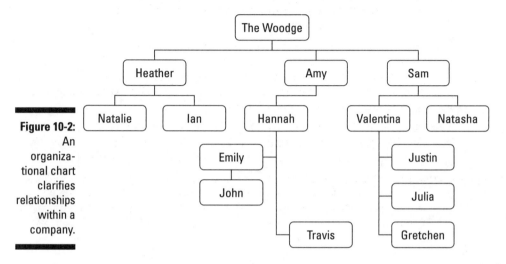

Organizational Chart for Laughter Inc.

**Figure 10-2:**
An
organiza-
tional chart
clarifies
relationships
within a
company.

# Tips and tricks for using charts and graphs

Here are a few pointers to keep in mind when you use a chart or graph:

- ✔ **Limit the data.** The more items included on a chart or graph, the harder it is to understand. If you have a lot of items that must be represented, rethink the graph. Maybe you can split the data into several graphs.

- ✔ **Size pie slices accurately.** The audience gets confused when you show a pie chart with a slice labeled "10 percent" that looks like a quarter of the pie. Make sure the slices of the pie correspond in size to the real numbers.

- ✔ **Make absolutely sure that the numbers are correct.** Check the numbers. Recheck them. And check them again. The accuracy of your numbers is a credibility issue. If one number is incorrect, it can undermine your entire presentation.

- ✔ **Avoid three-dimensional bars.** Don't make bar charts with three-dimensional bars. No one can tell exactly where they end, so no one knows what numbers they're supposed to represent.

- ✔ **Jazz them up.** Use graphics to add some pizzazz to your graphs and charts. Are you showing the trends for the wholesale price of rubber chickens? Put images of rubber chickens on the graph.

## A coverup that's *not* a crime

The court was in Dallas. The case involved an employee suing a large company for wrongful termination. The jury included Allatia Harris, district director, faculty development and core curriculum evaluation, Dallas County Community College District. The defendant company's attorneys produced a chart with a timeline of everything that allegedly happened.

"The chart was a great visual," Allatia says. "It was very impressive." But in cross-examination, the plaintiff's attorney pointed out that the timeline on the chart was inaccurate. It didn't represent the facts of the testimony, and the defendant company conceded that point. Unfortunately, the chart wasn't taken down. It remained in full view of the jury throughout the rest of the trial.

"When we deliberated in the jury room, I kept saying that the timeline on the chart wasn't factual," she says. "That we had to base our decision on the testimony. And even though the other jurors knew that, it didn't matter. Those visuals were implanted in their brains, and you couldn't undo it." So the plaintiff got shafted because of the chart. The plaintiff's attorney should have had the chart covered up as soon as the defendant conceded its inaccuracy.

Here's the lesson: If you're in a presentation situation where other presenters have preceded you, make sure their flip charts and other visuals are out of view before you begin. Even if those visuals don't directly attack your message (like the chart in the courtroom), they still distract your audience. (You don't want them reading the previous presenter's flip charts. You want them listening to you.)

# Selecting Slides and Overheads

Slides and overheads have emerged from a checkered past to become the two most popular visual aids of our time. Not that long ago, the bulk of these aids were associated with boring college lectures and recaps of family vacations. Their amateurish content was only exceeded by their amateurish quality. The high-powered slide or overhead presentation with snappy graphics was limited to top-level executives and their ilk. No one else could justify the expense. That all changed with the desktop-publishing revolution. Computers make slick, quality slides and overheads available to everyone. You can't attend a business presentation without tripping over the slides and overheads. (Measured at a per person rate of growth, the United States may soon have more slides and overheads than lawyers.)

## When to use slides

Well-designed slides can highlight your key points, add variety to your presentation, and capture audience attention. They also look slicker than overheads. But slides also have two big disadvantages. Projecting them requires you to darken at least part of the room. (That invites the audience to snooze.) And their order is inflexible after you place them in a carousel. (So you can't rearrange them as you're presenting.) A third, lesser disadvantage is that you can't use them until a photo lab has processed them.

Another disadvantage, which can be easily avoided, is the tendency some presenters have to run through slides too rapidly. "If you're flipping slides every two seconds, that's too fast," says Rachael Brune of Canyon Design, based in San Francisco, California. "You've got to leave them up long enough to register with the human eye." Her general rule: Allow at least 20 seconds for your audience to view and digest each slide. She also notes that people often rush through their slides, because they have too many of them. "Speakers who have a lot of slides will zip through them to make sure they get to show them all," she explains. "But if you're doing a 20-minute talk, perhaps having 150 slides is a bit much." Point taken.

## When overheads work best

When I have a choice between traditional slides (not a PowerPoint presentation) and overheads, I choose overheads every time. You can project them without turning down the room lights. (So the audience isn't invited to snooze.) You can write notes to yourself on the cardboard frames around the transparencies. And most important, you can change their order as you present. (You're not locked into the inflexible sequence of the slide carousel.)

I also like overheads because they're easier to create than slides. You don't need to send them out to a photo lab for development. You can make them yourself with a copy machine or with an inkjet printer.

Copy machines make great design tools. You can cut pictures, charts, and graphs out of a magazine or newspaper, and then resize them on a copier. Paste them in place on a piece of paper, add some text, and then copy it onto an overhead transparency. (Remember to get any necessary permission. Otherwise, you're practicing copyright infringement.) Want it in color? Use a color copier. Or apply colored markers directly to the transparency.

Overheads have one very major disadvantage: They don't work well for a large audience, because not everyone can see them clearly. You also have to make sure not to place the projector so that it cuts off the audience's view of the presenter or the overheads.

# How to work with designers and production people

If you don't want to create the slides and overheads yourself, you have to work with a designer. (If you *do* want to create your own, check out Chapter 14 for design tips.) After the designer creates the slides or overheads, you have to have them physically produced by other people (usually in a photo lab or service bureau). As in any creative collaboration, opinions can differ, miscommunications can occur, and tempers can flare. But Rachael believes much of that tension is easily avoidable. Here are her tips for working efficiently and effectively with designers and production people:

✔ **Let the designer design.** Many people have a tendency to micromanage the work of their designers. This behavior drives designers nuts and prevents them from giving you the full benefit of their creativity. If you hire experts to work on your visuals, let them be the experts.

✔ **Give the designer your bullet points.** The best input you can give to a designer is an outline of your bullet points — the text that you want on the slides or overheads. The designer can then make suggestions. ("Let's split these seven bullets into two slides, rather than one.") "What we don't want is the detailed outline of your entire speech," Rachael says. "It's not our job to figure out what the bullet points should be. The presenter has to make that decision. After the presenter decides on the bullet points, the designer arranges them so they look good on the visuals."

✔ **Be decisive.** Have you ever worked for people who kept changing their minds about what they wanted? Very frustrating, right? Even though you're getting paid for your time, you still get angry after a while. Well, join the designers' club. Designers may be the victims of customer indecisiveness more than members of any other occupation. "Designers aren't in a position to make the judgment calls on a presentation," Rachael says. "Only the presenter can do that. So we hate it when a presenter is indecisive. We know that revisions are part of the process. That's fine. But patience does wear out." The more decisive a presenter is, the less frustrating the production becomes.

✔ **Let the designer know what's coming.** Want to have a good working relationship with designers? Let them know what's coming ahead of time. "Charts and graphs tend to be last-minute items," Rachael says. "At least if we know what's coming, we can plan for it." Designers are only human. Want them to work all night tonight to finish the last-minute slides for your presentation tomorrow? They tend to be a lot more receptive if you tell them a day or two in advance instead of at 4 p.m. today.

✔ **Don't forget about imaging time.** No matter how fast you think you can force a designer to design, a physical limit, called *imaging time,* determines how fast the visuals can be produced. Forgetting about it is common. "Let's say you're doing 35mm slides from computer files,"

Rachael says. "Depending on how big the file is, one slide can take 10 or 15 minutes just to image on the camera. Just a plain-text file image takes 3 to 4 minutes. So multiply that by 30 slides." Even if your slides are being done in rush mode, you need to prepare for the minimum amount of time it takes to produce them. (You can also save yourself money if you plan ahead. Standard production of slides or overheads is 48 hours. If you want them in 24 hours, you pay a rush charge.)

## Neat ideas for slides and overheads

Tired of slide after slide of boring bullet points? You may want to try some of these less-conventional approaches as you create your slides and overheads. (For more do-it-yourself design tips, see Chapter 14.)

### Using cartoons

The common knowledge is that a funny cartoon that makes a point is usually a big hit with an audience. Well, the common knowledge is right for a change. (It can't be wrong every time.) So why don't more presenters use cartoons? Laziness. Lack of imagination. Stick-figure phobia. Who knows? The point is that it's worth taking time to find cartoons to use in your talk.

Many presenters who use cartoons do so illegally. They reproduce cartoons found in books, newspapers, and magazines without the permission of the copyright holder. One way around the problem is to license cartoons. For example, a wide selection of *New Yorker* cartoons is available inexpensively at www.cartoonbank.com. You can also create your own cartoons. Can't draw? No problem. You can compose a cartoon scene with computer clip art. Then add a caption, and you're in business. (See Figure 10-3 for an example.) You can also purchase many clip-art packages that include permission to use the cartoons they contain.

Are you giving a presentation that introduces a goal, mission, or vision? Write it as if it were a front-page headline on your favorite newspaper or magazine, and then make a slide or overhead that shows it that way.

Suppose that the goal is to diversify your company. You want to expand from manufacturing medical equipment in Hoboken to operating hospitals, running ambulance services, and distributing drugs around the world. A headline may say, "Thousands Cheer as Health Giant XYZ Corporation Opens a Third Office in China." You can make it look like it's on the cover of *Time*.

**Figure 10-3:**
With clip art
and text,
you can
create your
own
cartoon.

### Creating headlines of the future

Wouldn't it be simpler to just make the goal a bullet point instead of a head-line? Something like "Goal — open three offices in China." Yes, but the headline has more impact. Seeing the goal as a headline makes it seem attainable — and a lot more interesting to look at than another bullet point.

### Rearranging images

Have you ever had your photo taken while sticking your face through a giant cardboard scene? You know, the kind of thing you find at amusement parks. You end up with a photo that looks like you're some celebrity or historic figure. Or you're riding a surfboard or doing some other activity. Well, you can use this technique to liven up your slides and overheads. Just cut out the head from a photo of your organization's leader (or whomever), and attach it to a different body. (Yes, it sounds corny, but people love this stuff.)

## How to work with an overhead projector

Have you ever watched a presenter fumble around with an overhead projec-tor? Not a pretty sight! Just when it's time for the first overhead, the presen-ter realizes that the projector isn't plugged in, that it's out of focus, or that a bulb is burned out. (And my personal favorite: The presenter can't figure out where the on/off switch is located.)

Slick, well-designed overheads don't do much good if you don't know how to display them properly. The following subsections give you suggestions to ensure that your overhead delivery is as slick as your overhead content.

### Overhead basics

These rules can save you a lot of potential hassle. They also make the "overhead viewing experience" more enjoyable for your audience:

- ✔ **Use a projector with two bulbs.** You can instantly click the spare one into place if the first one burns out. (So make sure that both bulbs work before you begin.)

- ✔ **Bring an extension cord and an adapter.** You can't fit a square peg into a round hole, and you can't fit a three-pronged plug into a two-pronged outlet — especially if the projector cord is 10 feet long and the outlet is 12 feet away.

- ✔ **Avoid projector glare.** Put masking tape along the edges of the projector so that light doesn't glare out around the edges of your overheads. When there's no transparency on the projector, turn it off. Don't just leave the light glaring on the screen.

- ✔ **Use fewer overheads by showing only parts of them.** The buzzword in training circles is *gradual revelation:* You gradually reveal what's on the overhead. For example, I often talk about five types of humor anyone can use. I used to list them on five overheads — one per humor type. Now they're all on one overhead. When I put the overhead on the projector, I cover it with a piece of paper. Then as I talk about each type of humor, I slide the paper down to reveal the relevant section of the overhead. Why bother? The fewer overheads you need to make and handle, the fewer problems you'll have.

### Where to stand

According to Allen Weiner, president of Communication Development Associates, where you stand when you use an overhead projector makes a difference. "Our research says you have to be standing next to the screen, not the machine," he says. "If the audience members look up at the screen and you're not standing by it, they have to split their attention between you and the screen." And you don't want that. "The theory comes straight out of advertising," Allen says. "A driver going past a billboard is supposed to see the product and the celebrity in one glance. He shouldn't have to split his attention between the two." (For all you perceptual psychology buffs out there, it has to do with the theory of contiguity and splitting attention between figure and ground.)

### Talking to the visuals

The common knowledge is that you shouldn't talk to the visuals. It puts your back facing the audience, breaks off eye contact, and makes it difficult for the audience to hear you if you don't have a microphone. You know what? I don't think it's the big deal that everyone makes out of it. On the other hand, no, you shouldn't make a constant habit of talking to the visuals.

People instinctively look at whatever you're looking at. When I want to direct my audience's attention to something important on the screen, I twist my body to the side and talk to the visual. Guess what? Everyone looks at it. If you move onto a new point but don't have a corresponding visual aid, turn off the projector to keep the audience's attention.

### Using two overhead projectors

Try this great idea from Jim Lukaszewski: Use two overhead projectors at the same time. Just put one on each side of the room. "I use one for serious stuff and the other for funny stuff," he explains. (Of course, he breaks that routine every so often to keep the audience on its toes.) He also finds that two projectors help the audience take notes. "I cover a lot of material," he says. "With two projectors, I can keep up an overhead of important points for a long time. A lot longer than if I was using only one projector." Two projectors also allow him to design overheads using very large type. "If I have a list of seven items, I can put one through three on the left-hand overhead and four through seven on the right-hand overhead," he explains. "It makes it very easy for the audience to see." You can easily walk back and forth between the two projectors to change an overhead.

# Using a Flip Chart

A flip chart is a very large pad of paper that sits on an easel. Flip charts have become ubiquitous at business meetings — and for good reason. The flip chart is a very versatile visual aid. You can write on it as you present or have pages prepared in advance. A flip chart is easy to use: You don't have to find any on/off switches, electrical outlets, or replacements for burned out light bulbs. It always operates properly (unless your magic marker goes dry) and is easy to transport. Plus it's very inexpensive.

## When to use a flip chart

Flip charts make excellent visual aids for presentations that place a lot of emphasis on audience participation. Training presentations are a perfect example. You can write audience responses to questions and exercises on the flip chart, and tape them to the walls for later review. The flip chart is also useful for presentations in which detailed information is discussed and explained — such as a sales presentation. The presenter can draw diagrams and write numbers to enhance the sales pitch.

Flip charts aren't effective for audiences larger than 50 people. The people seated toward the back can't see what's on the chart. And if you don't write clearly, people in the front row can't decipher it either.

# Avoiding common flip-chart mistakes

Take a look at some common flip-chart mistakes to avoid:

- **Too many words:** I've seen flip charts covered with writing from top to bottom. It looks like a cave wall crammed with hieroglyphics and is about as easy to read. Do the audience a favor. Leave some white space.

- **Covering the entire sheet:** Restrict yourself to the top two-thirds.

- **Tiny writing:** Maybe some people in your audience can read the bottom line of an eye chart, but it's not your job to test them. Make your letters large enough so that they can be read easily from the back of the room. And leave a couple of inches between lines.

- **Skinny writing:** Even when the letters are large, they can be difficult to see if they're really skinny. So don't make letters that look like stick figures. Make them thick enough so that they can be read easily from the back of the room.

- **Colors that are difficult to see:** There must be something about flip charts that brings out the artist in presenters. Control the urge. Don't use a magenta marker to write notes on the flip chart. Yellow, pink, and orange are also bad. In fact, if you want to make sure that your audience can see what you're writing, stick with black or blue. Those two colors can always be seen from the back of the room.

- **Too many colors:** A rainbow is nice to look at in the sky but not on a flip chart. You can use a few different colors to highlight various points and add emphasis. But if you use too many colors, they lose their impact and become distracting. (Especially when the colors start vibrating in the audience's eyes. That's a clue that your color scheme is a tad busy.)

# Tips and tricks for using flip charts

Want to turn your flip chart into a powerful presentation tool? Try these tips and tricks that separate the masters from the disasters:

- **Use flip charts with paper divided into small squares.** Each page should look like a piece of graph paper. Here's the advantage: You can use the boxes as a guide when you write. That way, you know your writing is large enough for your audience to see. The boxes can also help you keep your writing evenly spaced. Don't forget to bring spare markers in case the one you're using runs out of ink.

- **Correct mistakes with correction fluid.** Have you ever spent a lot of time preparing a very detailed page in your flip-chart presentation only to make a minor mistake when you were just about done? Don't pull out your hair, and *don't* throw away the page. Put some correction fluid over the mistake just like you would on a sheet of typing paper. Then, make your correction. No one in the audience will be able to see it. (Unless you're presenting to Superman.)

✔ **Write secret notes on the flip-chart pages.** Worried that you may forget to discuss important points? Use your flip-chart pages as cheat sheets. Lightly pencil in a few key words or phrases on the appropriate page. No one in the audience will be able to see them.

✔ **Sketch out things you need to write or draw as you present.** Draw it lightly in pencil beforehand. When you come to that point in your presentation, you can just trace over it with a marker. (It will look a lot better than if you start it from scratch while you're presenting.)

✔ **Draw pictures from coloring books.** Drawing simple pictures can add a lot of interest to your flip charts. Can't draw? Children's coloring books are a great source of simple line drawings that are easy to copy.

✔ **Use human figures.** Are you drawing pictures on your flip charts? Use human figures whenever possible. People respond to humans. (We're a narcissistic species.)

✔ **Leave two blank sheets between each sheet you use.** If you prepare your flip chart in advance, don't use each page. Why? The paper is so thin that the audience can see through to the next sheet. And they can often see through that sheet also. So leave two blank sheets between each page that you use. Then you know you're safe.

When you move on to the next point but don't have a corresponding sheet on your flip chart, you can still flip to the first blank page so the audience isn't distracted by the info that you've already covered.

✔ **Save your flip-chart pages.** You put a lot of work into the ones you prepare in advance. So use them again. If you've torn them off the flip chart, don't worry. You can tape them up to a wall when you reuse them. There's no rule that they have to be *on* the flip chart. And here's another tip: Save the flip-chart pages that you haven't prepared in advance — the ones that you write on as you're presenting. (You know, the ones where you write down audience responses to exercises or make impromptu diagrams in response to audience questions.) They can be a very valuable source of information for improving your presentation. Bring them home and analyze them. (Then you can throw them away.)

✔ **Bring a roll of white duct tape.** It comes in handy: taping wires to the floor to prevent tripping, taping flip-chart pages to the wall so the audience can see them throughout your presentation, taping up the flip-chart easel in case it breaks, and so on.

Using two flip charts can be just as effective as using two overhead projectors. See "Using two overhead projectors," earlier in this chapter.

# Determining Whether Handouts Will Help

In today's self-reliant times, everyone says they don't want handouts. They don't want handouts from the government. They don't want handouts from the corporate world. They don't want handouts from the nonprofits. But when you make a presentation, *then* they want handouts. Consider the following things before you prepare and distribute handouts.

## Making handouts that get a hand

If you're going to make handouts, make them look good. It's not hard to do. Desktop-publishing programs give you many options for jazzing up handouts and making them look professional. Reproduce them on good-quality paper. If you can afford it, put them in a binder. Everyone likes to receive handouts, but giving out a few good-looking ones is better than a lot of hard-to-read, poorly designed ones. Remember, the handouts represent *you*.

## Including the right information

Are you using slides or overheads in your presentation? Your audience would probably appreciate hard copies of them. Put some in the handouts. (If you don't, you inevitably receive requests for them.) And while you're at it, throw in some presentation notes and outlines. They help your audience get more out of your presentation. Reprints of relevant articles, by you or others, are always popular items. (Be sure to get any needed permissions.) Checklists are also very good. People love checklists. And don't forget to include an agenda. If you give it out before you begin, it can help the audience keep track of your presentation. Your audience also wants to be able to contact you. So make sure you include your phone number, address, or e-mail. (Or something.)

And here's some uncommon knowledge from Rachael Brune: The more contact information you provide, the better people like your handouts. Did you recommend products or services in your presentation? Did you talk about sources of information for a particular topic? Include lists of contact names and numbers. (If appropriate, you may also want to provide a list of names and numbers of everyone who attended your presentation. Such lists are extremely popular at user conferences and similar meetings where a lot of networking takes place.)

## Knowing when to give them out

The common knowledge says never give out handouts before you present. They distract the audience. People read them instead of listening to you. Here's the uncommon knowledge: The appropriate time to distribute handouts depends on their function. If the handouts summarize your points and present supplemental information, then distribute them after your presentation. But if your handouts include audience-participation exercises or other materials that you want to reference while you're presenting, give them out *before* you begin. Handouts distributed before you present can also encourage the audience to take notes — especially when properly designed. Here's a tip from Allatia Harris: Instead of reproducing your slides or overheads to full-page size, print them so they occupy 25 to 50 percent of a page. Then the audience can use the rest of the page to take notes while you speak about each slide or overhead.

## Preparing Great Props

Throughout most of the 1950s, Senator Joe McCarthy gave stinging speeches from the Senate floor denouncing alleged Communists in the U.S. government. He always claimed to have a list of these offenders. His claim was always bolstered by the sheet of paper he waved in the air while making his accusations. It was a dramatic flourish that added authenticity to his claims. It wasn't until after his downfall that the sheet of paper was revealed to be blank.

McCarthy has long since become a discredited figure in American history. But I can say one thing for him: He knew how to use a prop. He also illustrated some uncommon knowledge about props: They don't have to be very elaborate.

## Using simple props for fancy effects

When people think about props, they frequently conjure up images of large, complex pieces of equipment. (Like the giant glass tank of water with a series of pulleys and chains used by Houdini-type escape artists.) But almost any simple household item can become a riveting object of attention if you use a little imagination.

Take a look at this list for some simple props:

✔ **Gag items:** Gag items can make good props — if they're used appropriately. Marketing consultant Marcia Lemmons recalls a meeting in which a new director was introduced to his group for the first time. "We presented him with gifts that we thought would be useful for his new job," she explains. These included a construction hard hat, a whip, a whistle, and a vest emblazoned with a firing-range target.

✔ **Hats:** Want to transform your public image instantly? Put on a hat. And if you really want to make an impression, put on several in rapid succession. That's how Marcia gained attention when she taught a seminar about how to land a job in marketing. "I'd open with a quick overview of the traits that employers were looking for," she recalls. "And I'd put on a hat to illustrate each trait." A baseball cap showed that you need to be a team player. A propeller hat showed flexibility. ("It goes where the wind blows," she explains.) A dunce hat showed a willingness to ask questions, no matter how stupid. And a two-visor hat (a baseball cap with a visor in front and back) showed the ability to move in two directions at once. "I spent about a minute wearing each hat and talking about what it represented," she says. "People always commented on it afterwards. They said it helped them remember the skills they needed."

✔ **Magic tricks:** Most people think that magic tricks are difficult to perform, because most of them are. So LexisNexis corporate trainer Loyd Auerbach says to forget about any trick involving sleight of hand. But here's his secret: You can find a good trick if you remember to always tell the magic-shop salespeople that you want a *self-working trick.* The phrase means just what you think it means — that the trick works by itself; it's a no-brainer.

The dove pan, a classic trick where the object in the pan turns into something else, is an example of a self-working trick. It's a great trick for introducing anything new — a new policy, a new product, a new procedure. "I'm holding page 12 of our personnel manual — the policy about vacation days. We've been reviewing it." Put the page into the pan. "We hired a consultant." Put consultant's business card into the pan. "Who did a survey." Put survey results into the pan. "And we took a hard look at the results." Put reading glasses into pan. "And we felt we'd covered everything." Put the cover on the pan. "Then we let it sit a while to see what developed." Remove the cover. "What's this? A pair of sunglasses." Take sunglasses out of the pan, and look at them. "Oh, I see. It's our new policy. Hourly employees will now be eligible for two weeks of paid vacation after only one year on the job instead of two years." (Wild applause from the audience.)

Check out *Magic For Dummies* by David Pogue (Wiley) for more magic tricks that will wow your audience.

✔ **Newspapers:** Here's some uncommon knowledge from Marcia: One of the most effective props you can use for any presentation is a current copy of a daily newspaper. "One of our business development directors begins every meeting by holding up *USA Today* and reading from it," she says. "He always finds something that he can tie into his talk." What's the advantage? "It makes everything that he's going to talk about seem fresh," she explains. "Holding up a newspaper makes his message seem timely and important."

# The do's and don'ts of using props

No matter what types of props you decide to use, a few general rules apply. Take a look at some do's and don'ts:

- **Do use them yourself if you want others to use them.** When it comes to props, you must walk a thin line between what's hokey and what works — particularly if you want your audience to use them. If you give out clown noses, don't expect anyone to put them on unless you're willing to do so yourself. "We had a meeting celebrating a 60 percent sales improvement," Marcia Lemmons says. "So we put sunglasses on each chair and played the song 'The Future's So Bright I Gotta Wear Shades.' As people arrived, we asked them to put on the sunglasses." And they did. Why? Marcia and her boss (who was running the meeting) were wearing giant wraparound sunglasses. "Leadership style makes a big difference," Marcia says. "The presenter has to lead the way."

- **Don't milk it.** A major mistake people tend to make with a prop is using it too long during a presentation. "Most props have a joke or point attached to them that the audience can get in under a minute," says computer executive Joe DiNucci. "But because the speaker goes to the trouble of preparing the prop and schlepping it to the presentation, there's a tendency to keep it center stage too long." Using a prop too long is like a baseball player who tries to stretch a triple into a home run and gets tagged out at home plate. So don't belabor your props. A triple is a lot better than an out.

- **Don't force it.** If your prop doesn't operate correctly, don't force it — especially if it could be hazardous. "I had a student who gave a demonstration of a Vegematic or some slicing-and-dicing gizmo," Allatia says. "And something didn't work, but he forced the blade in anyway. He sliced a big chunk out of his finger. And it's very distracting to the audience when you're bleeding all over the place."

# Part III
# Giving Your Presentation with Ease

# In this part . . .

It's show time! In this part, I show you how to deliver a presentation that wows your audience. To do that, you must know how to carry yourself, answer questions, and handle any audience, no matter how tough or wacky. You can also discover how to convey messages using your voice and body, how to deal with a podium, and how to produce commanding eye contact. And these chapters cover ways to get your audience involved and engaged.

# Chapter 11

# Making Body Talk: What's Out, What's In, and What's International

An old philosopher once said that presenters should speak up so they can be heard, stand up so they can be seen, and shut up so they can be enjoyed. That advice may be harsh, but it highlights an important aspect of presenting: Much of your presentation's impact comes from how you look and sound.

## Using Proper Nonverbal Speech in Any Language

Body language refers to the messages you send through facial expression, posture, and gesture. You don't need a course to learn this language. You already use it every day.

## Factoring in facial expressions

The single most important facial expression is the smile. Simply smiling at an audience creates instant rapport. Unfortunately, many presenters — particularly business presenters — feel they must wear their "game face" at all times. They're *serious* businesspeople. They have facts and figures. They have bottom-line responsibilities. If they smile, they may seem . . . human.

Use your face to accentuate key points. Act out what you're saying. Are you incredulous about a statistic you've just cited? Raise your eyebrows in disbelief. Are you briefing the audience on a business strategy that you disagree with? Frown. Are you telling a group of kindergarten students that they'll be getting more homework in first grade? Stick your tongue out at them. (Just kidding.)

## Seeing the point of posture

Your mother was right. You should always stand up straight — especially when you're making a presentation. Sloppy posture invites negative judgments from the audience.

The following tips can help you maintain perfect posture:

- ✔ **Do stand up straight with your feet slightly apart and your arms ready to gesture.** This is the basic, preferred posture for any presentation.

- ✔ **Do lean slightly toward the audience.** Leaning forward shows that you're actively engaged with audience members. Leaning back signals retreat.

- ✔ **Don't lean on the podium (if you're using one).** Once in a while for effect is okay. But planting yourself on the podium makes you look weak.

- ✔ **Don't stand with your hands on your hips.** You'll come across as a bossy gym teacher. Besides, doing so makes you look like you're leading a game of Simon Says.

- ✔ **Don't sway back and forth.** Unless you're giving a presentation about how to use a metronome or discussing the finer points of seasickness, no one wants to watch you sway back and forth.

- ✔ **Don't stand with your arms folded across your chest.** You'll look like a goon from a gangster movie. What are you going to do? Beat up the audience?

- ✔ **Don't stand with your arms behind your back.** It's a tad limiting on your ability to gesture. And if you clasp your hands together, it makes you look like you've been handcuffed and arrested.

✔ **Don't stand in the fig-leaf position.** That's when a presenter holds both hands together over his or her crotch — like the fig leaves that Adam and Eve wore. Go ahead and try it if you're posing for a Renaissance-style painting of blushing modesty. It looks really stupid in any other circumstance. It's like you've just discovered your nakedness (or lack of anything intelligent to say), and you want to hide it from your audience.

✔ **Don't bury your hands in your pockets.** People wonder what they're doing down there. Putting one hand in your pocket from time to time is okay. But don't park it there.

## *Taking a look at gestures*

Using gestures properly in a presentation means breaking one of your mother's basic rules: You *don't* want to keep your hands to yourself. You want to share them with your audience. How do you do that? Just follow these simple guidelines, and you'll do fine:

✔ **Do create opportunities to use gestures.** If you're worried that gestures won't occur to you naturally, then stack the deck in your favor. Include a few items in your presentation that beg for gestures. Talk about alternative courses of action — "on the one hand . . . and on the other hand." Talk about how large or small something is. Talk about how many points you'll make, and hold up your fingers.

✔ **Do vary your gestures.** If you make the same gestures over and over, you start to look like a robot. And the predictability lowers audience attention levels. Don't let your gestures fall into a pattern. Variation keeps audiences watching. You also look like a robot if you've "memorized" your gestures. Keep the audience guessing.

✔ **Do put your hands in the steeple position.** Your hands really will take care of themselves as you speak. But if you insist on guidance, here's what to do: Put your hands in the steeple position. Just put them together in front of you as if you're applauding. That's the steeple position. But don't keep them like that. It's just a rest stop. As you talk, your hands will naturally split apart from the steeple. Sometimes, they split widely. Sometimes, they split narrowly.

✔ **Do make your gestures fit the space.** A common mistake presenters make is transferring gestures used in small, intimate settings to large, formal settings. For example, people at a cocktail party gesture by moving their arms from the elbow to the end of the hand. But if you're presenting to a large audience in a large space, you must adjust your gestures. Are you going to emphasize a point? Move your arms from the *shoulders* to the ends of your hands instead of from the elbows.

✔ **Do make bold gestures.** Your gestures should communicate confidence and authority. Tentative, halfhearted attempts at gesturing make you look weak and indecisive. Get your hands up. (No, I'm not about to rob you.) You look more assured if your hands are higher than your elbows. Be bold. Don't use a finger if a fist is more dramatic. Watch the Sunday-morning evangelists on television. They know how to gesture with authority.

✔ **Don't forget to use gestures when using visual aids.** Using gestures is more difficult when you work with visual aids. (You may literally have your hands full.) But PowerPoint doesn't have to consume all your attention. In between changing slides, as you talk about what's on the screen, use gestures for emphasis.

✔ **Don't let your gestures turn you into any of these types of presenters:**

- **The banker:** These presenters keep rattling coins in their pockets. They sound like a change machine.

- **The beggar:** These presenters clasp their hands together and thrust them toward the audience as if they're begging for something.

- **The bug collector:** These presenters keep pulling at the hair on the backs of their necks or their heads. Yes, the audience knows it's just a nervous habit, but they still wonder when was the last time that you washed your hair.

- **The hygienist:** These presenters keep rubbing their hands together like they're washing them. It looks weird for a few reasons. There's no soap. No water. No sink. And a bunch of people called an audience is watching.

- **The jeweler:** These presenters fiddle with their jewelry. Necklaces are a big attraction for female presenters in this category. And you'll find ring twisters from both sexes.

- **The lonely lover:** These presenters hug themselves. It looks really weird. They stand up in front of the audience and hug themselves while they speak. They lose a lot of credibility.

- **The optician:** These presenters constantly adjust their glasses. They're on. They're off. They're slipping down their noses.

- **The tailor:** These presenters fiddle with their clothing. The tie is a big object of affection for male presenters in this category. They twist it. And pinch it. And rub it. No one listens to the presentation. Everyone is waiting to see if the presenter will choke himself.

- **The toy maker:** These presenters love to play with their little toys: pens, markers, pointers, whatever happens to be around. They turn them in their hands. They squeeze them. And they distract the audience.

# Making Eye Contact

*If looks could kill.* We've all been glad they can't, but what you may not know is that when you give a presentation, looks *can* kill. Depending on what you do or don't look at, looks can kill your entire presentation. Use the following rules to prevent yourself from committing a capital offense:

✔ **Do look at individuals.** As you gaze around the room, make eye contact with as many individuals as possible. A common recommendation is that you should pick out one friendly face and look at it. Don't try it. This poor person wonders why you're staring at him, and so does the rest of the audience. Look at a variety of individuals. You want to be a searchlight, not a laser beam.

✔ **Do establish eye contact at the end of a thought.** Allen Weiner, president of Communication Development Associates, says eye contact is most effective at the end of a thought. People nod their heads under the pressure of your gaze, and that's a big plus. Why? It has to do with English sentence structure. The important information is usually in the second half of the sentence, so making eye contact at the end of a thought emphasizes the important part. For example, a presenter says, "I think what we really need is a change around here." Allen explains that the "I think what we really need" is just setup. It's the "change around here" that requires the eye contact. In other words, you force people to nod when you make a point. That nodding doesn't automatically mean that they agree with you, but it subconsciously guides the audience in that direction.

✔ **Don't look out the window.** If you look out the window, so does your audience. This applies to looking at the ceiling, the walls, or the floor. The audience plays follow the leader, and you're the leader. Look at them so they'll look at you.

✔ **Don't look at one spot.** Make sure that you establish eye contact with all parts of your audience. Cover the entire room. Too many presenters face straight ahead and never look toward the sides. No, you don't want your head to look like a machine gun pivoting back and forth as it sprays eye contact at the crowd. But you do want to keep your gaze rotating from one part of the audience to another.

✔ **Don't forget to look at the back rows.** If you look only at people seated toward the front, you risk losing a major portion of your audience, because everyone in the back feels left out. Besides, as LexisNexis corporate trainer Loyd Auerbach explains, you get more bang for your eye-contact buck by looking at people in the back. "When you talk to a large group and catch someone's eye in the distance, the five people seated around that person also think you're looking at them," he says. "If you look at someone in the front, no one else thinks you're looking their way."

✔ **Don't let notes ruin your eye contact.** Some presenters get so hung up looking at their notes that they don't look at their audience. Big mistake. The notes aren't going to applaud when you're done. And neither will the audience if you haven't looked at them. What can you do? First, make sure your notes are easy to read — large print, legible, only a few key words per card. Second, watch how your favorite TV news anchors read from their notes. They look down. They read the notes. They look up. They look into the camera. They tell you one thought. Then they repeat the process. Head up. Head down. Head up. Head down. (Just don't do it too fast, or you'll look like one of those little statues you see in car rear windows.) For more on putting together presentation notes, see Chapter 4.

Keep the following advice in mind if you plan to read from notes:

- **Do begin without looking at your notes.** It gets you off to a much stronger start. You look at the audience and take command.

- **Do be familiar with your notes.** The first time you speak from your notes shouldn't be when you make your presentation. Your unfamiliarity with the notes will show. Rehearse with your notes so that you don't have to read them intently.

- **Do read quotes and statistics.** The audience appreciates your effort to get this type of material exactly right. Reading also makes the quote or statistic more credible, because the audience knows that you're not relying on the vagaries of memory.

  If the audience sees you read a quote from your notes, it justifies why you have the notes. (You don't need your notes for your outline. You just need them to get the quote correct.)

- **Don't pretend that you have no notes.** You don't want to draw undue attention to your notes, but acting as if you don't have any notes is silly. Yes, speakers who can deliver a great speech without notes impress audiences, but audiences know that most people can't do that. (Most people can give a really *bad* speech without notes.) So the notes provide a certain level of reassurance. They show the audience that you're prepared.

- **Don't keep your nose in your notes.** If you're just going to read your notes, you may as well have a script.

- **Don't play with your notes.** Playing with your notes just tells the audience that you're nervous or neurotic, and it increases the chances that you may drop them (the notes, not the audience).

✔ **Don't look over the heads of the audience.** A big myth is that gazing over the heads of your audience is okay. They won't know the difference. Wrong. People can tell if you're speaking to the clock on the back wall. And the smaller the audience, the more obvious this technique is. So what should you do if you're too nervous to look in their eyes? Look at the tips of their noses.

# Dressing to Impress

As the saying goes, clothes make the man (or woman). The question is, what do they make you? The answer: Credible — if you dress appropriately.

People make all kinds of judgments based on clothes. It's human nature. Many studies of retail outlets have shown that well-dressed customers receive better service than poorly dressed customers. Think about it: If someone walked up to you wearing checked pants, a striped jacket, white socks, and black shoes, you might make some assumptions, too. (And they wouldn't be very positive.)

The point is that your attire is part of your message. It should augment what you say, not detract from it.

## Image do's and don'ts

Use the following handy tips to dress appropriately for any presenting engagement:

- ✓ **Do dress conservatively.** You want your audience to focus on you — not on what you're wearing.

- ✓ **Do shine your shoes.** The audience will look at them — especially if you're on a stage.

- ✓ **Do wear comfortable clothes.** That doesn't mean old clothes or informal clothes. It means that maybe the time to break in that new pair of shoes isn't the day you're giving your presentation.

- ✓ **Don't have pencils, pens, and markers peeking out of your shirt or jacket pockets.** It makes you look like a nerd.

- ✓ **Don't wear distracting jewelry.** Distraction is defined as when your jewelry is louder than you are (both to the eye and ear).

- ✓ **Don't take a purse or briefcase to the podium or the presentation area.** It's a distraction. Ask a trusted member of the audience to guard it.

- ✓ **Don't keep bulky stuff in your pockets.** Remember Mae West's famous line, "Is that a gun in your pocket, or are you just glad to see me?" You don't want the audience wondering what's in your pockets; you want them wondering what you're going to say next.

# What about informal meetings?

Say that you're presenting at an event where the audience will be dressed casually — golf clothes, shorts, T-shirts, and maybe even bathing suits. Is it okay for you to dress casually? Great minds diverge, but when it's a business event, I say "No." Wear business clothes. I always do — even if the meeting planner says that it's not necessary, even if the whole audience is wearing beach attire. (Beach attire isn't that unusual. Many companies hold management or sales retreats at oceanfront hotels where meetings are followed by recreation.)

Here's why you ought to wear business clothes: The audience takes your message more seriously when you wear business clothes. And presenters who dress casually may fall into the trap of speaking too casually. Besides, I don't look that great in a bathing suit.

The exception is when you're also a member of the audience you're addressing. Say that a group of managers is dressed in golf clothes, because golf is scheduled right after the meeting. You're one of the managers in the meeting, so you'll be playing golf just like everyone else, and you're scheduled to make a presentation during the meeting. In that situation, you probably want to wear golf clothes. *Not* wearing them would seem odd and detract from your presentation.

Whatever the situation, always ask yourself what attire will most enhance your message. That's what you wear.

# Mastering Physical Positioning and Movement

Where do you stand? This question usually refers to a presenter's position on an issue. I'm posing it in reference to your position on stage or in the presentation area. Where do you stand? How do you get there? And how do you move from there? The answers to all of these questions have important consequences for your presentation.

## Knowing the basics of stage positioning

Assume the position. (No, don't put your hands behind your head and lie facedown on the ground. You're not under arrest.) I'm talking about the power position if you're presenting from a stage. What's the power position?

Divide the stage into a nine-square grid: back left, back center, back right, left center, center center, right center, front right, front center, front left. The power position is front center.

But don't just stand there. Move into different squares as you give your presentation. If you want a mechanical formula, find cues in your presentation that suggest moves. "I was in a cattle store looking at bulls. And over on the right, I saw [move to a square on the right] a beautiful set of china teacups. I took one to the proprietor [move into another square], and I said, 'Is this the famous china in a bull shop?'" Now you'd better move to a rear square, because with puns like that, the audience may start throwing things.

This process of moving from square to square is called *making an active stage picture*. It ensures that you don't just stand in one place, and it makes you more interesting for the audience to watch. Just remember to return frequently to the power square. Combine your movements naturally with logical gestures.

## *Working from a podium*

The common wisdom on podiums is that they act as a barrier between the presenter and the audience. The presenter is "hiding" behind the podium. Many public-speaking teachers, communication coaches, and other professional presenter types give this advice: Don't use a podium. And if you *do* use a podium, get out from behind it as often as possible.

The big deal that's made out of the podium being a barrier is a lot of baloney. My advice: If you want to use a podium, go right ahead. Why? Two reasons:

✔ **You may give a better presentation.** There's no point getting out from behind the podium to "eliminate a barrier with your audience" if doing so creates a bigger barrier — stage fright. (It's interesting how the same people who say the podium is a barrier also say that most people fear public speaking more than death. Don't they realize that presenting without a podium is even scarier? The lack of internal logic never ceases to amaze me.)

✔ **The "barrier" argument is a myth.** Allen Weiner, president of Communication Development Associates, says that a presenter's first connections with an audience are facial expression and eye contact. "I've seen studies," he says, "where the speaker's facial expressions and eye contact were so good that two weeks later, the audience didn't remember whether a podium had been used." What about the argument that stepping away from the podium every so often gets attention, because it eliminates the barrier? Allen's response: "It doesn't get attention because they can now see your whole body. It gets attention because it's a change. Any change gets attention."

Here are some tips for using the podium.

- ✔ **Do look at your notes while you're moving behind the podium.** Want to disguise your reliance on notes? Look at your notes whenever you move. When you make a gesture, shift position, or turn your head, take a quick peek at your notes. The audience focuses on your movement rather than the fact that you're reading.

- ✔ **Do use a podium to "hide" when appropriate.** Even if you don't like to stay behind a podium, sometimes you may need to draw audience attention to something other than yourself. Are you using slides, overheads, or a volunteer from the audience? Standing behind a podium makes perfect sense for these situations, especially if the podium is placed off to the side.

- ✔ **Don't press or grip the podium.** Go ahead and use a podium — but not as a crutch. Clutching the podium distracts your audience, because it's an obvious indication of stage fright.

## Handling visual aids with ease

The most common visual aid in a business presentation is a PowerPoint show projected onto a screen. But sometimes, figuring out where to stand isn't easy. Or when to point at things. Here are a few tips from Allen:

- ✔ Stand close to the image, not close to the computer.
- ✔ Point with your hand or the palm of your hand.
- ✔ Don't use a pointer (unless it's a laser pointer).
- ✔ Briefly touch the point of interest on the screen, turn to your audience, and talk about it.

He calls this the *touch, turn, and talk* method. Want a free clinic in how to use this method properly? Turn on your television and watch the weather forecaster on the evening news.

# Understanding What Your Voice Says about You

A popular radio commercial says that people judge you by the words you use. Well, they also judge by how you use them. Do you say the words loudly? Rapidly? Monotonously? Do you have an accent? Do you mispronounce them? All these factors — *how* you say things, not *what* you say — are known as *paralanguage*.

# Tricks and tips for using your voice

Loyd Auerbach is a corporate trainer, as well as a professional mentalist, so he makes a lot of presentations. The following are some of his tricks and tips for using your voice:

✔ **Warm up your voice.** You're about to speak. Your opening line is a gem. People will be quoting it for years. You're introduced. You get to the podium. You open your mouth to deliver your bon mots, and . . . your voice cracks. So much for the brilliant opening.

Now you know why you need to warm up your voice. Go into the bathroom before you give your presentation, and do some vocal exercises. Hum. Talk to yourself. Get your voice going.

✔ **Don't be monotonous.** Monotony refers to more than just tone of voice. Yes, a monotonous voice may be the result of speaking in one tone. But it may also result from speaking at one rate of speed, in one volume, or in one pitch. If you're monotonous in any of those ways, you have a problem. If you're monotonous in all of those ways, your audience will fall asleep. The cure is vocal variety.

✔ **Use your voice for emphasis.** You can completely alter the meaning of a sentence simply by changing the words you emphasize. Say the following line aloud, and emphasize the word in italics. "Are you talking to *me?*", "Are *you* talking to me?", and "Are you *talking* to me?" All right, enough with the Robert De Niro impressions. You get the idea. Use vocal emphasis to reinforce the meanings you want to communicate.

✔ **Slow down for flubs.** Inevitably, you will mispronounce a word or stumble through a tongue-twisting phrase. The natural instinct is to speed up when you make a mistake. Don't. It highlights your error and increases your chances for making additional errors. Just slow down.

✔ **Don't discount volume.** Volume is a powerful tool that's easy to manipulate. It may be tough to change your pitch or tone, but anyone can speak more loudly or softly.

Many presenters think you should never speak softly. Wrong. Speaking softly can be incredibly effective. I've seen presenters whisper and draw in an entire audience. People lean forward in their seats. If you're speaking into a microphone, it doesn't matter if you occasionally speak softly. That's the whole point of using the microphone — it allows you to speak in a full range of volumes.

✔ **Don't be afraid to pause.** A common mistake inexperienced (and nervous) presenters make is speaking without pauses. The pause is a vital part of the communication process. "It leaves time for the meaning of what's been said to sink in," explains speech guru Jim Lukaszewski.

# Using a microphone

The late comedy coach John Cantu worked with a wide variety of presenters. Here are some of his tips for using a microphone.

### Choosing the right mike

The type of microphone you use dictates many other aspects of your presentation. For example, a wireless mike lets you walk into the crowd. A mike with a cord puts you at the end of a leash. And a mike built into the podium means that you can't move at all. Choose one that fits your needs:

- **Built-in podium mike:** Many podiums come with a built-in mike. This kind of mike has a major disadvantage, because it limits your movements severely. You can't walk around. You can't even come out from behind the podium. You're stuck there. When Loyd gets into this situation, he lets the audience know: "I'd love to move around here, folks, but carrying this podium just isn't going to make it for me." The line gets a laugh and absolves him of potential criticism for not walking around. Another problem with built-in podium mikes is that their physical dimensions limit you. If you're tall and the mike is short, you have to bend down to speak into it. Kind of an awkward-looking way to give a presentation, but what's your choice? The choice, as always, is advance planning. Tell the meeting organizers you want a detachable mike. Even if the podium has a built-in mike, they can still get you another one. I do this all the time. I speak from a podium with a built-in, but I use a lavaliere or wireless mike. (One thing to remember if you do this: Turn off the built-in podium mike. Otherwise, you may get ear-splitting feedback when you get near it with the mike you're using.)

- **Hand-held mike:** A hand-held mike lets you move around. Many speakers like this type of mike, because it gives them a place to put one of their hands. But that cuts both ways. It means that you can't gesture with both hands while you're speaking. (Otherwise, the audience can't hear you, because the mike is away from your mouth.) You also have to contend with a cord, which limits how far you can move and requires you to avoid tripping over it. But what bugs me the most about hand-held mikes is that you always have to be aware of how far you're holding the mike from your mouth. If you hold it a fraction of an inch out of range, the mike won't pick up anything you say.

- **Lavaliere mike:** The *lavaliere mike* (also called a lapel mike) clips onto your shirt, blouse, jacket, or tie. Sometimes, you can wear it necklace-style. The mike is attached to a loop of string that is placed over your head. The mike then rests on your chest like a pendant. In either case, a cord runs from the mike back to a power source. The cord is the only disadvantage of the lavaliere mike. It acts like a leash, letting you move only as far as its length. And you have to avoid tripping over it. I've seen speakers who, while moving back and forth as they speak, completely tangle their legs in lavaliere mike cords. Then they have to disentangle themselves while still speaking and hope that no one notices. (All right, I admit it — I've done this more than once.) The big advantages of the lavaliere mike are that you can gesture with both hands, you don't have to worry about where it is in relation to your mouth after its initial positioning, and you can walk around — even if it's a limited distance.

✔ **Wireless mike:** The wireless mike is like a lavaliere mike but without the cord. The mike clips onto your shirt, blouse, jacket, or tie. A thin wire runs from the mike to a small box (like a beeper) that clips onto your belt or pocket. The wireless is always my first choice. There's no cord to trip over or limit your movements. Both your hands are free to gesture. And you don't have to worry about whether the mike is close enough to your mouth (assuming you've clipped it on properly). If anyone ever tries to talk you out of using a wireless mike, be suspicious. They often cost more to rent, and the person running the meeting may just be trying to save money. That isn't your problem.

### Checking the mike

Familiarize yourself with the sound system well in advance of your presentation. Find out how the mike turns on and off and how far you can hold it from your mouth and still be heard. Test to make sure the sound system and mike are actually on. Sometimes, the switch is on, but the mike doesn't work. (Check out Chapter 26, which includes several things to check out before you give a presentation.)

### Taking control of the mike

The presenter, who is 6 feet tall, is introduced and walks on stage. The mike is adjusted only to a height of 5 feet, 8 inches. What happens next is critical. The presenter should adjust the mike to the proper height. But what often happens is that the presenter bends over to speak into the mike — and stays that way for the entire presentation. It makes the presenter look weak and silly.

### Holding the mike in relation to your face

If you stick the microphone right in front of your face, it creates a barrier with the audience. Remember that you're trying to have a conversation with them. Hold the microphone about a half-inch below your chin to avoid problems.

### Gesturing while holding a mike

If you're using a hand-held mike, gesturing can be a problem. Don't worry. You have two choices for handling the situation. You can use only one arm and hand to gesture with. (The other hand holds the mike to your mouth). Or you can gesture with both arms and hands — *if you stop talking while you're gesturing*. If you don't stop talking, no one can hear you because the mike is away from your mouth (in one of your gesturing hands).

### Speaking without a mike

If the mike goes dead and you continue without one, you must speak loudly enough to be heard by the entire audience. But how loud do you need to be? Sometimes, judging is difficult. Try this: Look out at the last row, and speak as if you were having a conversation with someone in that row. Use whatever volume you would use if you were both separated by the length of the room. Even if it seems too loud to you, it will sound natural to the audience. If you speak to the last row, everyone else can also hear.

# Remembering Tips for Successful Global Communications

Body language takes on a whole new level of difficulty when you address audiences from other nations. Cultural differences come into play. So how do you know if your body language is appropriate?

To answer that question, I spoke with Allen Weiner, president of Communication Development Associates in Woodland Hills, California. For the past 25 years, he has coached executives around the world to become more effective communicators. He also runs www.essessnet.com, an online tool that provides executives, managers, and employees with feedback about their communication abilities. "If you compare the feedback from Americans, Europeans, and Asians, the differences stand out immediately," he says.

Here are his general guidelines for using body language successfully when you present around the globe:

- European audiences prefer a more formal style, and that's reflected in a low-key use of body language. "Europeans don't like the high-energy style with emphatic gestures and lots of walking back and forth across the stage favored by Americans," he explains. "They consider that type of delivery shallow, and it lowers the speaker's credibility."

- Europeans always stand when making presentations. "In the U.S., it's becoming common for a speaker to speak from a sitting position at a conference table while showing PowerPoint slides," Allen says. "A European presenter would never do that."

- With a European audience, don't worry that you won't be considered upbeat if your facial expression isn't pleasant enough. If Europeans find you too upbeat, they perceive you as not having enough depth.

- North American audiences appreciate an animated style of delivery. "Think of a bell-shaped curve going from flat to carbonated to overcarbonated," explains Allen. "With a North American audience, you can approach the overcarbonated zone. That means your gestures can be bigger and more passionate." A good example is how far you should move your hands apart to emphasize a point. According to Weiner, you could move your hands apart to the width of a basketball when presenting to North Americans. For a European audience, move your hands to the width of a baseball.

✔ The body-language rules that apply when presenting to North American audience also generally apply to Asian audiences. "Asians like the North American style," he says.

✔ North Americans make eye contact during last few words of a sentence and then hold it for a second or two. When presenting to Asian audiences, it's better to drop eye contact before the end of a sentence, because it looks more self-effacing and humble.

✔ Asian audiences are attentive and respectful even if the presenter isn't good.

✔ South American audiences prefer a decisive presenter, Weiner says. That means gestures and movement can be expansive and emphatic. "You can spread your hands apart a little more than the width of a basketball while gesturing," he says. "On my 'carbonation curve,' you can move into slightly overcarbonated."

✔ For a North American audience, end your thought upbeat: "We don't believe it's feasible currently, but we're very enthusiastic about the idea." For a European audience, end thoughts cautiously: "We're very enthusiastic about the idea, but we don't believe it's feasible currently."

These general guidelines can help you plan a presentation to global audiences, but the only way to be sure that specific body language is appropriate is to talk with people from that culture before your presentation.

# Chapter 12

# Appreciating Your Audience

. . . . . . . . . . . . . . . . . . . . . . . . . . . . . . . . . . . . . . . . . . . .

## In This Chapter

▶ Assessing audience response

▶ Making audiences comfortable during presentations

▶ Dealing with hecklers and other distractions

▶ Keeping the attention of the audience

▶ Getting the audience involved

. . . . . . . . . . . . . . . . . . . . . . . . . . . . . . . . . . . . . . . . . . . .

*Y*ou can have the world's greatest presentation, but that may not mean very much if you have the world's worst audience. An audience is like a thorny, long-stemmed rose. Handled properly, it's a thing of beauty that can blossom as you give a presentation. Handled improperly, it can make you bleed.

# Reading Your Audience's Reaction

Many professional speakers claim they can read an audience like a book. I've always wondered what that means. They read a little of the audience at bedtime, drift off to sleep, and read some more the next day? They mark up the audience with a yellow highlighter? They put a bookmark down the audience's throat? In any event, it makes a lot more sense to read an audience like an audience — a group of people who have to listen to your presentation. What follows are a few ways to gauge their reactions. (For more on analyzing an audience, see Chapter 2.)

## Checking the energy level

One of the easiest ways to read an audience is by observing its energy level. Are people talking and laughing as they wait for the event to begin? If so, you're looking at a high-energy audience. This type of audience is much more receptive to your presentation. A high-energy audience is basically yours to lose. They're already energized. You don't have to wake them up, but don't put them to sleep. If you have a high-energy audience, you don't have to be high-energy yourself. (Although it doesn't hurt.)

I want to share a tip from the late San Francisco comedy coach John Cantu: A high-energy audience laughs and applauds longer than a low-energy audience. Therefore, if your audience is high energy, you need to allow extra time for laughter and applause when you calculate how much you can say in the time you've been allotted.

A low-energy audience is just the opposite. No one's talking, and the mood is kind of blah. (This mood often correlates to specific times of the day and week. For example, an audience that has just returned from lunch is typically low energy.) This audience is tough. You have to be high energy. You have to ignite the audience. Monday evening is another low-energy time.

## Noticing body language

Your audience's nonverbal behavior can tell you a lot about the effectiveness of your presentation. Are people nodding at what you say? Are they looking up at you? Are they leaning forward? Are they smiling? Or are they squirming in their seats, nudging one another, looking at their watches, and staring out the windows? (You don't need a PhD to interpret these signals.)

Don't judge the entire audience by the reactions of a single person. If you see one sourpuss who won't crack a smile, don't become obsessed with this person and make all your presentation decisions based on her reaction. Nothing you do works with the sourpuss, and you get nervous, feel you're bombing, and screw up. If you look at the other 99 percent of the audience members, you can see that they're enjoying your presentation — at least until you screw it up by focusing on the sourpuss.

## Asking questions to gauge the audience

If you don't know whether an audience agrees with you, disagrees with you, or even understands you, just ask. That's the direct method of reading audience reaction. ("How many of you are familiar with the marketing test that I just talked about?", "How many of you disagree with the results of the customer survey?", or "How many of you have never seen these numbers?")

# *Helping Your Audience Get Comfortable*

Most people are cautious in an unfamiliar situation. If they're interacting with a stranger, they assume a conservative demeanor. They don't let their guards down until they're sure they can do so safely. Audiences react in much the same way. If Robin Williams steps up to a podium, the audience members know they have permission to laugh. If someone the audience doesn't know steps up to the podium, people in the audience don't know how they're expected to behave. You have to tell them.

Management communication counselor Jim Lukaszewski calls this process *giving permission.* "Most of us are strangers in front of crowds," he explains. "So you have to give the audience permission to enjoy your speech." Jim likens this process to having a continuing side conversation with the audience. "I give them substantive information in my speeches," he explains. "But I also keep giving them permission to react in various ways."

What kind of permissions must audiences receive? It depends on what you want to accomplish and how you want the audience to react. The following list shows you three important permissions you can bestow on your listeners:

- ✔ **Permission to laugh:** Do you want to use humor successfully in your presentation? One of the most important permissions you can give your audience is permission to laugh. Joe DiNucci, vice president of sales at Immersion, is famous for his humor-filled talks to customers and employees. He starts by telling them it's okay to enjoy themselves. He'll say something like, "I intend to communicate and inform and enlighten and bring insight, but it is an explicit goal that you be entertained. So loosen up your tie. Loosen up your mind. Turn off the immune system that rejects anything that's amusing. I promise you there's a lot of meat in this material, but we also put some fun in with it too."

- ✔ **Permission to learn:** Jim Lukaszewski likes to give his audiences permission to learn. He says, "I believe this is a really important speech. I'm going to be talking about three sensitive, important topics. I'll go into more detail later. But I think when you leave here today, the things you'll really remember about this talk are these key areas . . ." By telling the audience what's important, he gives the audience insight into his interpretation of his own talk. "I've given them permission to enter my psychological being," he explains. "Now they can actively follow the outline with me — not just react to it as I dump it out there."

- ✔ **Permission to write:** Here's some uncommon knowledge from Jim — one of the most important permissions that you can give is permission to take notes. He starts by saying something like "My speech is packed with information you'll want to remember. That's why there are pencils and paper at your seats. And if you don't have some, please make friends immediately with someone who does, because you'll need them."

This permission flies in the face of the traditional wisdom that considers writing to be a distraction. "A lot of trainers believe you can't have people writing and paying attention to you at the same time," Jim says. "That's dumb. What is greater than having hundreds of people writing things down as you speak?" How does he make sure they don't miss anything? "I shut up and let them write," he explains. "And guess what — if I stop talking, they start writing." Encouraging your audience to take notes is especially helpful when you present information they need to remember: new office procedures, technical directions, and so on.

# Taming a Tough Audience

The audience was so tough that when they gave the presenter a standing ovation, they were standing on his chest. When the presenter began to talk, the audience took its seat — and everything else that wasn't nailed down. When the presenter asked, "Am I on target?" the audience said, "Bull's-eye!" and took aim.

Not every audience you ever address will be an absolute delight. When you face a tough crowd, you have some choices. You can figure out the problem and handle it, or you can wait for a standing ovation — on your chest.

## Handling hecklers and other pains in the neck

The traditional notion of a heckler is someone who interrupts a presenter by shouting out hostile remarks or questions. (Of course, that definition could also apply to the White House press corps.) I'm going to define heckling a little more broadly. My definition of heckling is anything that someone does purposely to distract you or the audience from your presentation. You may encounter some of the following hecklers:

✔ **The nonheckler:** I want to start with some uncommon knowledge from John Cantu. *The most common distractions caused by audience members may seem like heckling, but they're not.* Don't assume you're being heckled. Your audience is innocent until proved otherwise.

✔ **The dweeb:** The dweeb unintentionally engages in distracting behavior. Suppose you ask a rhetorical question about what you can do when faced with an unethical competitor. The dweeb shouts out an answer. Technically, it's not heckling, because dweebs aren't purposely trying to disrupt the proceedings. They just don't know any better.

✔ **The one-upper:** The one-upper wants attention. If you ask the audience for questions, the one-upper jumps in with a sarcastic comment or tough question designed to embarrass you. It's not that the one-upper dislikes you personally or even disagrees with your positions. You're just a prop for the one-upper to manipulate in an unending quest for attention.

# The do's and don'ts of dealing with hecklers

Although many presenters worry about facing hecklers, the situation isn't all that common. If you're not talking about outsourcing or another controversial business issue, the problem usually doesn't arise. But if you ever have to confront hecklers, use these do's and don'ts for handling them:

- **Do identify the type of heckler.** Why are you being heckled? Is the heckler a rival trying to undermine your talk? Is he opposed to you or your views on corporate strategy? Does he simply want attention? You must know why the heckling started so you can determine how to end it.

- **Do be empathetic.** Sometimes, you can defuse a heckler just by acknowledging her point of view. Let her know that you understand her position, even though you don't agree with it.

- **Do suggest that the heckler speak with you after your presentation.** You can say: "Listen, my friend, this is my presentation. If you want to argue with me afterwards, you're more than welcome. I'll be glad to talk to you later, but right now, you're insulting the rest of the audience."

- **Do look for help.** You shouldn't have to deal with audience members who are out of control. Seek help from the person running the meeting or the person who invited you to present. You can also appeal to the audience members for assistance. (Let them tell the heckler to shut up.)

- **Don't argue.** It just gives legitimacy to the heckler and makes you look bad. And that's exactly what the heckler wants.

- **Don't get angry.** Hecklers want control. If you get angry, you give them what they want — a negative reaction (and confirmation that you've lost control). So always stay calm. If nothing else, it drives the heckler nuts.

# Dealing with other distractions

Hecklers will probably remain a rare occurrence at your presentations; other distractions are far more common. If you're giving a presentation at a business lunch or dinner, a waiter will inevitably drop some dishes during your talk. If there are high-level executives present, one of them will be called out. The audience member with the loudest cell phone will receive a call while you're presenting. The list goes on.

## Heckling the hecklers

The greatest nightmare for many presenters is the prospect of being interrupted by a heckler. But don't overlook the fact that being heckled provides a great opportunity for the presenter to respond with wit and acumen. In fact, a good retort is usually remembered long after the actual presentation is forgotten. Following are some examples.

Al Smith was a popular governor of New York and a presidential candidate. During a campaign speech, he was interrupted by a heckler who yelled, "Tell 'em what's on your mind, Al. It shouldn't take long." Smith didn't miss a beat. He replied, "I'll tell 'em what's on both of our minds. It won't take any longer."

William Gladstone and Benjamin Disraeli were archrivals in the British Parliament. During one of their many debates, Gladstone yelled at Disraeli, "You, sir, will die either on the gallows or of some loathsome disease." Disraeli responded, "That, sir, depends upon whether I embrace your principles or your mistress."

President William Howard Taft received the ultimate heckle during a campaign appearance. Someone threw a cabbage at him. Taft evaded the projectile and said, "One of my opponents has apparently lost his head."

Nancy Astor, the first woman to sit in the British House of Commons, was an outspoken proponent of women's rights. During one of her speeches on the subject, a heckler interrupted with comments about Lady Astor's numerous bracelets and necklace. The heckler said, "You have enough brass on you, Lady Astor, to make a kettle." Astor's reply was quick and devastating: "And you have enough water in your head to fill it."

During a campaign speech, Al Smith was repeatedly interrupted by a heckler who shouted, "Liar!" After ignoring the heckler proved fruitless, Smith replied, "If the gentleman would be so kind as to give us his name as well as his calling, we should be happy to hear from him."

When these types of distractions occur, an audience often reacts with laughter. If that happens, laugh right along with the audience. You have to show the audience that you're handling the problem, and that you remain in control. (It's analogous to skidding while driving a car. If you steer into the skid, you regain control.) If you get upset about the distraction, the audience becomes uncomfortable, and you lose momentum.

Anticipate things that can go wrong, and have some quips ready to deal with them. For example, assume the room lights go out because of a power failure. You can say, "Now I'm really going to have to shed some light on the subject." (No it's not hilarious, but it doesn't have to be. It communicates that you're not upset and that you're still in control.)

# *Energizing a Dull Audience*

You can pick up subtle clues that tell you when you're not clicking with an audience. (People don't nod in agreement, but they do nod out.) If you want to save your presentation, then you have to take charge and provide some audience first aid — before it's too late. The following sections look at some resuscitation techniques for nonresponsive audiences.

# What to do if you're losing them

An audience first-aid kit includes a variety of devices for reviving interest in your presentation. Like the contents of a real first-aid kit, these devices range in strength. You have to know how to use the appropriate device for the audience in front of you. I find it convenient to diagnose a dying audience by sorting it into one of three categories, which I refer to as levels.

### Level one: You have audience members' attention, but they look bored or puzzled

The audience members are watching you present, but you sense that you're not connecting with them. They're fidgeting. They're not responding. What can you do? You must break out of the pattern you're in. Talk directly to the audience like it's a real conversation. Ask if they understand what you're talking about. Ask if they want you to give another example. Or tell them that what you're about to say is very important. Emphasize a key benefit that really puts them in the picture. ("Now I'd like to tell you the only guaranteed way to prevent yourself from being laid off in the next two years.")

Or you can say something that you feel is guaranteed to get applause. (The energy of their hands clapping helps prevent the onset of lethargy.) What if you're waiting for applause, and you don't get it? Say something like, "Oh, I guess you didn't think that was as important as I did." If they laugh, you've connected with them. If they don't, you're not any worse off.

John Cantu says that if you want to maximize your chances of getting applause, you should ask the audience some questions and tell them to respond with applause instead of a show of hands. ("How many of you can't wait until my presentation is finished?" Thundering ovation.)

### Level two: Audience attention is definitely waning

The audience is starting to drift off. People are staring at the ceiling, out the windows, and at their watches. The only thing they're not looking at is you. One of the simplest things you can do to revive this audience is also one of the most effective; just ask the audience members to stand up. Say something like, "You've been sitting down for a while now. And I think we could all use a short stretch. Everyone stand up. . . . Okay, sit back down. Feel better?" It's amazing how a stretch can transform the energy level in the room. (That's why they have a seventh-inning stretch at baseball games.) But let me add a word of caution: The effect is temporary. When the audience members sit back down, they pay attention for a minute or two, and you have a chance to get your presentation back on track with some exciting, dynamic stuff. If you don't, you lose the audience again.

### *Level three: Code blue — the audience is about to become comatose*

The audience is falling asleep or in a trancelike state or just plain dazed. You don't have time to ask them to stand up or applaud. You need to do something immediately to jar audience members out of their stupor. It must be loud or dramatic or both. Consider these tips:

- ✔ Pound your fist on the podium
- ✔ Move the mike toward a sound-system speaker to cause loud feedback
- ✔ Wave a $20 bill in the air and then rip it up
- ✔ Throw your notes on the floor
- ✔ Light the podium on fire

Any of these should wake up the audience. But here's the trick: You need to tie these actions into your talk so that they make a point. Otherwise, it looks like you were just trying to wake up the audience members. (You can't admit that your goal was to wake them up. They would resent that. It has to appear that you were giving your talk, and part of it happened to revive them.)

For example, you pound your fist on the podium. (Do it near the mike so it makes a loud noise.) Then you tie it into your topic. "That's the sound of customers beating their heads against the wall of our service department.", "That's the sound of your heart beating when you go on a job interview.", or "That's the sound of jobs being outsourced to another continent."

When you're planning your presentation, think of a few tactics to use in case you need to get your audience's attention back to your talk.

## Get a volunteer from the audience

One of the best ways to coax a response is to put people from the audience into your act. The rest of the audience identifies with the member who stands before them. Suddenly, your presentation becomes a lot more personal. (Using volunteers in training presentations is quite common to demonstrate some skill or exercise in front of the whole group.)

Talking with members of your audience before you give a presentation helps you get a volunteer. Whenever I've had to beg for a volunteer, the person who volunteered has always been someone I'd spoken with earlier. Why does this happen? Your guess is as good as mine. Maybe some kind of bonding takes place. The person now feels like we're friends and feels obligated to help out. Who knows? I can only tell you that it happens consistently.

# Adopting Surefire Audience Involvement Techniques

An old Chinese proverb says, "I hear and I forget, I see and I remember, I do and I understand." The point is that your presentation is more successful if you get your audience members involved. They learn more and remember more — two of your major objectives.

## Using psychological involvement

Involving audience members isn't limited to having them perform physical activities. You can also do things to get an audience psychologically involved.

The late San Francisco comedy coach John Cantu suggests involving your audience by activating their emotional connections. "There are certain things that mean a lot to people — their high school, their first car, their first date," he says. "Find a way to bring those things into your talk." It can be as simple as telling the audience to think about the first person they ever dated. "Anyone who hears you will automatically start thinking about this person," John explains. "They'll become very involved in your talk."

There's just one catch — you have to have a reason to ask the audience to think about the emotional subject. "It must relate to your talk and make a point," says John. Fortunately, that's easy to do. Just find something in your presentation that evokes similar emotions and link it to what you've asked the audience to think about. ("Think about your first date. Remember how you felt excited, scared, and happy, all at the same time? That's how I felt when I went to the bank to apply for a loan to start my company. . . .")

## Choosing icebreakers and other gimmicks

Many presenters rely on audience participation exercises and other gimmicks to keep their audiences engaged. Why bother? "Once you get audience members to speak, they become much more receptive to you," says Loyd Auerbach. That's why many of these gimmicks are called icebreakers. They warm up the audience. You may want to try a few of the following gimmicks.

### The table card

Are you presenting at a business breakfast, lunch, or dinner? Your audience will be sitting around tables, talking and eating before you begin. Put a card on each table or at each place setting. The card should contain something to provoke a discussion about your topic — a quote, a question, a prediction. Your audience becomes involved in your talk before you even speak.

### The greeting

Ask audience members to turn to the person next to them and say hello or shake hands. Is this corny? Absolutely. Does it work? Most of the time. It depends a lot on the type of audience and event. If you have a bunch of yuppie types who think they're too sophisticated for this icebreaker, make an adjustment. Instead of asking them to shake hands with their neighbors, ask them to exchange business cards. They'll think you're a genius.

### The question

One of the simplest ways to involve people in an audience is to ask for a show of hands in response to a nonthreatening question. Just the physical act of raising their hands can boost their energy level and receptivity. (It may be the most exercise they've had all day — especially if you're the last in a series of presenters.)

What should you ask? Many presenters like to ask questions that give them a better handle on the audience. "How many of you are here from our company's field offices? How many of you work in high tech?" (How many of you wish the presenter would stop asking dumb questions?) As trite as this survey technique may seem, it works.

But here's an important reminder from Allatia Harris, district director, faculty development and core curriculum evaluation Dallas County Community College District: After people in an audience respond to your questions, you have to acknowledge their response. "Some speakers ask questions, don't pay attention to the answers, and just plow ahead with their next scripted comment," she explains. "That's a big turn-off. It makes the audience feel like they're just props in your slick presentation."

### The invitation

You've given your presentation. You've asked for questions. No one responds. Here's some uncommon knowledge from Loyd Auerbach: Expand your invitation. Don't just ask for questions. Invite questions *and* comments. "Your speech may have been so great that no one has any questions," he says. That's why he always says something like "I'll be happy to take questions now. And if anyone has an experience that's related to the subject matter that you would like me to comment on, please speak up, because I'm sure other people here would like to hear about it." The invitation for comments often sparks a discussion.

Handling an audience is like handling a porcupine — you've got to do both with great care. But neither is really as frightening as it may first appear. After all, underneath that prickly exterior, both audience members and porcupines are soft and cuddly creatures. Keep them involved and deal with them fairly, and they won't stick it to you.

# Chapter 13

# What Did You Say? Fielding Questions

**M**any presenters let their guard down during the question-and-answer period. But doing so is a big mistake. Even if you gave a great presentation, a poor performance during the Q&A can totally change the audience's perceptions of you and your topic. That's the bad news. The good news is that if your presentation was mediocre, a strong performance during the Q&A can leave the audience with a very positive impression.

## Reviewing the Basics of a Q&A Session

Want to give a sparkling performance during a question-and-answer session? You can stack the odds in your favor by following a few basic rules.

## Anticipate questions

As any high school student can tell you, the secret to giving brilliant answers is knowing the questions in advance. In high school, this is called cheating. After you grow up, it's called anticipating the questions that you'll be asked.

How do you anticipate questions? Just use your common sense. Think about your presentation and your audience. Then generate a list of every possible question that the audience may ask. Don't pull any punches. Think of the toughest questions that may come up. Then ask your friends and colleagues to think of the toughest questions they can devise.

After you've compiled a comprehensive list of questions, prepare an answer for each one. Practice until you've got them down cold. Unfortunately, you may not anticipate every single question the audience is going to come up with, but you can think of some of them.

## Answer questions at the end

 Take questions *after* your presentation, rather than while you're giving it. If you take questions during your talk, it distracts both you and the audience, it makes your presentation harder to follow, and it ruins your rhythm. Tell the audience in the beginning that you plan to take questions at the end.

## Don't let a few people dominate

Don't let a few people ask all the questions (unless they're the only ones with questions). Why? It frustrates everyone else who wants to ask you something.

You want to take questions from as many different audience members as time permits. And be fair. Don't favor one section of the room over another. Try to call on people in the order in which they raised their hands. (Yes, it's tough to do it, but try anyway.) Don't give in to bullies who don't wait their turn and instead shout out questions.

 Establish the ground rules early. When you open the session up for questions, tell the audience that everyone is initially limited to a single question. Then, if time permits, you may take a second round of questions. If only the same few people keep raising their hands, ask if anyone else has questions.

## Don't let the questioner give a speech

You just asked for questions. Despite the fact that you're standing at a podium, and you've just made a lengthy presentation, someone in the audience may want to give another speech.

*You're* the presenter. You opened up the session for questions — not speeches. When one of these people starts giving a speech, you must cut it off. How do you do it? Watch CNN star Larry King. Callers to his show are supposed to ask questions. If a caller launches into a speech, King immediately asks, "Will you state your question, please?" Want to be more diplomatic? Say, "Do you have a question?"

## Listen to the question

If you want to be successful in a Q&A period, you must listen. I mean *really* listen. By *really listening,* I mean going below the surface of the words used by the questioner. Read between the lines. Watch the body language. Listen to the tone of voice. What is the questioner really asking? That's the question that you want to identify and answer.

For example, say you're leading a meeting of your department. After your presentation, you take questions. One person nervously asks about the company's strategy for the next quarter in light of its poor performance for the past few quarters. "Specifically, how does the company plan to become profitable?" After observing the questioner and knowing the context of the question, you respond, "I think what you're really asking is will the company be having any layoffs?" And, of course, that's exactly what is being asked.

## Repeat the question

One of the biggest mistakes presenters make is *not* repeating the question. And it's an enormous mistake. There's nothing more frustrating than giving a brilliant answer to a question that wasn't asked. You get frustrated because it's a waste of a brilliant answer. Your audience gets frustrated because you didn't answer the question.

There are three major reasons why you should *always* repeat the question:

- ✔ You make sure that everyone in the audience heard the question.
- ✔ You make sure that *you* heard the question correctly.
- ✔ You buy yourself some time to think about your answer. (If you want even more time, rephrase the question slightly and ask, "Is that the essence of what you're asking?")

## Don't guess

If you don't know the answer to a question, never guess. *Never.* It's a one-way ticket to zero credibility. Once in a while, you may get lucky, beat the odds, and bluff the audience. But most of the time, someone calls your bluff. Then you have a big problem. First, you're exposed as not knowing the answer you claim to know. More important, the audience members wonder if you bluffed about anything else. And they project their doubts backward to encompass your entire presentation.

If you don't know, admit it. Then take one, some, or all of the following actions:

- ✔ Ask if anyone in the audience can answer the question.
- ✔ Suggest a resource where the questioner can find the answer.
- ✔ Offer to find out the answer yourself and get it to the questioner.

Remember, nobody knows everything (except my grandmother).

## End the Q&A strongly

The Q&A session is your last chance to influence audience opinion of your topic, your ideas, and you. So you want a strong ending. To achieve that, avoid the following:

- ✔ **Don't wait for audience questions to peter out and say, "Well, I guess that's it."** You look weak and not in control.
- ✔ **Don't say, "We only have time for one more question."** It may be a question you can't answer or handle well. Again, this makes you look weak.

How do you achieve a forceful finish? Wait till you get a question that you answer brilliantly. Then announce that time has run out. (Of course, you'll be happy to stick around and speak with anyone who still has a question.)

What if you don't get any questions that you can answer brilliantly? Don't worry. Just make the last question one that you ask yourself. "Thank you. We've run out of time. Well, actually, you're probably still wondering about [fill in your question]." Then give your brilliant answer. It works every time.

End the Q&A session on time. Some audience members come solely for your talk. They don't care about the Q&A. They just want to get back to work or go to the next seminar, but they're too polite to go before it's all over.

## Coming Up with a Perfect Answer Every Time

Experts are people who know all the right answers — if they're asked the right questions. Unfortunately, your audience may not always ask the right questions. This section presents some ways to make sure your answers are expert, no matter what you're asked.

# Knowing how to treat the questioner

Questioners may be rude, obnoxious, opinionated, egomaniacal, inane, obtuse, antagonistic, befuddled, illiterate, or incomprehensible. You still have to treat them nicely. Why? Because they're members of the audience, and the audience identifies with them — at least initially. Use these suggestions for dealing with someone who asks you a question:

✔ **Do assist a nervous questioner.** Some audience members who ask questions may suffer from stage fright. They stammer and stutter, lose their train of thought, and make the rest of the audience extremely uncomfortable. So help these people out. Finish asking their questions for them if you can. Otherwise, offer some gentle encouragement. By breaking in and speaking yourself, you give nervous questioners time to collect themselves. They'll be grateful. And so will everyone else.

✔ **Do recognize the questioner by name.** If you know the name of the person asking the question, use it. This has a powerful effect on the audience. It makes you seem much more knowledgeable and in control. And the people whose names you say love the recognition.

✔ **Do compliment the questioner, if appropriate.** If the question is particularly interesting or intelligent, it's okay to say so. But be specific and say why. Some communication gurus advise never to say, "Good question," because it implies that the other questions weren't. If you're worried about this, then say, "That's an especially interesting question because . . . " This statement implies that the other questions were also interesting — a compliment. It also eliminates all the value judgments attached to the word "good."

✔ **Don't make the questioner feel embarrassed or stupid.** Remember your grade school teacher saying there's no such thing as a dumb question? She was wrong. There are plenty of dumb questions, and presenters get asked them all the time. But you don't want to be the one to point them out. No matter how idiotic the query, treat the questioner with dignity. If you go into a scathing riff about the stupidity of the question, you make yourself look bad, generate sympathy for the questioner, and discourage anyone else from asking a question.

✔ **Don't send the questioner a negative, nonverbal message.** It can take a lot of guts to rise out of the anonymity of the audience to ask a question, so don't discourage questioners by looking bored or condescending while they're speaking. Even if you think the question is imbecilic, look fascinated. Shower each questioner with attention. Give full eye contact. Lean forward. Show that your most important priority is listening to the question. Nothing is more insulting or dispiriting than a presenter who looks around the audience for the next question while the current question is being asked. And the questioner isn't the only one who gets offended. The whole audience picks up on it.

✔ **Don't attack the questioner.** No matter how offensive the question or questioner, stay calm and in control. Use diplomacy and finesse to dispose of such annoyances. If the questioner is a major jerk, the audience can see it. Don't become a jerk yourself by getting defensive. The questioner wants to provoke you. Don't take the bait. (See Chapter 12 for more on handling hecklers.)

## Designing your answer

You never know exactly how to answer until you hear the question, but I do have some general guidelines to help you prepare:

✔ **Do keep it brief.** Your answer should be a simple, succinct response to the question asked. Too many presenters use their answer as an excuse to give a second talk. Give everyone a break. If the audience wanted an encore, it would have asked for one. And remember, many members of the audience may not even be interested in the question you're answering. They're waiting to hear the next question — or to ask one.

✔ **Do refer back to your presentation.** Tying your answers back to your presentation reinforces the points you made earlier. This tactic also makes you seem omniscient. (You somehow foresaw these questions and planted the seeds of their answers in your presentation.)

✔ **Do refer to your experience.** You're not bragging when you make referrals to your personal and professional experience in your answer. That experience is one of the reasons you've been invited to give a presentation and is part of what makes an expert. The audience *wants* to hear about your experience.

✔ **Don't assume that you know the question.** Unless the questioners are rambling or need help, let them finish asking their questions. Too many presenters jump in before the question is fully stated. They *think* they know what the question is and start giving an answer. They look foolish when the questioner interrupts, saying, "That's not what I was asking."

✔ **Don't let the questioner define your position.** An alarm should go off when you hear a questioner say something like "Well, based on your presentation, it's obvious that you think . . ." Typically, what the questioner says that you think *isn't* what you think at all. Don't let anyone put words in your mouth. If this occurs, address the problem immediately — as soon as the questioner finishes asking the question. Point out the misconception contained in the question, and then firmly state your actual position.

✔ **Don't get locked into the questioner's facts or premises.** If the questioner makes assumptions with which you disagree, politely say so. If you dispute the questioner's statistics, say so. Don't build a nice answer on a faulty question. Start by dismantling the question.

✔ **Don't make promises you won't keep.** Don't say that anyone can call you at your office to ask questions if you know you won't take their calls. Don't say you'll find out the answer to a question if you know you won't. Don't offer to send information to someone if you know you'll never get around to it.

✔ **Don't evade questions by acting like you're answering them.** You're not obligated to answer every question. (You're *really not* under interrogation, although it may sometimes seem that way.) But if you evade questions, you lose credibility. It looks like you're ducking the issues. If you don't want to answer a question, say so firmly and politely. State the reasons why, and move on to the next question. Reasons may include advice from a lawyer, the information is a trade secret, or the information is confidential.

✔ **Don't depend on being asked a particular question.** It may not get asked. And definitely don't leave important points out of your presentation because you want to save them for the Q&A session. You may never get a chance to raise them.

## Delivering your answer

Having the perfect answer doesn't mean much if you can't deliver it effectively. But don't worry. The following simple rules ensure that your response will be — well, perfect:

✔ **Do be appropriate.** Match your demeanor to the substance of the question and your answer. If someone is confused, be understanding. If someone is blatantly offensive, be forceful and disapproving (without counterattacking). If someone is seeking information, be professorial. Never lose control of yourself. Never be discourteous.

✔ **Don't assume a new persona.** Many presenters undergo a transformation at the end of their talks. I call it the Cinderella effect. The presenter's brilliant, thoughtful, formal persona of the presentation is stripped away to reveal someone who is relieved to be done. It's like the clock struck 12, and the spell wore off. What happened to that confident expert who just delivered the presentation? All that's left is a glass slipper, which the presenter is rapidly putting in her mouth. The moral of this story is to stay in character. If you assume a new persona during the Q&A, you lose credibility. Which is the real you? Are you a chameleon? Was the confidence you showed during your talk fake?

✔ **Don't limit eye contact to the questioner.** Start by looking at the questioner, but as you give your answer, direct your eye contact to the entire audience. You're speaking to everyone — not just the questioner.

✔ **Don't be smug.** Smugness doesn't win any accolades from the audience, and it just creates a barrier. It can also backfire in a big way: The audience starts rooting for you to screw up. The first time you fumble an answer — even if you just misstate an insignificant detail — smugness comes back to haunt you.

# Seizing Six Great Question-Handling Techniques

How do you become an expert in deftly fielding questions? Practice. Practice. Practice. Practice what? The following six basic techniques (some of which were provided by my old friend Dr. Barbara Howard, a Denver-based corporate facilitator) can help you build your question-handling skills.

## Building a bridge

Watch a CEO evade a question in the following example. "Mr. Executive, are you going to increase the number of outside directors on your board's compensation committee?" "Well, sir, you want to know if I'm going to increase the number of outside directors on the board's compensation committee. What you're really asking is how we can make the board more responsive to shareholders. Let me tell you about my 12-step plan for a new corporate ethics program . . . "

The CEO has built a bridge. He's constructed a phrase that allows him to move from a question he wants to ignore to a topic he wants to address. In this case, the bridge is, "What you're really asking is . . ." You can use lots of bridges of this sort:

"It makes much more sense to talk about . . . "

"The real issue is . . . "

"The essential question is . . . "

"What you should be asking is . . . "

"If you look at the big picture, your question becomes . . . "

A word of caution about using a bridge: Use it to move a short distance away from a question you dislike, rather than to evade it completely. You lose credibility when you evade a question. (Politicians don't care because they have none to lose.) You have to give the appearance of at least attempting to answer.

# Exposing a hidden agenda

Sometimes, a question contains a hidden (or not-so-hidden) agenda. It may be a loaded question. It may be some other type of trick question. It may be a question containing an accusation. ("How could anyone in good conscience possibly suggest cutting funds for the human resources department?") No matter the method, the question has a "hook" in it. The questioner wants to provoke a certain answer so that he or she can argue with it. The question is just a setup for a fight.

Don't fall for this trap. Instead of launching into an answer, acknowledge your suspicions. Say something like "Wow, that one feels like it's got a hook in it. Tell me, what's your stake in this question? What's of interest to you in it?" This forces questioners to put their agenda on the table. Then you can deal with it in a straightforward manner.

Other responses that work well for this type of question include the following:

> "Do you have some thoughts on that?"

> "It sounds like you're expecting me to give you a certain answer. What is it you're trying to get me to say?"

The point is to expose the hidden agenda politely, and get the questioner to speak about it first.

# Putting the question in context

"Isn't it true that you were in the boardroom the night the chairman was found there stabbed to death?" This is known as a loaded question. It's framed in a way that makes the audience members jump to very specific conclusions that make you look bad. Your response has to broaden their frames of reference. You have to provide the missing information that "unloads" the question. "Well, yes, as the company's chief janitor, I did go to the boardroom a few hours after the chairman died and the police were finished, so I could clean up the mess. That's why I was in the boardroom the night he was stabbed to death." The meaning of any words or behaviors can be distorted if they're taken out of context. It's up to you to give a context to any question that needs one.

# Redirecting the question

Someone asks a question. You don't have the vaguest idea how to answer it. What can you do? Get the audience involved. Redirect the question to the entire group. "That's an interesting question about the industry's long-term direction. Does anyone have any thoughts on the subject?" or, "Does anyone have any experience with testifying in a wrongful-termination lawsuit?"

If you can't respond to a question, admit that you don't know, and encourage someone in your audience to answer it. The audience is a tremendous resource — a veritable repository of knowledge. Take advantage of it.

If you know that someone in your audience is particularly well qualified to answer a question, find out if that person is willing to weigh in on the matter. For example, you get a question about what fees are due an employment agency if you want to offer a permanent job to a temporary worker. You may say, "Well, Sheila, our HR guru, is sitting right here. Can you help us out?"

## Rephrasing the question

"Last week's indictment of your chief lobbyist for bribing a senator has finally revealed how your parasitic company got federal approval for a drug that's already killed 200 people. Will you now issue a recall to remove it from the market?" Hmmm. Are you really supposed to repeat this question for the audience? I don't think so. In fact, you never want to repeat a question that presents a problem — doing so is embarrassing, difficult, hard to follow, and a bad idea. Here's the solution: Don't repeat the question word for word. Rephrase it to your advantage. "The question is about how we plan to convert our concern for public safety into action. Here are the steps we are taking to protect the public . . . "

Keep in mind that a question can be a problem just because it's too wordy. "In your opinion, will the actions of the Federal Reserve Board to control inflation through monetary policy, combined with global financial trends — particularly the devaluation of the Mexican peso — result in economic forces that validate or prove wrong the Wall Street bulls in the short term?" Huh? Rephrase the question so that the audience can understand it (assuming *you* can understand it). "The question is whether the stock market will go up or down in the next few months."

## Reversing the question

Someone in your audience may ask you a question for the express purpose of putting you on the spot. No sweat. Just reverse it. For example, the questioner makes a big show of appearing bored and asks, "What time are we going to take a break?" Don't get defensive. Just respond, "What time would you like to take a break?" It's mental judo. You use the weight of the questioner's own question against him.

# *Responding to Special Situations*

Handling questions from the audience is a very delicate situation. You often need to take a firm hand, but you don't want to alienate your listeners. Use the following tips to handle common problem situations:

- ✔ **A questioner interrupts you while you're answering.** Stop talking, and let this boor finish what he's saying. Then say something like "Please wait until I've finished." Then complete your answer. If the person interrupts again, repeat the process. Don't get into a fight. If the interrupter continues, other members of the audience will eventually intercede on your behalf. (If they don't, then they don't deserve to hear your pearls of wisdom.)

- ✔ **Someone asks about something you covered in your presentation.** Don't say, "I already covered that in my presentation." Perhaps you did, but maybe you didn't cover it clearly. If the person asking the question missed the answer in your presentation, then others may have missed it too. And if it was important enough to include in your initial presentation, then you can spend time going over it again. So answer the question. Try explaining it a different way this time.

- ✔ **Someone asks a question that was already asked.** If your answer will take more than ten seconds, politely refuse to answer. Say something like "We've already addressed that question." This situation is completely different from getting a question about something covered in your presentation. Here, the audience member simply hasn't been paying attention. If you answer the question, you're being rude to the rest of the audience. You're wasting their time. Want to be nice? Offer to talk with the questioner individually after the Q&A session is over.

- ✔ **Someone asks a completely irrelevant question.** You can say that it's not germane to the discussion, and go on to the next questioner. You can give the questioner a chance to ask a relevant question, or you can use the question as a springboard to raise a topic you want to discuss.

- ✔ **Someone asks a completely disorganized question.** You have a couple of choices. You can ask the person to restate the question (not a good idea, because you'll probably get a question more disorganized than the first attempt). You can respond to part of the question (a part that you liked), or you can offer to talk with the person individually after the Q&A session is concluded.

- ✔ **Someone asks multiple questions.** You have a few options for handling this situation. You can tell the questioner that you can answer only one of the questions due to time constraints and fairness to other audience members. (Offer to answer the other questions later, after everyone else has had a turn to ask one.) You can answer all of the questions in the order asked, or you can answer all of them in an order you choose. (Exercise these last two options when you feel that answering the questions is to your advantage.)

✔ **Someone asks a long, rambling question.** If you see where the question is going, gently interrupt (citing time considerations), and pose the question concisely in your own words. Confirm that you've understood what the questioner wants to know. Then answer it. If you don't see where it's going, use the Larry King technique. Ask, "Can you state your question, please?"

# Handling Tough Questions

Certain types of questions are designed to put you at a disadvantage. What follows are some tough questions you must be ready to identify and handle:

✔ **The yes-or-no question:** "Is your company going to form an alliance with the Okkie Corporation, yes or no?" Don't get trapped by this type of question. Unless you're under oath on a witness stand, you're not required to provide a yes-or-no answer. If the question requires a more complex answer, don't hesitate to say what needs to be said. "The formation of an alliance between our company and Okkie depends on a number of factors . . . " Does this kind of response evade the question? Not really. It evades *the form of the question* that the questioner is trying to force on you, but your answer does address the question.

✔ **The forced-choice question:** This is a close relative of the yes-or-no question. Here, the questioner wants to force you to choose between two alternatives, but you're not obligated to do so. Sometimes, both alternatives offered are bad. ("Does your plan omit security guards at company headquarters because they're too expensive or because you forgot to include them?" "Neither. I didn't include them because they're not needed.") Sometimes, you just don't want to choose between the alternatives. ("What is the main focus of your growth strategy — developing new products or cutting costs?" "Actually, we intend to do both of those and more. We will also be acquiring new products, expanding our sales force . . . ")

The classic response to a forced-choice question is contained in an old joke. A senator is asked, "Are you for the war or against the war?" He replies, "Some of my friends are for it, and some of my friends are against it. I stand with my friends." (Of course, this response evades the question, but it was a senator answering.)

✔ **The hypothetical question:** What if . . . the product doesn't sell up to your expectations? . . . the board turns down your proposal? . . . pigs could fly? Don't get sucked into the morass of hypothetical questions. You've got enough real things to worry about. Just say something like "I don't anticipate that happening, so we'll cross that bridge if we come to it."

✔ **The top question:** Someone asks, "What are the top five challenges facing your industry?", "Which will be the best ten fields for finding a job ten years from now?", or "What are the three most useful features of your software?" Your answer will be "wrong" no matter what choices you make, because someone will argue about your selections. Here's an easy fix for this problem: Any time you get this type of question, purge the number from your answer. "Well, we can debate all day about what the top five challenges are, but I can tell you that some of the major challenges facing the industry include . . . "

✔ **The false-assumption question:** The classic example is "Have you stopped beating your wife yet?" The question assumes that you've been beating your wife. (And you may not even be married.) False assumptions can also include incorrect facts and statistics, as well as incorrect conclusions that the questioner has drawn from your talk. The solution: Point out the false assumption, and correct it immediately.

✔ **The implied question:** "The time frame you outlined for the product release just doesn't seem like it will work." This is a comment, not a question, but that's okay. Many Q&A sessions begin with a request for questions *or comments.* In some cases — like this one — the comment will imply a question. It's your job to flush it out. "It sounds like you really want to know how we'll get the product fully tested in only two months. Here's our plan . . . "

✔ **The multipart question:** "Could you tell me if we'll be receiving raises this year, and if not, why not, and if so, how big will they be?" Whoa. Slow down there, pardner. That's what's known as a multipart question. When you get one like this, divide it up, and answer one part at a time.

# Handling Hostile Questions

One of the great fears facing many presenters is the prospect of dealing with hostile questions. Stop worrying. You can use tried-and-true techniques for handling this problem. In fact, a little planning can significantly reduce your chance of receiving these pesky questions.

## Identifying hostile questions

Don't put a chip on your shoulder and assume that anyone who disagrees with you is hostile. Even people who disagree can have legitimate questions. They don't necessarily want to argue with you. They may just want information.

Also, don't assume that someone who asks pointed questions disagrees with you. The exact opposite may be true. Someone who agrees with you may ask a tough question, hoping that your answer can persuade others in the audience. So some of your toughest questions can come from your biggest allies. Don't assume that these audience members are hostile.

If someone asks you a trick question — that's hostile. "Have you stopped kicking back money to your customers yet?", "Do you still make your vendors pay bribes before you give them a contract?", or "Isn't this an amazing business achievement — for a woman?" It's safe to assume these questioners are out to get you.

## Heading hostile questions off at the pass

The simplest way to handle hostile questions is to not get any. Unfortunately, I can't guarantee that you won't, but these techniques can help you minimize the number you do receive:

- ✔ **The inoculation:** Can you anticipate specific hostile questions that you may receive? Then raise them and answer them during your presentation. By beating your antagonists to the punch, you leave them with nothing to ask you.

- ✔ **The admission:** Admit at the outset of the Q&A session that you're not the world authority on everything. Set audience expectations properly about the extent and areas of your expertise. Tell the audience what you don't know. This helps defuse potential hostility and disappointment resulting from your inability to answer specific questions.

- ✔ **The revelation:** At the outset of the Q&A session, announce that the people who ask questions must begin by identifying themselves. They must reveal their name, company department, and anything else you want to require. Having to reveal this information is a major barrier to hostile questioners. They don't like losing the cloak of audience anonymity. Acting like a jerk, being hostile, or getting confrontational with the presenter is a lot easier if no one knows who you are.

## Dealing with hostile questions

Receiving a hostile question is like being tossed a bomb. You need to know how to defuse it before it blows up in your face. Use the following tactics:

- ✔ **Empathize with the questioner.** Start by recognizing that the questioner is upset, and assert that you *understand* her point of view even if you don't agree with it. Make sure you communicate that you bear no personal animosity toward the questioner. Your disagreement is solely about the issue in question. "I can see that you feel strongly about the new corporate logo, and I understand where you're coming from. Let me give you a few more facts that may affect your opinion. . . . "

✔ **Establish common ground.** Find an area where you and the questioner can agree, and build your answer from there. "Then we agree that the budget will have to be limited to 75 percent of what we spent last year. We just differ on how to allocate the money. . . . " If you just can't find any common ground, try this all-purpose (albeit somewhat lame) response that works for any hostile question: "Well, at least we agree that this is a controversial issue. . . . "

✔ **Put the question in neutral.** If you get a question loaded with emotionally charged words or phrases, rephrase the question in neutral terms. (See "Rephrasing the question," earlier in this chapter.)

✔ **Be very specific.** Talk about specific facts and figures. Be concrete. The more you get into theory, speculation, and opinion, the more opportunity you provide for disagreement. You want to limit the opportunities for arguments.

✔ **Ask why they're asking.** What if you're on the receiving end of a loaded question or any other blatantly hostile query? Don't even bother giving an answer. Just ask, "Why did you ask that?" This can go a long way toward defusing the situation. The questioner, often embarrassed that you spotted the trap, may withdraw or modify the question. (See "Exposing a hidden agenda," earlier in this chapter.)

✔ **Elude the jerks.** Don't allow continued follow-up questions from people who just want to interrogate you in a hostile manner. (Unless they've got a badge.) You should be giving everyone in the audience a chance to ask questions. And if you're going to let one person dominate (which you shouldn't), why on earth would you give this opportunity to a hostile questioner? If you want to go one-on-one with someone, do it one-on-one — after the Q&A session is concluded.

# *Persuading a Silent Audience to Ask Questions*

Every question-and-answer session requires one item: questions. If you make a big deal of asking for questions and no one responds, it seems like you've somehow failed. You can use these tips to eliminate this problem:

✔ **Plant a question.** Arrange in advance for someone in the audience to ask you a question. (Just make sure it's someone you can trust.) Or go all out and plant several people throughout the audience. (For maximum impact, don't tell them about one another.)

✔ **Ask yourself a question.** No one wants to break the ice? Break it yourself. "When I talk about this topic, the one thing everyone usually wants to know is . . ."

✔ **Ask a question you were asked privately by an audience member.** If you get to the site of your presentation well in advance of your talk (as you should), you may get to speak with members of your audience — the early arrivers. And you'll certainly touch base with the person responsible for your presentation. During these conversations, you may receive questions about your topic. Just because they're asked before you speak doesn't mean they can't be used after. "When I arrived here today, I had an opportunity to meet some of you and chat a little bit. And someone asked me . . ."

✔ **Solicit written questions in advance.** Want to guarantee that you get questions? Arrange for the audience to submit written questions before you start giving your presentation. This arrangement has several benefits. Audience members who are uncomfortable asking a question in public have no problem submitting anonymous questions. Also, you get to pick the questions that you want to answer. And you can "submit" your own questions (and act like they came from the audience).

If you're presenting within your own company or organization, ask potential audience members to submit advance questions by e-mail. If you're presenting to a group from various organizations, ask audience members to write and submit advance questions while they're waiting for your presentation to begin.

✔ **Ask the audience a question.** Involve the audience in the question process in a nonthreatening way. Ask a survey-type question that can be answered with a show of hands. Then use the response to generate a discussion. "By a show of hands, how many of you think the mainframe computer will become a commodity item in the next ten years?"

✔ **Offer to take questions privately.** Sometimes, a lack of questions stems from the nature of your topic. If you're dealing with a sensitive issue — layoffs, personnel matters, workplace harassment, and so on — don't expect people to discuss their questions and concerns in public.

# Part IV
# Mastering the Power of PowerPoint

The 5th Wave          By Rich Tennant

"Nothing serious. I'm still trying to use a pair of nun-chucks in my PowerPoint presentations."

# In this part . . .

**H**ey, we live in the age of computers. So even if you don't present on a regular basis, you need to know how to use PowerPoint. In this part of the book, I describe the basic techniques for designing and creating PowerPoint slides that look good. You can also find out how to use advanced features like animation, video, audio, and other special effects — the stuff that wows an audience. Most importantly, I tell you how to avoid the common PowerPoint mistakes that really annoy people.

# Chapter 14

# Employing Stunningly Simple Design Techniques

* * * * * * * * * * * * * * * * * * * * * * * * * * * * * * * * * * * * * * * * * * *

*In This Chapter*

▶ Designing effective slides

▶ Checking out templates

▶ Wowing with technical tricks

* * * * * * * * * * * * * * * * * * * * * * * * * * * * * * * * * * * * * * * * * * *

Some people think PowerPoint is the greatest thing since sliced bread — especially if they're making a presentation about bread. Other people are less charitable in their opinions. But no matter where you stand on the subject, PowerPoint has become a ubiquitous presentation tool in the business world. For better or worse, you're now expected to have PowerPoint slides to accompany almost anything you say. So you'd better know how to use this tool effectively. But don't worry. In this chapter, I show you some basic design techniques for creating a polished PowerPoint presentation.

For more details on PowerPoint, check out the latest version of *PowerPoint For Dummies* by Doug Lowe (Wiley).

## Detailing the Do's and Don'ts of Design

Following a few basic rules of design ensures that your PowerPoint slides read well, look good, and don't make your audience think they're watching a tribute to the psychedelic '60s. The following subsections go over some things you should keep in mind.

All the PowerPoint design tips in this section work for regular slides and overheads as well. See Chapter 10 for more details on slides, overheads, and other visual aids.

# Tailoring text

Snappy text on your slides doesn't do much if no one knows what it says. Here are some rules to make your words stand out.

### Do make text large enough to read

The size of the room where you present affects how large the text should be. As a general rule, don't make the text size smaller than 30 point.

### Do keep the text style simple

Many speakers feel compelled to "pretty up" their visuals with fancy text. Don't fall prey to this temptation; fancy text can make your slides and overheads difficult to read. "I'd rather look at a simple blocky type than something artsy like old-English lettering," says Rachael Brune of Canyon Design in San Francisco, California. And here's another reason to keep it simple: "An artsy text style that works on a white background may be unreadable on a colored background," she says. "Then your points don't come across." Three fonts that display well when projected are Arial, Helvetica, and Verdana. Consider using one of them for your text.

Two text effects that are common in printed material should be avoided in PowerPoint presentations: italics and underlines. They're difficult to read when projected.

### Do check for spelling errors

Nothing is more embarrassing than a typo projected onto a large screen. So make absolutely sure to eliminate all spelling errors from your slides. (PowerPoint has a spell checker under the Tools menu.) And no matter how many times *you* proof them, have someone else take a look at them.

### Do use builds

A *build* is a series of slides or overheads in which each successive slide contains the bullet points from the preceding slides plus a new bullet point. Builds have become a standard part of business presentations. They provide a good way to emphasize key points. (The downside is that you need more slides. For example, say you want to make six points. You can put all six points on one slide. Or you can do them as a build, which means using six slides.)

Before you go berserk with builds, here's a warning from Rachael: Don't overdo them or put them into your talk just for the sake of having them. "Builds should be used only to emphasize important points," she says. "Otherwise, it's just a waste of slides and audience attention." She also says the points on the build should relate to one another. Don't create a build that's just a random list of things. "If it's the four components of your business, that makes sense," she explains. "But if it's just four points that happen to follow each other, then don't do a build."

### Don't use all uppercase or lowercase text

A mix of uppercase and lowercase text is easier to read. All uppercase text may be okay for headings or subheadings, but don't use it for the body of the text.

### Don't use too much text

"Speakers tend to think everything they say has to be on a slide or overhead," Rachael says. "But if it's too text-intensive, people won't read it — no matter how nice it looks. It's just too overwhelming. You don't want to ask your audience to read a novel on the screen."

So what should you do? "Let the slides or overheads reflect the basic outline," Rachael advises. "Just put down the key things, and then fill in the blanks as you speak." Marketing consultant Marcia Lemmons calls this the 4 x 4 rule. Don't put more than four lines on a slide or four words in a line. Other authorities place the numbers as 6 x 6. The rule isn't set in cement. Just don't cram too much information onto one slide or overhead. And make sure you write key words, not full sentences.

### Don't mix a lot of fonts

"Try not to use more than two fonts," Rachael says. "It just clutters things up too much." Her major exception: slides that display a company logo, product name, or similar item that's identified by a specific font. Those items don't count toward your limit of two fonts.

## Going with graphics

It's been said that one picture is worth a thousand words. Of course, the wrong picture can be worth a thousand inappropriate words — words that are pointless, redundant, stupid, useless, and so on. That's why using graphics properly is essential for any PowerPoint presentation.

### Do use consistent templates

Visually, you need to strive to be consistent. It shows organization. Or as Rachael says, "If your visuals are kind of scattered, you can come off as scattered." What does being consistent mean? Don't mix and match slides or overheads from different presentations if they have different design templates. "You're showing one type of template, and then all of a sudden, there's a different kind," Rachael says. "It's jarring and distracting." If you use color overheads, don't suddenly throw in a black-and-white one.

### Do left justify your bullet points

Have you ever seen a slide where the bulleted items were centered? I rest my case. It looks terrible, and it forces the eye to work harder than it has to.

### Do appeal to both sides of the brain

A popular bumper sticker claims, "Guns don't kill, bullets kill." But in the case of presentations, bullet *points* kill. (Too many, that is.) "All these computer programs make it very simple to create lots of bullet points for visuals," says Rachael. "That's great for the left side of the brain — the logical, analytical side. But too many speakers starve the right side of their audience's brains. When they don't use drawings, graphs, cartoons, charts, or other graphics, they miss out on a great opportunity to connect with the audience."

### Do use relevant graphics

Graphics are good but only if they support a point. "You need a reason for using them other than that they're pretty," Rachael says. "Too many people throw graphics onto a text slide just to fill space. The image draws your eye to it. But if it doesn't relate to the bullet points, then it doesn't make any sense." Want some examples? "I've seen text slides that had silhouettes of people or stick figures in the corner," she says. "But those graphics didn't really say anything. They were just distracting."

### Don't overemphasize your logo

If you're going to use a logo on every slide, make it small. "It shouldn't be screaming at everyone," Rachael says. "Otherwise, that's all they'll notice, slide after slide." A logo should simply be a little element that says this is a presentation from your company or organization.

### Don't mix different types of clip art

Clip-art images can make your presentation more interesting and entertaining. But if they're not properly chosen, they can make you look disorganized and amateurish. The key is stylistic consistency. "If you use different styles of clip art, then your presentation will look like it's been patched together," observes Willy Keats, a Mountain View, California–based PowerPoint consultant and designer. "One slide shows a cartoon person. Another slide shows a realistic person. Another slide shows a photo of a person. And they're all supposed to represent the idea of a person." The problem: Your presentation doesn't communicate a unified message.

"Use clip art from one style for one presentation," advises Willy. "It gives your message a consistent image."

The clip art that comes with PowerPoint represents a variety of styles. "Go through them and use the ones that go together stylistically," Willy says. "That will help you tie your presentation together." You can find this clip art by going to the Insert menu, clicking on **Picture,** and then clicking on **Clip Art.**

# Cramming a quick course in color

Color can make or break your presentation. Colors can set the mood, convey information, and provide psychological comfort or distress. Most important, they can make it easier or harder to read the text on your slides. Here are some basic guidelines.

### Do look at the big picture

Philosophers often claim that the whole is greater than the sum of its parts. With slide and overhead shows, the whole can be *worse* than the sum of its parts. "You can have slides that look good individually," Rachael says. "But when you click through them, they don't work well together. They make your eyes bounce all over the place." How can you prevent this problem? PowerPoint has a slide-show feature that runs your slides on the computer screen. (You can find it in the View menu.) Use it to get an overall impression of your presentation.

### Do consider how your presentation will be used

Many PowerPoint presentations survive beyond the time they're projected onto a screen. Will you print out copies to distribute as handouts? Will you fax copies to people who couldn't attend your presentation? "Some things that work in color won't work in black and white," Willy says. For example, color type on a color background doesn't show up on a fax. "Black type and a light background is best if you're faxing your presentation," he says.

Want to preview what your presentation will look like in black and white? Click on **View.** Now you see a menu that gives you an option to convert your presentation to black and white. The exact wording of the menu option varies depending on what version of PowerPoint you're using.

### Don't emphasize everything

Have you ever seen college students who use a yellow highlighter to mark up 95 percent of every page in a textbook? What are they trying to emphasize — the stuff that's not yellowed in? If you want to visually direct attention to certain points with color, go ahead. But don't dilute your message by emphasizing everything.

### Don't use too many colors

The general rule is a maximum of four colors per visual — one color for the background, one color for headlines, one color for body copy, and perhaps a color for emphasis. (Graphs and complex images are exceptions to this rule. You may need more colors to make a pie chart or line graph understandable.) "Use a dark color for the background — maybe blue or purple — with yellow headlines and white body copy," Rachael says. "And you might use red bullets for emphasis, but don't get insane."

# Using Templates

You're not an artist or designer, so how are you supposed to know what colors go together? Or of you're using too many fonts? Or if the text is spaced properly on your slide? Don't worry. Templates to the rescue! They automatically make your design decisions and lay out your slide for you.

## Taking advantage of existing templates

PowerPoint includes many predesigned templates for creating your presentation. You just choose a style, and the program cranks out all your slides in that design. "Take advantage of the templates if you're a beginner," Rachael says. "They'll help you achieve consistency."

Willy agrees. "Your goal is visual consistency," he explains. "So if you stick with one template, you'll be okay. The problem comes when you want to integrate other material into your design. The artwork in the PowerPoint templates is so stylistically distinct it probably won't go with anything else you have."

Where do you find the templates? They appear in a menu on the right-hand side of your computer screen when you open PowerPoint 2002.

## Making your own templates

What if you want to make your own template? It's easy to do. And I highly recommend it, because it saves a lot of time. You don't have to keep reinventing the wheel — or, in this case, the slide. For example, instead of inserting and placing your corporate logo on each of your 40 slides, you do it once in a template. Then all your slides automatically have your logo. You can also use a template to set all your other design elements: fonts, type size and color, background color, and so on. In other words, you do the heavy design lifting just once instead of over and over again for each slide.

Here's how you do it:

1. Click **View.**
2. Click **Master.**
3. Click **Slide Master.**

That's it. Anything you put on the master slide will appear on all your slides.

# Transforming with Technical Tricks

Now that you know some basic design techniques, why not go the extra distance and turn your presentation into something really impressive? Here are some PowerPoint tricks that are easy for you to do and hard for your audience to resist.

## Controlling file size

Small is beautiful when it comes to file size. Unfortunately, PowerPoint presentation files can get very large. Here are two tricks for decreasing their bulk if you have PowerPoint 2000 or later editions:

✔ Turn off Allow Fast Saves. Here's how:

1. Click **Tools.**

2. Then click **Options.**

   Now you'll see the Save menu.

3. Make sure that the box next to Allow Fast Saves isn't checked.

✔ Don't use images with file formats such as BMP, TIFF, and PNG. They are very large.

Keep in mind that audio and video clips increase the overall size of your presentation file. Plan accordingly.

## Choosing JPEG or GIF

Want to keep your PowerPoint presentation file size under control? Use images that are JPEG or GIF. (JPEG is also known as JPG.) Both of these file formats are much smaller than other image formats such as BMP, TIFF, or PNG. But how do you decide between the two?

JPEG compresses smaller than GIF. It can also handle millions of subtle color variations, whereas GIF is limited to 256 colors. So use JPEG if you have an image with lots of colors and color patterns. Use GIF if your image has a few colors spread over large flat fields. In that situation, a GIF image looks better than a JPEG. A general rule says to use JPEG for photos and GIF for line art.

Use GIF if you want to animate an image or make it transparent. You can't do those things with JPEG.

## Creating a letterbox view

Here's an easy effect that will wow your Hollywood-minded audience members. You know that letterbox view of movies that you sometimes see on TV? Film snobs love it because it duplicates the rectangular dimensions of a movie screen. Otherwise, they'd have to watch the movie in the square shape of a television — heaven forbid! Anyway, you can easily format your PowerPoint presentation in a letterbox view to give it a different look and to make it stand out from the crowd. Here's how:

1. Go to the **File** menu, and select **Page Setup.**

2. You'll see a Page Setup dialog box (see Figure 14-1). Look at the Height. It will probably be 7.5 inches — the default number. That's how tall your screen will be. So change it to 5 or less.

3. Click **OK.** You now have a letterbox view (see Figure 14-2).

Don't like how it looks? Repeat the process, but change the number you put in Height.

Use images that have a landscape (horizontal) orientation.

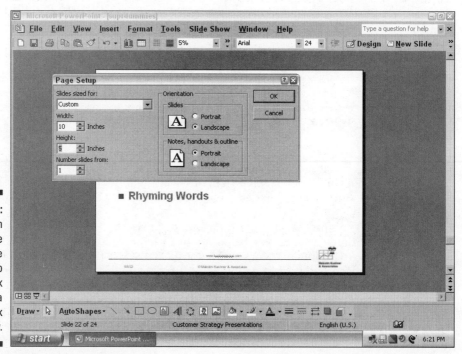

**Figure 14-1:**
You can
change the
height in the
Page Setup
dialog box
to create a
letterbox
view.

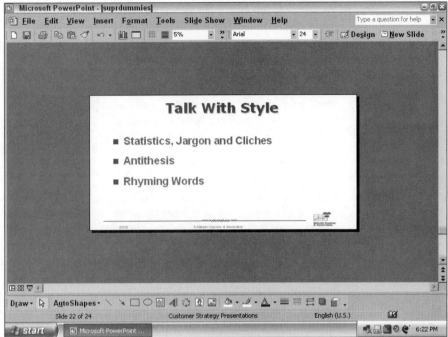

**Figure 14-2:**
A letterbox
view is
rectangular,
not square.

# Using screen captures

Want to talk about your Web site? The user interface on your hot new software product? Or anything else that appears on a computer? Then display an image of that particular computer screen in your PowerPoint presentation. It's easy:

1. Get your computer to show the screen that you want to capture.

2. Click **Print Screen,** and press the **Alt** key on your keyboard.

3. Open PowerPoint, and open the slide where you want the screen capture.

4. Go to the **Edit** menu, and click **Paste.**

   You can also use the shortcut by just going where you want to place the item and pressing **Control** and **v.**

How does it look? If it's too big, just adjust the size like you would any other image in PowerPoint. If it shows more than you wanted, just crop it like you would any other image in PowerPoint. (After selecting the picture, go to the **Picture** toolbar, and click on the **Crop** icon — it looks like two diagonal Xs. Crop marks appear on your picture, and you can resize it to your needs.)

## *Putting photos into words and objects*

Ever see a postcard with the name of a city spelled out in thick letters that are filled with images of that city? It's a very cool effect. And you can do it easily with PowerPoint. Of course, you don't have to use the name of a city. You can use any word you want. The word "success" filled with images of your company's products. Or your company's name filled with the smiling faces of your coworkers. You get the idea.

Here's how you do it:

1. Use WordArt to create your word.

   WordArt is a PowerPoint feature that lets you create fancy-looking text. It's on the **Draw** toolbar at the bottom of your PowerPoint screen when you're in editing mode. Just click on the icon of the crooked capital letter **A.**

2. Select the word you've created, and then click **the arrow next to Fill Color** on the Drawing toolbar.

3. Select **Fill Effects.**

4. Click on the **Picture** tab.

5. Click on **Select Picture.**

6. Find the picture you want to use, and click **Insert.** (See Figure 14-3.)

7. Click **OK.**

   You now have a photo included in a word (see Figure 14-4).

Pretty cool, huh? And there's more. This technique isn't limited to WordArt. You can also use it to put photos inside objects. Just go to the Drawing toolbar, and create an object. Click on the **square** or **circle** or **draw your own shape.** Or click on **AutoShapes** for a large selection of objects already drawn for you. Then proceed from step 2 above, substituting your object for the word.

## *Making stuff look three-dimensional*

Want to make a word or image 3-D? No problem. Create the object that you want to be 3-D: a line, a shape, a word written with WordArt. Now follow these steps:

1. Select the object.

2. Click the **3-D** button on the Drawing toolbar.

3. Choose a 3-D effect from the menu, and click on it.

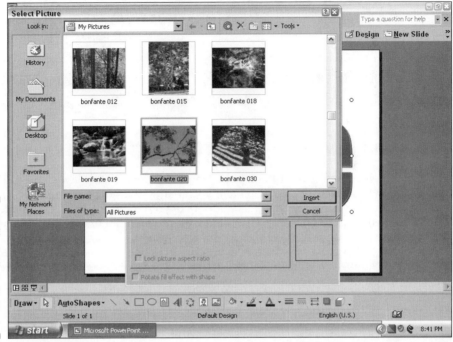

**Figure 14-3:** In the Select Picture box, you can choose a photo to insert into a word.

**Figure 14-4:** Including a photo in a word is a cool trick to use in a PowerPoint presentation.

Want to play with the image some more? Repeat steps 1 and 2. Then click on **3-D Settings.** This reveals a toolbar that lets you make further adjustments to the 3-D image: tilt its angle, change its color, lighten or darken it, change its thickness.

Although 3-D is fun to play with, it can get in the way of your message if used indiscriminately. Apply it carefully and sparingly.

## Numbering your slides

If you have to refer back to slides you've already displayed, number them — in both your presentation and your handouts. This step is particularly important if your audience has handouts of your slides as you're presenting. If you tell them to go back to the slide with the diagram of the improved widget maker, they will have to hunt for it, producing delay and confusion. If you tell them to go back to slide number 9, they will be able to do so instantly. (Numbering works for PowerPoint 97 through PowerPoint 2002.) Here's how you do it:

1. Go to the Insert menu, and click **Slide Number.**

2. You see a box called **Header and Footer**. It displays a menu for the tab called Slide. Down the menu is a box labeled **Slide Number.** Click the box so a checkmark appears.

3. Up at the top-right corner of the menu is a box labeled **Apply to All.** Click it.

That's it. Your slides in your presentation are numbered.

## Spell checking more than one language

In today's global economy, the chances are great that you'll eventually give a presentation to people from another country or culture. (See Chapter 22 for information about international presentations.) That means you may want to include some foreign words or phrases on your PowerPoint slides. If you do, you want to make sure they're spelled correctly. And PowerPoint will help you do that. Here's how:

1. Select the foreign text that you want to spell check.

2. Go to the **Tools** menu, and click **Language.**

3. Choose the language that you want, and click **OK.**

# Using the summary slide feature

Summary slides are good at the beginning or end of a presentation or any-where else you need a summary. And PowerPoint gives you a quick way to create them. (It works for PowerPoint 97 through PowerPoint 2002.)

Here's how you do it:

1. Open your PowerPoint presentation.

2. Click the **View** menu.

3. Click **Slide Sorter**.

4. Now you'll see small versions of all your slides. Select the ones that you want included in the summary slide. (See Figure 14-5.)

5. Click the **Summary Slide** button on the toolbar.

6. Now you get a summary slide called Summary Slide, and it will have a bulleted list of titles from the slides you selected. (See Figure 14-6 for an example.) Want to edit it? Just double-click it, and you can make any changes you want. For example, you can change the title "Summary Slide" to "Agenda" or "Conclusion."

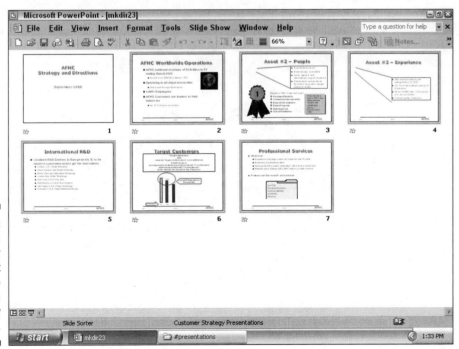

**Figure 14-5:**
You can use Slide Sorter to select slides to include in a summary slide.

# Summary Slide

- AFHC Worldwide Operations
- Asset #2 – People
- Asset #3 – Experience
- International R&D
- Target Customers
- Professional Services

**Figure 14-6:**
A summary slide contains a bulleted list of titles from selected slides.

SS/2 © AFHC **AFHC**

The summary-slide feature doesn't work if you haven't used PowerPoint's slide format to create your slide titles. (It's the format that automatically appears when you want to create a new presentation.)

## *Writing on your slides as you're talking*

You're in the middle of your presentation, and you get a question. You could give a great answer by modifying your slide. Wouldn't it be great if you could write on it as if it were a blackboard? Well, you can. PowerPoint lets you change the pointer to a pen. (It works for PowerPoint 97 through PowerPoint 2002.) Here's how:

1. Right click on your slide.

2. Select **Pointer Options.**

3. Click **Pen.** (See Figure 14-7.)

Want to change the pen color? Repeat steps 1 and 2, click **Pen Color,** and select a color.

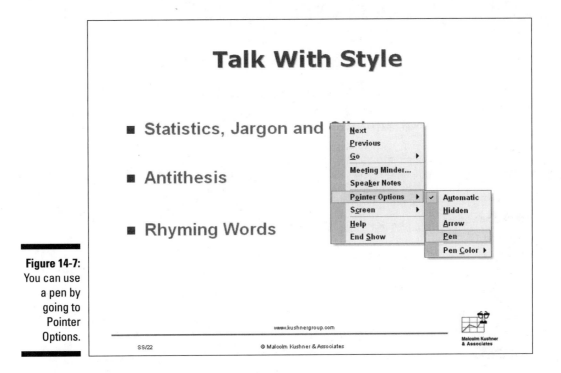

**Figure 14-7:**
You can use a pen by going to Pointer Options.

Want to change the pen back to a pointer? Repeat steps 1 and 2, then click **Arrow.**

Check out Figure 14-8 for an example of a pen in action.

## Directing diagram builds

Many business presenters like to use diagrams. You know, those pictures of all kinds of parts and lines and arrows and stuff connecting to each other. Examples include a model of a new product, an illustration of a channel marketing strategy — basically, anything. However, no matter what diagram you use, ensure that it makes a point. "If the point isn't clear from the diagram, then the diagram is too complex," Willy Keats says. "It should be broken down into smaller components." That's where the build comes in. Instead of beginning with a picture of the entire diagram, start with a component. Then add components one at a time until you finish with the entire diagram. The audience will understand the diagram more fully by seeing the relationships build gradually.

**Talk With Style**

- Statistics, Jargon and Cliches

- Antithesis  = OPPOSITES

- Rhyming Words

www.kushnergroup.com

SS/22                    © Malcolm Kushner & Associates

Malcolm Kushner
& Associates

**Figure 14-8:**
Presenters
can answer
questions
or clarify
points on
slides by
using the
Pen option.

## Creating a semitransparent background

Want to create an effect that makes your slides seem like a professional
designer made them? Use PowerPoint's semitransparent feature. It lets you
make images look like they're partially transparent. They're great to use as
backgrounds for your slides. Here's how you do it:

1. Click on **Insert.**

2. Click on **Picture.**

3. Click on **From File.**

4. Choose a photo to insert, and insert it.

5. Click on **View.**

6. Click on **Toolbars.**

7. Click on **Picture.** Now the **Picture** toolbar will appear.

8. Click on the **Color** icon, and you see a pop-up menu. (The Color icon is a picture of two vertical rectangles. It's the second image from the left on the toolbar.)

9. Click on **Washout** (for PowerPoint 2002). In older versions (PowerPoint 97), it's called **Watermark.**

You've now got a semitransparent background image that will contrast well with any text you put on top of it. How cool is that?

## *Making your ending look good*

You've given a great PowerPoint presentation. The audience is on its feet. And then you advance your presentation one screen too far. Here's the mistake: You were already on your last screen. So now the audience is looking at PowerPoint in its edit mode, with all the Windows toolbars and everything else. Congratulations. You've just pulled defeat from the mouth of victory.

But don't worry. There's a simple solution to ensure this doesn't happen. Put a black slide at the end of your presentation. In fact, put two of them there. (Just make a box, and shade it all in black.) That's what I do. Then if you advance the presentation too far at the end, all the audience sees is a black screen. And if you get nervous and advance it again, they'll still see a black screen. If you're so nervous that you advance it a third time, then you didn't read Chapter 5.

# Chapter 15

# Considering Cool Tricks to Whip Your Audience Into a Frenzy

*W*ant to go beyond the basics with PowerPoint? Good. Because in this chapter, you find a bunch of tricks that can take your presentation from super to superb. And here's the best part: Most of them require you only to hit some computer keys or click your mouse. Read on.

For more information on PowerPoint, check out the latest version of *PowerPoint For Dummies* by Doug Lowe (Wiley).

## Keeping the Flow Going

Have you ever watched someone fumble through a PowerPoint presentation? It's not pretty. Well, the slides may be pretty, but the presenter doesn't know how to show them correctly. And that's the problem. The message gets lost, because the presenter is inept using the PowerPoint technology. In this section, I give you some tips to make sure it doesn't happen to you.

## Starting the presentation from your desktop

You're introduced. You leap out of your seat. You walk briskly to the front of the room. You say, "Good morning." The audience answers, "Good morning." They're energized with anticipation about your presentation.

But that energy won't last long if they sit around waiting for you to get PowerPoint going. You know the routine. You double-click the PowerPoint icon on your computer desktop screen. Then you have to find the right presentation file. And when you click on it, PowerPoint opens it in edit mode. So you have to click the Slide Show button. Finally, you're ready to give your presentation. But the spell is broken.

Here's what you should have done: prepared your presentation so it would start automatically. You go up to the computer, click a button, and there's the first slide. No fuss. No muss. And your audience is still excited. Here's how you do it for PowerPoint 97 and later versions:

1. Open your PowerPoint presentation in edit mode. (It's the default mode when you open PowerPoint.)

2. Click **File.**

3. Click **Save As.**

4. Select **PowerPoint Show** from the menu options.

5. Click **Save.**

   If you double-click on this new file, it goes directly into Screen Show mode.

   Okay, that's a start, but you still haven't solved the problem. Because you still have to play with your computer to get to the new file before you can double-click it. So here's what you do:

6. Start Windows Explorer, and find your new file.

7. Click on it using the right mouse button.

8. Click on **Create Shortcut.** A new shortcut appears in Windows Explorer, as shown in Figure 15-1.

9. Drag the shortcut onto your computer desktop screen.

10. Click on the **shortcut,** and it's showtime.

**Figure 15-1:**
You can drag a shortcut from Windows Explorer to start your presentation from the desktop.

# Hitting shortcut keys

Another way to keep a PowerPoint 97 (or later version) presentation moving at a good pace is to use the shortcut keys available on your keyboard. Here are two that you should memorize:

- ✔ **B:** Pressing the **b** key once replaces your slide with a black screen. Pressing **b** again replaces the black screen with the slide you had there before.

- ✔ **W:** Pressing the **w** key once replaces your slide with a white screen. Pressing **w** again replaces the white screen with the slide you had there before.

The screen-blanking shortcut keys come in handy when you get a question that takes you away from discussing the slide you're projecting. Instead of having the audience look at a slide that has nothing to do with what you're talking about, you can just blank it. You can find out about additional shortcut keys in the latest version of *PowerPoint For Dummies* by Doug Lowe (Wiley).

## Showing your slides out of order

Here are some shortcuts that let you show your slides in any order you wish for PowerPoint 97 and later versions:

- ✔ Pressing **Home** takes you to the first slide in your show.
- ✔ Pressing **End** takes you to the last slide.
- ✔ Pressing **12** and **Enter** takes you to slide number 12. (And so on.)

This last one — entering the number of a slide — is particularly useful. It gives you a lot of flexibility. You can decide as you're presenting which slides you want to use depending on audience reaction and interests. Just prepare a slide for every possible contingency.

You probably don't have the time to memorize the numbers of all your slides if you want to use them out of order. So don't bother. Just keep a list that you can glance at as you're presenting. Include the slide number and the slide topic. Problem solved.

What if you planned a half-hour presentation, and just before you start, you're told you're getting only 15 minutes? It happens all the time. Don't worry. You can be prepared for this situation. Here's how: Create your show in modules. A *module* is a group of slides that addresses a particular topic. Then write down the slide number that starts each module. Now you can easily shorten your presentation. Just jump past the modules you decide not to use. And make sure you have a good concluding module. You never know when you may just want to go straight into your conclusion.

## Using hidden slides

Do you have some slides you're not sure whether to use? Hide them. Then you can decide as you're giving your presentation whether to show them. Here's how for PowerPoint 97 and later versions:

1. Go to the slide that you want to hide.
2. Click **Slide Show.**
3. Click **Hide Slide.**

That's it. The slide is still in your presentation, but it won't show unless you want it to. Want to show it? When you're at the slide immediately before the hidden slide, press the **h** key. The hidden slide appears. After you talk about it, advancing the presentation takes you to your next slide. Jot down the slides you've skipped to save time.

If you go backwards, you will show the hidden slide even if you didn't show it going forward.

Hidden slides are great for detail information that you may or may not want to get into. For example, you're doing a presentation about next year's budget from a 50,000-foot viewpoint — basic expenses like R&D, sales and marketing, and so on. Someone wants to know more about the cost of the company's television advertising campaign. You can have a hidden slide about advertising costs ready to go. You weren't planning to use it, but you were ready.

## Linking to other documents and the Web

*Hyperlinks* (connections to a Web page or file or another slide or PowerPoint presentation) provide another way to change the order of your presentation. They let you move to documents outside your PowerPoint show. For example, say you were talking about contract language in sales agreements. You get to a bulleted item that says, "Use simple language." Instead of just talking about it, you could click on that text, and suddenly, the entire contract would be projected on the screen. How? You hyperlinked the text to a Microsoft Word document of the contract.

### Linking to documents

Text or image in a PowerPoint slide can be hyperlinked to another document. Here's how you do it.

1. Select the word or image that you want to hyperlink. (With a word, you can just put the cursor on it. With an image, you have to select it all.)

2. Click on it.

3. Click on **Insert.** (You can right mouse click for a shortcut.)

4. Click on **Hyperlink.**

5. You can see an **Insert Hyperlink** dialog window. Click on the link to button called **Existing File or Web Page** window. (This is the language in PowerPoint 2002. Older versions have a different wording and layout, but it works pretty much the same way. Believe me, you'll know what to do.)

6. Choose the file that you want. Use the browse feature to find the file you want to link to.

7. Click **OK.**

That's it. If you hyperlinked an image, you won't see any change on your slide. If you hyperlinked text, it will change color and be underlined, like in Figure 15-2.

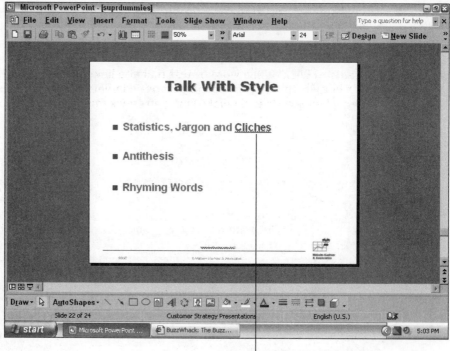

**Figure 15-2:**
A hyper-
linked word
is under-
lined and a
different
color.

A hyperlinked word

How do you get back to your presentation from the linked file? Just close the file. Then you're back at the slide you linked from.

You can also hyperlink to another PowerPoint presentation. Then you can play that presentation until you want to return to your original presentation. Just hit the **Escape** key, and you're back on the slide you linked from in your primary presentation.

Why would you want to link PowerPoint presentations? One reason is if you want to display pictures in both landscape and portrait orientation. PowerPoint forces you to choose one or the other. So you can create two PowerPoint presentations, one in each orientation, and link them together.

### Linking to Web sites

Want to give a tour of a Web site during your presentation? Hyperlinks make it easy.

1. Repeat steps 1 through 5 in "Linking to documents."

2. Find the window labeled Address:.

3. Type in the URL of the Web site you want to link to, as shown in Figure 15-3.

4. Click **OK.**

You can now click on the word or text that you linked and jump to that Web site. Of course, this step works only if your computer has a live Internet connection when you do it. So make sure you check that in advance.

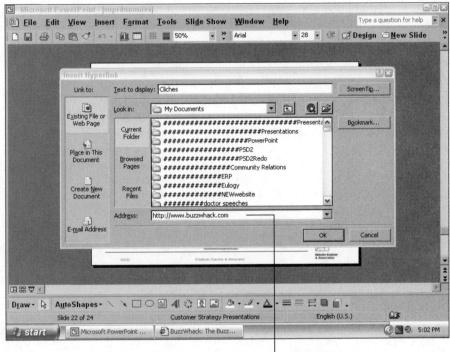

**Figure 15-3:**
You can link to a Web site by typing its address.

Type a Web address here.

# Using Audio

Most people associate PowerPoint with visuals, chiefly because most people use only PowerPoint's visual capabilities. And that's a shame, because PowerPoint is also a great tool for adding sound to your presentation. One picture may be worth a thousand words. But the right sound at the right time can really make a picture come to life, especially if it's a picture of a customer and the sound is a recording of the customer praising your products. In this section, I show you some simple ways to jazz up your presentations with sound.

# Knowing when to use different sounds

Using sounds in PowerPoint can add another dimension to your presentation — if you don't overdo them. Sounds can range from sound effects to music to recordings of someone talking. Here are a few ideas to get you started.

### Sound effects

Small touches can have a large effect in the quality of your presentation. Say you're giving a sales training presentation with a game-show-style question-and-answer board. Whenever you give the correct answer, a "bing" sound gives the proceedings an authentic TV feel. It's a small detail, but audiences love it. Use your best judgment when selecting a sound for each specific business presentation.

### Music

Music can set the tone for your presentation. In one of my presentations about American presidential humor, I have an opening slide that contains the "Washington Post March." After introducing my topic, I click the sound icon, and the march starts playing. Inevitably, the audience claps along. It's a great way to get them ready to hear about presidential stuff. (Don't play the music when you're actually speaking. It's distracting when the audience is trying to listen to you make your presentation.)

Music is good for filling time when you're not talking. For example, say that you've asked the audience to do an exercise. Silence may make them uncomfortable. (It's too reminiscent of grade school. "There will be no talking while you're taking the test!") Instead, you can click a sound icon on your slide and play an appropriate tune.

By the way, don't forget to get any necessary permissions for the music you use. Several companies sell royalty-free music. You pay for it once and then use it as much as you desire. I got the "Washington Post March" in that type of deal.

### Voices

Recordings of customers praising you, your company, or your products provide a great way to spice up a presentation. Keep them short — a minute or less. And, if possible, put a photo of the person speaking onto the slide. This helps "bring the testimonial to life." You can also use this technique for experts who agree with your opinions. There's no better way to convince an audience. And when your audience actually hears it from the third party (rather than you quoting it), that's even more convincing. One caveat: Don't overuse other voices. The audience came to hear *you* talk.

## Putting sounds into slide transitions

The easiest way to use sound is in transitions between slides. *Transitions* refer to what you see when one slide changes to the next in your presentation. If you add sound every time your slides change, you hear something. What? You get to decide. Here's how you do it for PowerPoint 97 and later versions:

1. Go to the slide that you want to work on.

2. Click **Slide Show.**

3. Click **Slide Transition.**

4. Look in the **Sound** window, and choose a sound from the menu. PowerPoint gives you some sound effect choices: Applause, Arrow, Bomb, Breeze, Camera, Cash Register, Chime, Click, Coin, Drum Roll, Explosion, Hammer, Laser, Push, Suction, Typewriter, Voltage, Whoosh, and Wind. But you don't have to use them. At the end of the menu, you see a choice called **Other Sound.** Click that and you can insert any sound file that's on your computer — music, voices, and so on.

5. Click on the sound you want.

If you want the sound to play on the transitions for all of your slides, then click the Apply to All Slides window.

Sounds in slide transitions get old fast. They can also become annoying. So if you use them, choose carefully.

## Adding sounds to slides

Have you ever watched a Three Stooges film? Imagine it without sound effects. It loses a lot. And that's my point. Used creatively, sound can add a lot to your PowerPoint presentations. You can play audio clips of customers praising your company. You can play dramatic music that underscores a point. You can literally have all the bells and whistles. Here's how you do it:

1. Select the slide you want the sound on.

2. Click on **Insert.**

3. Click on **Movies and Sounds.**

4. Click on **Sound from File.**

5. Find a sound file that you want to use.

6. Double click on the sound file.

7. Now you get a message: "Do you want your sound to play automatically in the slide show? If not, it will play when you click it." Click **Yes** or **No.** (This step doesn't occur in PowerPoint 97. It does occur in PowerPoint 2002.)

8. Then you get a sound icon on your slide. (See Figure 15-4.) You can move it anywhere on your slide or out of view off your slide. (Of course, if you're going to play it by clicking it, then you need to keep it on your slide, or you won't have anything to click.)

9. Want to play your sound? Put your slide show in presentation mode. If it's an automatic sound, it will play automatically. If it's not automatic, then click on the sound icon to hear it. (The sound won't play in edit mode unless you take some extra steps.)

**Figure 15-4:**
You can
move a
sound icon
anywhere
on your
slide.

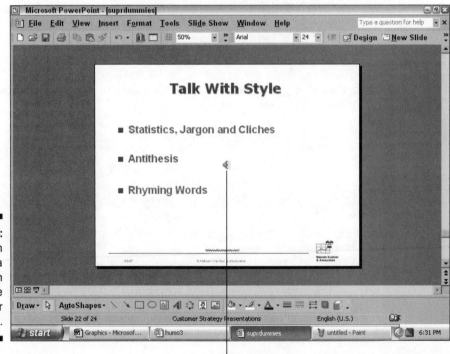

A sound icon

# Using sounds beyond PowerPoint

You're not limited to the sound files that come with PowerPoint. You can find lots of sound files on the Web or even create your own.

### Finding sounds on the Web

You can find free WAV files on the Web. Here are a few sites to get you started:

✔ www.wavsource.com

✔ www.findsounds.com

✔ www.soundamerica.com

✔ www.wavplanet.com

These sites provide a combination of sound effects, music, voices, and so on.

Just download the files you want to use to your desktop. Create one folder, and keep all the downloaded files for your particular presentation together in that folder. And don't forget to obtain any permission required to use them. Want to purchase sound files that are already legally cleared for you to use? Lots of sites on the Web provide this service. One that I like is www.soundrangers.com.

### Recording voices and other good stuff

Want some really cool audio for your PowerPoint presentation? Record it yourself. Call up a customer, and ask for a testimonial. You can record it over the phone. Record your company's CEO or other executives talking about key issues. Or record familiar sounds from your workplace, and use them as sound effects. The possibilities are limited only by your imagination. Make sure you get written permission before making the recording.

Here's how you can do it with a PC:

1. Attach a microphone to the microphone jack on the side of your PC.
2. Click the **Start** button.
3. Click **All Programs.**
4. Click **Accessories.**
5. Click **Entertainment.**
6. Click **Sound Recorder.** Now you see the Sound-Sound Recorder dialog window, as shown in Figure 15-5.

**Figure 15-5:**
You can
record with
the Sound-
Sound
Recorder
window.

7. Click the **record button** (the window with the filled-in red circle) when you're ready to start recording.

8. Click the **stop** button (the window with the filled-in black rectangle) when you're finished recording.

9. Click **File** in the Sound-Sound Recorder dialog window.

10. Click **Save As.**

11. Now you see the Save As dialog window. Give your file a name and click **Save.** (Don't forget to see what folder you're saving it to so you can find it later.)

12. Now you're back in the Sound-Sound Recorder dialog window. You can make another sound file or close the dialog window.

That's it. You've now have a WAV file that you can play in a PowerPoint presentation.

What if you want to use sound you already recorded on an audiocassette recorder? (A customer interview or whatever.) No problem. Instead of plugging a microphone into your computer, plug in the audiocassette recorder. Follow steps 1 through 7. Then turn on your audiocassette player to play what you want recorded on the computer. Now follow steps 8 through 11.

# Using Video

Are you giving a presentation about a new hotel with facilities that are perfect for your company's annual customer convention? You can talk about them all day. But showing a video clip is more effective. Then your audience can see for themselves. That's why video is so powerful. We're accustomed to accepting it as reality. In this section, I give you some ideas for making your presentation more vital with video.

## Preparing video for your presentation

It's beyond the scope of this book to give you all the technical details for preparing a video file to use with PowerPoint. You can find that in *Digital Video For Dummies* or *Adobe Premiere For Dummies* both by Keith Underdahl (Wiley). Instead, I give you a quick overview of what you need to do.

### Finding video to use

You can find video in many places: video stores, libraries, corporate archives, on the Web, and so on.

But remember: No matter where you get it from, make sure that you get written permission to use it. Getting the written permission eliminates much of what you find in video stores. In libraries, look for videos made by federal or state governments. These videos are often in the public domain and available for use without licensing.

An overlooked source of video is the corporate public relations department. Many companies shoot a wide array of professional-quality videos that end up warehoused in a corporate archive after one-time use at trade shows or other events. Ask what's available and whether you can have permission to use it.

Another choice is to videotape the video yourself. This way, you can create customized material. You can film your customers praising your products. You can tape your products in action. You can film company events. You get the idea. By the way, you don't have to use big-bucks, professional equipment. A good camcorder turns out video good enough to use in a PowerPoint presentation.

### Manipulating video on your computer

After you have your video, you need to get it into your computer. Doing so is relatively easy if you shoot it with a digital camcorder, because it's already in a digital format. The transfer is a little more complicated if the video is in analog format. (If you don't know how to convert video from analog to digital, just take it to a local merchant who will do it for a fee. Many photo shops now provide this service.) After it's in your computer, you can use an appropriate program to edit it and save it as a file compatible with PowerPoint. For all those technical details, see *Digital Video For Dummies* or *Adobe Premiere For Dummies* both by Keith Underdahl (Wiley).

## Adding video to a slide

In today's television-addicted society, a video clip really captures audience attention. Video clips can really spice up a presentation — if they're used judiciously *and to make a point*. Here's how you put a video clip into a PowerPoint slide:

1. Display the slide you want to add the video to.

2. Click **Insert.**

3. Click **Movies and Sounds.**

4. Click **Movie from File.**

5. Find a video file that you want to use.

6. Double click on the video file.

7. Now you get a message: "Do you want your movie to play automatically in the slide show? If not, it will play when you click it." Click **Yes** or **No.** (This step doesn't occur in PowerPoint 97. It does occur in PowerPoint 2002.)

8. You get a picture on your slide — a rectangle containing the first image in your video clip. You can move it around on your slide until you like where it's located. (Check out Figure 15-6 for an example.)

Don't panic if you insert a video and end up with a black window on your slide. The first frame of the video may be black — many videos play black for a few seconds before an image appears. If that's what you've got and you don't like it, edit the video file so it starts on an image. For all the technical details, check out *Digital Video For Dummies* or *Adobe Premiere For Dummies* both by Keith Underdahl (Wiley).

Resizing the image window that appears on your slide after you insert a video affects the quality of the video's appearance.

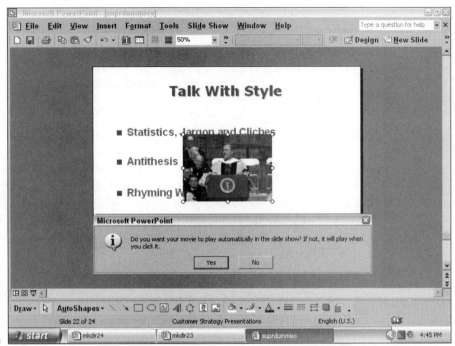

**Figure 15-6:**
You can add
a video clip
to a slide
and place it
wherever
you want it.

## Checking out a few do's and don'ts

Want to make your life simpler when you use video clips in a presentation?
Here are a few do's and don'ts that may help:

- ✔ **Do create one folder for your PowerPoint presentation file and all the video files that it uses.** Doing so makes it easier for the computer to find them when you're ready to show them. It's also easier for you to find material if you want to change something.

- ✔ **Do consider using a video without its soundtrack.** If you like the images on a video clip but not the sounds — edit out the sounds. You can add a different soundtrack. Or talk about the video while it's playing. For more details, see *Digital Video For Dummies* or *Adobe Premiere For Dummies* both by Keith Underdahl (Wiley).

- ✔ **Do consider animating your video "object."** Do you have a video clip of a customer calling you a genius? You can make it seem even more important by giving it a grand entrance. Animate it so it flies onto your slide. Just follow the directions for adding animation in the "Adding Animation" section later in this chapter.

- ✔ **Don't use too many video clips**. They're cool at first, but your audience will get bored with them. Use them sporadically throughout your presentation. Then they remain surprising and entertaining.

- ✔ **Don't use video clips longer than 30 seconds**. Most of them should be shorter. (Think about television ads — many of them are only 15 seconds.) You can make an exception for the beginning and end of the presentation if you want to use the video as an introduction or conclusion.

# Adding Animation

Remember the first time you saw a PowerPoint presentation that used animation? Text flew onto the screen out of nowhere. There were slick dissolves between slides — like one slide exploding to reveal another. You know what I'm talking about. It was unbelievably cool. You can do that stuff too. It's easy.

Build the animation into your text. For example, you have your first bullet point fly in, and then you talk about it. You have your second bullet point fly in, and then you talk about it. Just don't overuse animation.

## Transforming transitions

Transitions refer to what you see when one slide changes to the next in your presentation. The default setting is nothing — literally. Nothing special happens. A full view of one slide is simply replaced by a full view of the next slide. Want to jazz that up a little? Here's how:

1. Go to the slide that you want to work on.

2. Click **Slide Show.**

3. Click **Slide Transition.**

4. Now you see a Slide Transition dialog window. In the window labeled Apply to Selected Slides, you find a menu of options for transition effects. Click on the effect that you want. (The language and layout are slightly different for PowerPoint 97 and other older versions, but it's basically the same procedure.)

5. Go to the window labeled **Speed:**, and click the **down arrow.**

6. Choose a speed (**Fast, Medium,** or **Slow**), and click on it.

Now you've got a fancy transition for that slide. Want the same effect on all your slides? Just click the **Apply to All Slides** window at the bottom of the Slide Transition dialog window.

## Animating text

Want your text to do tricks as it appears on your slide? No problem. Here's what you do for PowerPoint 2002. (The language and layout are slightly different for PowerPoint 97 and other older versions, but just follow the same basic steps.):

1. Go to the slide you want to work on.

2. Select the text that you want to animate.

3. Click on **Slide Show.**

4. Click on **Custom Animation.**

5. Click on **Add Effect.**

6. Click on **Entrance.**

7. Choose an effect, and click on it. For this example, I'm choosing **Fly In.** (See Figure 15-7.)

8. Look in the window labeled **Direction:,** and click on the **down arrow.** You get a menu of direction. Choose one, and click on it. I've clicked on **From Left.**

9. Look in the window labeled **Speed:,** and click on the **down arrow.** You get a menu of speeds. Choose one, and click on it. I've clicked on **Very Fast.** (See Figure 15-8.)

   Your text will now fly in from the left at a very fast speed.

   Repeat steps 1 through 9 for other text that you want to animate — for example, additional lines of bulleted text. Now you're almost done.

10. Look in the window labeled **Start:,** and choose one of three options: **On Click, With Previous,** or **After Previous.** Here's what they do:

    *On Click* means your slide comes on without the animated text. When you click the mouse, a line of text will fly in. You've got to click the mouse separately for each line of text to appear.

    *With Previous* means that the lines of text will automatically fly in together at the same time when your slide comes on. You don't have to click the mouse.

    *After Previous* means that your lines of text will automatically fly in one after the other when your slide comes on. You don't have to click the mouse.

11. Go into **Slide Show** mode, and watch your text fly onto the screen.

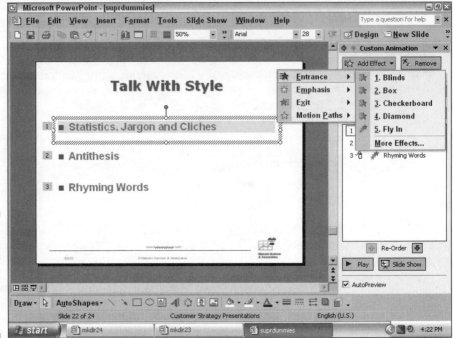

**Figure 15-7:**
You can use
one of
several
animation
effects in
PowerPoint.

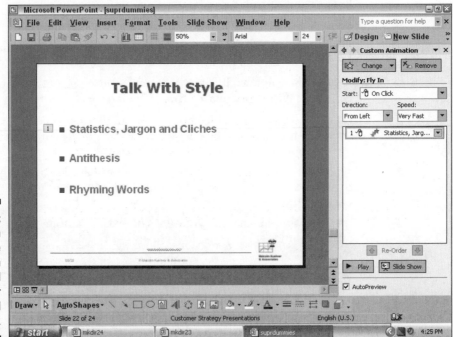

**Figure 15-8:**
You can
choose the
direction
and speed
of your
animated
text.

## Animating images

Want to animate an image? It's pretty much the same as animating text. But in this section, I run through it anyway. (Again, these directions are for PowerPoint 2002. The language and layout are slightly different for PowerPoint 97 and other older versions, but you can just follow the same basic steps.):

1. Put an image on your slide: a photo, a piece of clip art, or an object you've drawn. Want to make it really easy? For this example, use the **Drawing** toolbar at the bottom of your PowerPoint screen to add an oval to your slide.

2. After it's on your slide, select it.

3. Click on **Slide Show.**

4. Click on **Custom Animation.**

5. Click on **Add Effect.**

6. Click **Motion Paths.** (The motion paths include down, left, right, diagonal up right, diagonal down right, and customized.)

7. Click **Up.**

8. Look in the **Speed:** window. I'm setting mine at **Medium.**

9. Look in the **Start:** window. I'm setting mine at **On Click.**

10. Go into Slide Show mode.

11. Click the mouse once.

Now you should see your oval go up at medium speed.

 The best way to become familiar with PowerPoint's animation function is to play with it. You can create many interesting effects. Just don't use them all at once in your presentation. If your audience wanted to see that much animation, they would have stayed home and watched cartoons.

# Mining Miscellaneous Impressive Stuff

You've added sound, video, and animation. But that's not enough. You want more. Okay. This section goes over a few more things you can do to impress your audience.

## Keeping track of action items

As your presentation progresses, various issues come up. You discuss them with members of the audience, and action items are assigned. Wouldn't it be great to keep track of them with PowerPoint? Hey, guess what? You can. Here's how for PowerPoint 97 and later versions:

1. While you're in slide show mode giving your presentation, right click on your computer screen.

2. Click on **Meeting Minder.** You see a Meeting Minder dialog window.

3. Click on the **Action Items** tab.

4. Enter the appropriate information into the windows labeled Description, Assigned To, and Due Date.

5. Click **Add.**

6. Click **OK.**

You can repeat this process as needed throughout your presentation. Here's what PowerPoint does. It creates a new slide that contains all the action items, and it puts the slide at the very end of your presentation. That lets you remind each volunteer what she committed to do. Pretty slick, huh?

## Customizing your bullets

The bulleted list is a staple of PowerPoint presentations. Everyone uses them. Everyone is going to keep using them. So how can you make yours stand out? One way is to change the look of the bullets that PowerPoint automatically provides. Here's how for PowerPoint 2002. (The language and layout is slightly different for PowerPoint 97 and older versions, but you can basically follow the same steps.):

1. Select the bullets you want to change.

2. Click **Format.**

3. Click **Bullets and Numbering.**

4. You get a dialog window that's open to Bulleted. In the lower-right corner of the dialog window is a window labeled **Customize.** Click on it.

5. Now you see a dialog window called **Symbol.** Near the top is a window labeled **Font:** with a **down arrow** next to it. Click on the arrow.

6. Choose a font from the menu. I'm choosing **Wingdings.**

7. Now you see a bunch of Wingding images. Choose one that you want to use as your bullet, and select it. I'm choosing the **skull and crossbones.** (See Figure 15-9.)

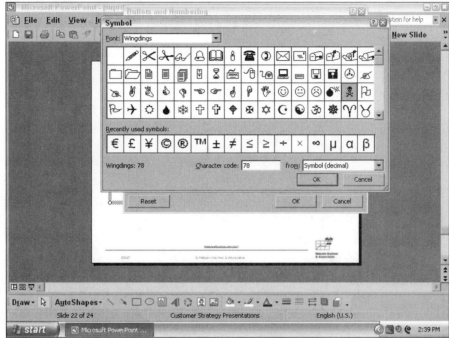

**Figure 15-9:**
You can
choose from
many
images to
create a
customized
bullet.

8. Click **OK.** That takes you back to the Bulleted dialog window.

9. Click **OK.**

You've now got a skull-and-crossbones bullet, as shown in Figure 15-10.

Want to really get creative? Use an image as a bullet. Here's how:

1. Repeat steps 1 through 3.

2. You get a dialog window that's open to Bulleted. In the lower-right corner of the dialog window is a window labeled **Picture.** Click on it.

3. Now you see a dialog window called Picture Bullet. It has pictures that you can use for bullets. Don't like any of them? No problem. In the lower-left corner of the dialog window is a window labeled **Import.** Click on it.

4. Now you're in a dialog window labeled **Clip Organizer.** Navigate to the image file that you want to use for your bullet. Select the file. Click **Add.**

5. The image appears in the dialog window called **Picture Bullet.** Select it. Then click **OK.**

That's it. That image is now your bullet.

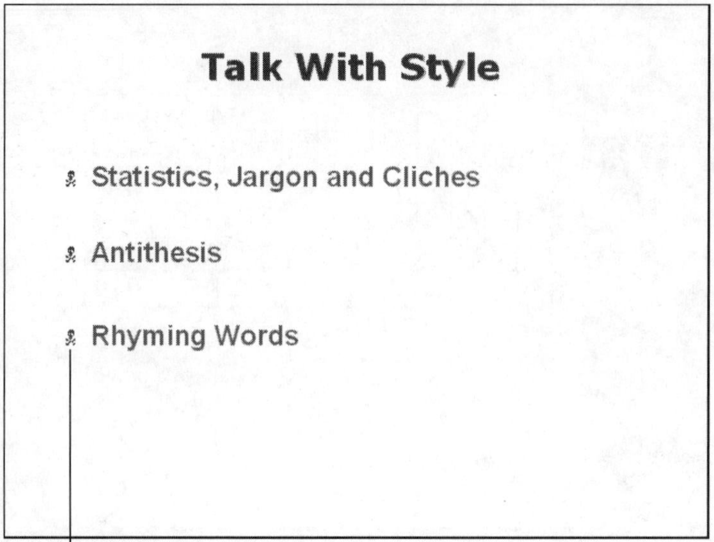

**Talk With Style**

    🦋 Statistics, Jargon and Cliches

    🦋 Antithesis

    🦋 Rhyming Words

**Figure 15-10:**
Customized
bullets
really stand
out in a
PowerPoint
presen-
tation.

A customized bullet

# Chapter 16

# Avoiding Common Mistakes with PowerPoint

. . . . . . . . . . . . . . . . . . . . . . . . . . . . . . . . . . . . . . . . . . . . . .

*In This Chapter*

▶ Ferreting out mistakes while preparing your slide show

▶ Avoiding blunders while giving your presentation

▶ Knowing whether PowerPoint is too overpowering

. . . . . . . . . . . . . . . . . . . . . . . . . . . . . . . . . . . . . . . . . . . . . .

**A** cartoon in *The New Yorker* magazine showed a job interview conducted in hell: "I need someone well versed in the art of torture," the devil says. "Do you know PowerPoint?"

The clever cartoonist may be overstating the case, but not by much. Most of us have sat through PowerPoint presentations that were less than exciting. You know what I mean — by the time the presenter is done, you'd rather have real bullets fired at you than PowerPoint bullets. In this chapter, I tell you about some common PowerPoint mistakes and how to avoid them, as well as discuss whether you need to use PowerPoint at all in certain situations.

## Recognizing Mistakes When Prepping Your Presentation

Many mistakes can pop up when you're first developing a PowerPoint presentation. Blunders range from talking about the wrong things to overdoing the special effects.

## Creating the wrong message

PowerPoint slide designer Willy Keats sees this mistake more often than he'd like. "Sometimes, people develop a big, one-size-fits-all presentation with slides for every conceivable topic related to their subject," he observes. "The problem is they don't edit it before they give it." And that's a mistake, because one size doesn't fit all. "You've got to adapt your message for a articular audience at a particular time," he explains. "You can't show everything to everyone."

His advice: Be flexible, and remove slides that won't further your message with a particular audience. If you're presenting to executives, pull the slides with lots of technology details. And move the summary slides to the front of the presentation. Presenting to engineers? Load up on slides with lots of technical details. You get the idea.

Check out Chapter 2 for details on customizing the best presentation for your audience.

## Undermining your message

If a picture is worth a thousand words, then you'd better be sure your PowerPoint visuals support your message. If you're talking about your company's attention to detail, then your slides shouldn't be riddled with errors. If you're discussing the good taste that goes into development of your company's products, then don't show ugly slides. If you want to appear organized and in command, don't use slides that are out of order, irrelevant, or both. And if you're talking about important, serious stuff, don't use lighthearted clip art and playful fonts. (It would be like writing a legal document in crayon.)

## Prettifying without purpose

In the early levels of elementary school — kindergarten and first grade, for example — a phenomenon I'll call *crayon color mania* often pops up. Most kids have the basic box of 10 crayons. Then one day, some kid brings in the super-size box of 64 crayons, and the 54 extra colors create mania. Every kid wants to use them to make his pictures *prettier*.

The same phenomenon occurs in adults exposed to PowerPoint for the first time. They want to use fancy fonts. Lots of clip art. Beautiful color schemes. So here's my advice: Do all that. Get it out of your system. Then start over again. And keep in mind that anything that goes on the slide must enhance your message. Remove anything that could potentially distract or confuse your audience — even if it's *pretty*. That means any picture you use must relate to the concepts discussed on a particular slide. Even better is when the picture helps explain the concepts and allows you to eliminate some text.

## Passing poor design

Using badly designed slides is one of the biggest mistakes that presenters make with PowerPoint. Specific errors to watch out for include:

- ✓ **Too much information:** Use only key words on slides, not full sentences. And don't cram too much onto one slide. It's hard to read and looks cluttered. If you've got that much information to communicate, use multiple slides. Figure 16-1 shows a slide with too much information, and Figure 16-2 shows a slide that's not so crowded.

- ✓ **Misspelled words:** Use the spell checker *and* a colleague who knows how to spell. Check the grammar also.

- ✓ **Creepy colors:** Don't use hideous color combinations. And make sure enough contrast exists between the text and background so that the slide is readable.

See Chapter 14 for more suggestions on designing effective PowerPoint slides.

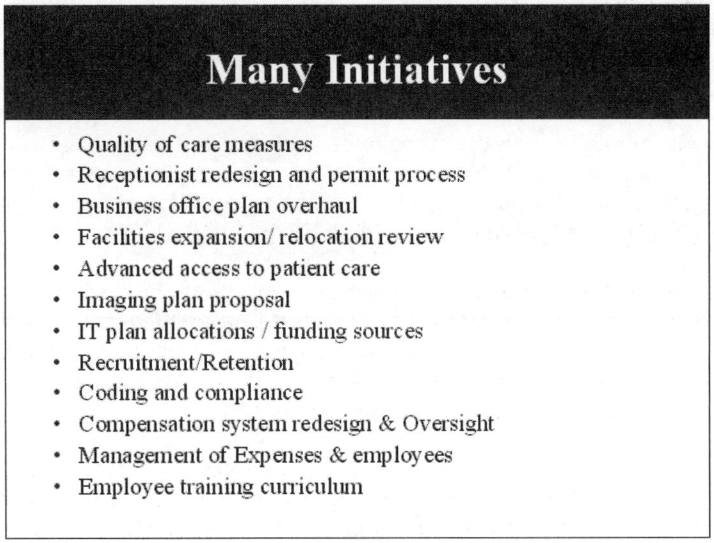

## Many Initiatives

- Quality of care measures
- Receptionist redesign and permit process
- Business office plan overhaul
- Facilities expansion/ relocation review
- Advanced access to patient care
- Imaging plan proposal
- IT plan allocations / funding sources
- Recruitment/Retention
- Coding and compliance
- Compensation system redesign & Oversight
- Management of Expenses & employees
- Employee training curriculum

**Figure 16-1:**
Avoid putting too much information on one slide.

## Many Initiatives

- Quality of care measures

- Receptionist redesign and permit process

- Business office plan overhaul

- Facilities expansion/ relocation review

- Advanced access to patient care

- Imaging plan proposal

**Figure 16-2:**
A slide with just a few important points is much easier for your audience to read.

## Using too many special effects

When it comes to PowerPoint special effects, many presenters can't avoid the temptation to use lots and lots of them. You know what I'm talking about. Every slide change features a different animated transition with a different accompanying sound. Animated images move all over the slides, and videos automatically pop up everywhere. Enough, already. Is your purpose to communicate a message or to make your audience think it took hallucinogenic drugs?

Yes, you can use PowerPoint to create a lot of cool special effects. But go easy on them; you don't want to overwhelm and distract from your message. And distraction is all too common when presenters start playing with the audio, video, and animation possibilities of PowerPoint. Think of it this way: When Sir Edmund Hillary was asked why he climbed Mount Everest, he replied, "Because it was there." With PowerPoint special effects, the opposite is true — just because they're there, you don't have to use them. (To find out how to use cool tricks correctly, check out Chapter 15.)

## Forgetting to practice

Practice makes perfect, and not practicing your presentation with the actual technology you'll be using is one of the biggest presentation mistakes. Run through all of your PowerPoint slides to make sure everything works, the sounds and videos play, and the transitions are correct. You've spent a lot of time creating the perfect slides, and that's why you should invest a little more time to run your whole show in Slide Show View mode. I find it amazing that many people don't do a dry run — and regret it later. How else can you explain all the presenters who fumble around trying to get their show started? Or waste time looking for the right file? Or push a key that closes their presentation when they're trying to advance to the next slide? Aside from the embarrassment, amateur operation of PowerPoint distracts from your message.

If you're giving your presentation on a computer other than the one you created it on, make sure that the computer can display your fonts. Be sure to check to make sure the fonts you used are loaded onto the computer, embed the fonts in your presentation, or stick with a basic font that's on most computers — like Arial or Times New Roman.

If possible, you should also practice with the projector that you will use during your presentation. Remember, you'll need an LCD projector to show images from your computer. (It's a special projector that attaches to your computer.) Like everything else in our digitized age, LCD projectors are notoriously finicky about functioning properly when hooked to a computer for the first time. So be sure you leave lots of time to get the projector running smoothly. Does it connect properly to your computer? Does it recognize your PowerPoint program? Is it properly focused? The time to answer all these questions isn't when you're standing in front of an audience. Also, don't forget to test the volume settings on your computer to make sure any music, voice, or sound effects aren't too soft or too loud. And bring an extension cord — you'll be glad you did.

# Avoiding Mistakes When Presenting

Even with a perfect set of slides, you can still mess up your presentation when you're standing in front of your audience. The following subsections go over some common mistakes made during PowerPoint presentations.

## Ignoring your audience

If you want your message to get through to your audience, you need to connect with them. That doesn't happen when you ignore them. Unfortunately, presenters using PowerPoint have a tendency to ignore the audience. They're so busy working the controls on their computers that they never look up. They ignore the audience. They don't connect. They talk to their computers instead of to the audience.

When used properly, PowerPoint should be a bridge to your audience, not a barrier. You're using the program only to emphasize your points and make them easier to understand. PowerPoint is never a substitute for eye contact with your audience.

One of the biggest advantages of PowerPoint over traditional slides is that you *don't* have to run your presentation in the dark. So turn the lights on. Look at the audience. Let the audience look at you. Don't give them an opportunity to fall asleep by darkening the room.

## Reading the slides

Audiences hate this. If you're just going to read your slides, then you don't even need to be there — just set up the computer and projector, and set PowerPoint to automatically forward your slides every 30 seconds. When designed properly, PowerPoint slides have key words or phrases that help keep the audience on track with where you are in your presentation. But they don't replace the presentation. That's what you're there for.

Also, if you can just read your slides to the audience, then you've put too many words on them. (See "Passing poor design," earlier in this chapter, for more design problems to avoid.)

## Not talking about what's on the slide

Audience members get really confused when they're looking at bullet points on the screen, and the presenter is talking about something else. Sound far-fetched? It happens all the time. The presenter moves on to the next point without advancing the PowerPoint slides. Or the presenter doesn't stick to the script and goes off on a tangent. Either way, the audience ends up looking at a visual that's irrelevant to what the presenter is saying.

What can you do to avoid this? First, pay attention to your presentation. Keep your slides in sync with what you're talking about. And if you go off on a tangent, then blank the screen. Hit the computer keys **b** or **w** to make the screen go black or white. Then, when you return to your regularly scheduled programming, show the audience your slides again. (For the scoop on other cool tricks, see Chapter 15.)

## Having bad timing

PowerPoint's timer feature changes your slides automatically after a set period of time. Don't use it. Why? What if you take longer to discuss a point than you'd planned to? What if you get a question from the audience? What if a disturbance, like a loud noise, momentarily draws attention away from your presentation? Any of these scenarios means that you'll still be talking about one slide while PowerPoint automatically switches to another. So set your slides to change with a mouse click — then you can change them when you're ready. By the way, changing your slides with a mouse click is PowerPoint's default setting. So just leave it that way. Want to see where this stuff is? Click **Slide Show** and then **Slide Transition,** and you'll see a big menu on the right side of your screen. Look toward the bottom, and you'll find Advance Slide. It will provide two choices: On Mouse Click and Automatically After. The box adjacent to On Mouse Click should be checked.

## Using someone else's slides

Busy colleagues sometimes trade PowerPoint presentations. The reason you shouldn't do this is the same as the reason you want to: You're busy, and it saves time. The problem is that too often, you're so busy that you don't find out exactly what's in the presentation before you give it. Then you get a big surprise as you're presenting — a slide is missing, an extra slide is present, or the slides are in a different order than you're used to. So build your own presentation. Then you know exactly what to expect. And if you borrow a slide show from someone else, make sure you have plenty of time to become familiar with it.

# Overpowering with PowerPoint: How Much Is Too Much?

Since its inception in the mid-1980s, PowerPoint has spread through the global business world faster than an epidemic. In fact, some pundits consider *epidemic* the perfect word to describe PowerPoint's wave of popularity. You can't go into a business meeting without someone pulling out a PowerPoint presentation. And if you don't have one, you're viewed as odd or unprepared. Or both.

So it shouldn't be surprising that a backlash has begun. Critics of PowerPoint see it as a barrier between presenter and audience and a tool that weakens rather than strengthens the message. Or as technology guru Vint Cerf put it, "Power corrupts, and PowerPoint corrupts absolutely."

What exactly is the problem? And what, if anything, can be done about it?

## Defining the problem

One of the chief criticisms of PowerPoint is that it emphasizes form over content. As a result, it reduces the importance of the message. Perhaps the best example of this charge is a PowerPoint parody of the *Gettysburg Address* created by computer guru Peter Norvig. Its agenda slide includes bullet point versions of Abraham Lincoln's great lines. (You can view it at `www.norvig.com/Gettysburg`.) It's funny, and it makes its point: PowerPoint tends to give every message a sameness that makes it hard to distinguish between the important and the trivial.

Another major criticism is that PowerPoint keeps presenters from connecting with the audience. It gets in the way. Everyone is so focused on the slides that no real exchange of ideas occurs. In fact, critics say that PowerPoint discourages discussion, and its templates symbolically represent words set in stone and ideas not subject to change. Critics also argue that PowerPoint encourages presenters to develop slides instead of a message. They just read their slides to the audience instead of sharing a message that motivates, informs, or entertains. (For more on deciding what a presentation should do, check out Chapter 2.)

So what's a presenter to do? Current business customs suggest that audiences expect PowerPoint presentations. But many of the executives who expect one claim that PowerPoint presentations are ineffective and boring. You're faced with a classic dilemma — whichever choice you make, you lose. Is there no way out of this morass?

## Finding an innovative solution

Joe DiNucci is a legendary sales and marketing executive in Silicon Valley. He spent the bulk of his career at two Fortune 500 companies, and he's currently a sales vice president with Immersion, a haptic technology company in San Jose, California. Joe has a reputation as an innovator, so I asked for his opinion about PowerPoint and the backlash. Not surprisingly, he had already thought about it in great detail. He also had a solution to the dilemma.

"I love PowerPoint," says Joe. "I think it's one of the best sales tools ever created." Despite that opinion, Joe has banned his sales force from using PowerPoint on many sales calls, especially on executives. Why? He believes that PowerPoint is a "conversation killer." Its capabilities are now so powerful that presenters get wrapped up in the medium and lose control of the conversation.

"You always think you're going to get through your slides in a third of the time it actually takes," explains Joe. "But you get bogged down on one slide. Then 18 minutes have gone by, and you're only on the fourth slide. And your really good stuff is still eight slides away. Then you get bogged down again. And the next thing you know, you've lost control of the conversation."

And that's not his only objection: Joe doesn't like the power relationship it establishes. "You're standing and pointing at a screen," he observes. "And the audience is reading what's on the screen or looking at your graphics. If that floats your boat, fine. But you've got to remember, especially when you're selling to senior executives — they want to have a conversation with you."

So how does Joe handle the fact that many executives *expect* a PowerPoint presentation? Simple. He makes one but doesn't show it.

Here's how he and his team handled a sales presentation for top executives at a major car manufacturer. "We created the PowerPoint as though we were going to show it," Joe recalls. "It was big — 45 slides. The whole works — photographs, diagrams, quotes — powerful, punchy stuff." When it was done, the team had it printed in color and spiral bound, with enough copies for everyone at the meeting.

When the time came for the sales call, they walked into a room full of executives, and Joe said, "The bad news is, we have a 45-slide PowerPoint presentation. The good news is, we're not going to show it to you." What was the audience reaction? Applause. Then Joe's team fanned the printed PowerPoint presentation to show the work they'd put into it. "We told them that we'd brought copies for everyone," Joe recalls, "and that they contained everything we were going to talk about, plus a lot of background information. It really was a spectacular presentation. But we didn't project it. We just talked. We had a conversation."

Joe believes that his approach strikes the proper balance. If his team had walked in without anything, they would have been perceived as lazy or unprepared. But by having the PowerPoint presentation and not showing it, they became heroes to the audience.

Not ready to totally give up PowerPoint? Joe has an alternative. Tell your audience that you have 45 slides, but you're going to show only the 2 or 3 that really matter. They can see the rest in your PowerPoint handout.

# Part V

# Checking Out Tips and Tricks for Common Presentations

The 5th Wave    By Rich Tennant

"I was giving them a rousing motivational speech from my college football days, at the end of which everyone jumped up and butted heads."

# In this part . . .

When you work in the business world, you're expected to deliver certain presentations. Whether or not you're in sales, you'll eventually have to give a sales presentation. Even if you're not in finance, you'll have to present numbers. You'll also have to train a colleague, customer, or vendor. And you can count on having to communicate technical information at some point in your career. In this part of the book, I describe all of these situations and how to handle them.

You can find tips on everything from how you should present a business plan to a venture capitalist to how to make presentations to an international audience. I also cover impromptu and motivational presentations, informational briefings, serving on panels and roundtables, and participating in virtual meetings.

# Chapter 17

# Succeeding in Sales and Other Motivational Presentations

. . . . . . . . . . . . . . . . . . . . . . . . . . . . . . . . . . . . . . . .

## In This Chapter

▶ Making an effective sales presentation

▶ Motivating a business audience with ease

. . . . . . . . . . . . . . . . . . . . . . . . . . . . . . . . . . . . . . . .

*O*ne winter day, a grade school teacher was trying to motivate her students to avoid catching colds. So she told them a heartbreaking story about her little brother, when he was the same age as the kids in the class. He went out in the snow with his sled. He stayed out too long. And he caught a cold. The cold turned into pneumonia. Three days later, he was dead. When she finished speaking, there was absolute silence in the room. And she figured she had really gotten through to them. Then a voice from the back of the room asked, "Where's his sled?"

Motivation is a tricky business — especially when it's done with words. (It's much easier to motivate someone with a baseball bat, but often illegal.) Whether you're trying to talk someone into doing something, not doing something, or just thinking about something, you've got your work cut out for you. In this chapter, I discuss some techniques you can use to make your motivational presentations more motivating — especially sales presentations.

## Giving a Sales Presentation

The most common type of motivational presentation in the business world is the sales presentation. It's also the most difficult to carry off successfully. Why? Hey, motivating people to fork over their hard-earned cash for your products or services is difficult. In this section, I give you some ideas for crafting a sales presentation that sells.

## Doing your homework

As with so much in life, the key to a successful sales presentation is preparation. You've got to find out everything you can about the people you'll be talking to. How does their business operate? What are their problems? How can your product or service specifically help them?

Any personal information you can obtain in advance is also useful, because it helps you create rapport. What are your prospects' favorite sports teams? Where did they go to school? Where have they worked? This type of information can help you establish a connection with your audience.

You also need to find out how much they already know about your product or service and exactly what aspects they're interested in. Do they want the 50,000-foot view or nuts and bolts? These details are critical for constructing a presentation to meet their specific needs. You don't want to waste their time talking about stuff they already know. And you definitely don't want to emphasize product capabilities that they couldn't care less about.

How do you get this information? Any way you can. Ask contact people, do research on the Web, and obtain company promotional materials. There's no magic formula. (Check out Chapter 2 for more on audience analysis. For more insight into research, see Chapter 3.)

## Developing and delivering the presentation

After you've done your homework, you need to create your presentation. The following subsections go over a few tips to help you make your presentation more effective in development and delivery.

### Try the DiNucci test

Joe DiNucci is a legendary sales and marketing executive in Silicon Valley. He spent the bulk of his career at two Fortune 500 companies, and he's currently a sales vice president with Immersion, a haptic technology company in San Jose, California. He has a one-question test for determining what belongs in a sales presentation: What will you say or show that you couldn't just as well communicate in an e-mail? "If the answer is nothing," says Joe, "then don't waste your time. Put it in an e-mail." Here's his reasoning: "It costs money and time to get people together," he notes. "And you have to take advantage of the fact that you're physically present in front of people. There's a huge payoff if you play it right, if you go for the chemistry and connect."

## Make a good impression with the opening

As with any presentation, the opening to a sales presentation is critical. It's when people get to know you. It's also when they start forming opinions about you and your presentation. (Check out Chapter 9 for an introduction to introductions.) That's why Joe believes you've got to communicate two things in the first sixty seconds.

"First, you have to show that you've done some research," he explains. "That you know something about them that's relevant to what you're trying to get them to do." In other words, that you know enough about their business problems to offer a solution.

"Second, tell them something they don't know," says Joe. "There's no better way to ingratiate yourself with a prospect than to bring them information they don't have. About a competitor. About technologies that are relevant to them. About government regulation. Something that's relevant to their business. That's so often overlooked." How do you get that information? Hey, that's the hard part. It takes a lot of work and research. That's why new information is so powerful when you use it in your opening. (For more on researching, see "Doing your homework," earlier in this chapter.)

## Communicate your objective

Why are you there? The answer isn't as obvious as you may think. Are you just getting acquainted? Are you giving initial information that may lead to a sale down the road? Are you planning to get a signed order at the conclusion of your presentation? Whatever your objective — and you should have one — you need to communicate it to your audience early on. Let them know what it is you want them to do and why it would be good for them. Everything in your presentation should support your objective. (For the scoop on figuring out what your presentation should do, see Chapter 2.)

However, preserving your relationship is more important than accomplishing your objective. "Relationship is more important than anything," says Joe. "Maybe you go in with the goal of closing them today. But if you can't, you don't burn any bridges. You're going to be closer to the goal line next time than if you hadn't made this particular sales call. It's all about the relationship." In other words, don't make them mad.

## Differentiate yourself from the competition

Congratulations if you have no competitors. I'd like to get into your business. However, because most people do have competitors, assume that they're also presenting to your prospect. That means your presentation should emphasize your unique capabilities — the stuff your competition doesn't have and can't do. How are you different? And how can those differences benefit your audience? The more compelling you make the answers to those questions, the closer you get to a sale.

### Distinguish features from benefits

A basic rule of sales presentations is to sell benefits, not features. It's the difference between saying, "This car has a turbocharged engine that can go up to 150 miles per hour" (feature) and "This car is so fast, you'll be able to outrun the police" (benefit — depending on your line of work). Pointing out benefits is much more persuasive. In fact, the distinction is important for any type of message, not just sales presentations. How do the audience members benefit if they purchase your product or service? Tell them.

Don't forget that your audience's point of view determines what gets defined as a benefit. You may not think something is a benefit. Almost no one else in the world may think something is a benefit. But if your audience thinks something is a benefit, then it is. And conversely, you may think something *is* a benefit, but if the audience doesn't, it's not. (See Chapter 2 for more information on relating to your audience.)

### Suggest small, specific steps

Be realistic about what you can talk someone into. You have a far greater chance of success if you advocate a small change rather than a large one. For example, say you're trying to persuade a company to purchase a new enterprise-wide computer system. If you tell them to cough up hundreds of millions of dollars to do it all this year, you've got a tough sell. Instead, you can suggest implementing one module at a time over a period of years at a lower initial cost.

### Anticipate questions and objections

You don't want questions and objections to come as a surprise. As you're preparing your presentation, put yourself in the position of your audience. What questions or objections would you have to what you're saying? Make a list, and have an answer ready for each one. (For more on fielding questions, see Chapter 13.)

### Show empathy

"The most important thing, besides knowing what you're talking about, is empathy," says Joe DiNucci. "To do a good job, you have to care about the audience — who they are, why they're there, and what they want." And you have to let them know it. How do you do that? Aside from being responsive to audience concerns during your presentation, you can show your empathy by extensive preparation. A major research effort while preparing your presentation translates into a statement of empathy, because it shows that you care about your audience.

You can be polite and have no empathy. Empathy means you understand the other people's problems from their point of view. You show that by what you say in your presentation. And the only way to know that stuff is to do a lot of research. If I talk about overworked human resources personnel who have to conform to idiotic internal procedures (and name specific procedures), that shows empathy.

### Be enthusiastic

If you're not excited about your pitch, why should anyone else be? You don't have to be loud or excessively extroverted. But you must radiate confidence and energy. The style depends on your personality. It can be low-key or high-pitched. Either way, you've got to be enthusiastic about what you're talking about. Remember, enthusiasm is contagious. For some information on how to convey enthusiasm by using body language, see Chapter 11.

### Ask the audience questions

Asking questions keeps your audience involved and lets you know that they're with you. It's also a nice way to break up your presentation so they don't just hear your voice droning on and on. Questions such as "Does that make sense?" and "Is that clear?" should be peppered throughout your presentation.

Always ask how much time you have and whether anyone in the audience has to leave before you finish. That way, you can recalibrate your presentation to make sure the important points are covered while the important people are there.

## Avoiding common mistakes

Selling something is hard enough when your presentation goes right. So don't make it tougher on yourself. Don't make the following mistakes.

### Talking too much

Yes, we know that you're excited about what you sell and that you've got a lot to say about it. But please, don't go over your allotted time — some of us have other things to do today. And please leave time for questions. We may have a few — especially if you try to cram in too much technical information.

### Trashing the competition

Your mother probably told you, "If you can't say something nice about some-one, don't say anything at all." This is particularly true in sales presentations. And it applies to talking about your competition. You don't make yourself look good by making your competition look bad, especially if you're trying to sell to someone who already uses your competition. In that case, you're implying that your prospect is stupid. Otherwise, they wouldn't have gone with your competition in the first place. Just take the high road. Keep your pitch focused on how great your products and services are. You can acknowledge the competition, but don't trash them. Doing so says more about you than about them.

Want to communicate the faults of your competition without trashing them? Emphasize your company's good points to imply competitors' bad points. For example:

- ✔ When you go with us, we're in for the long haul. (Translation: We won't sell and run like our competitors.)

- ✔ We manufacture our products from the highest-quality materials. (Translation: It's not junk like our competitors' stuff.)

You get the idea. Your potential customers will figure out what you're saying.

### Ignoring part of the audience

You've done it. Your audience includes the top executive, the Big Cheese herself. So you aim your entire presentation, all your wit and charm, directly at the Head Honcho as if no one else is in the room. Unfortunately, other people *are* in the room. And they don't like being treated like they don't exist. Guess what? They have input in the purchasing decision. That's why they're in the room. Duh! And now they don't like you, because you ignored them. So give your presentation to everyone. You'll be glad you did.

### Being inflexible

You've put in a lot of time to do your homework and prepare a brilliant presentation. But it's not working. One of the key audience members keeps glancing at his watch. Or one of them keeps interrupting you with questions about things you were going to discuss later. Or one of them keeps taking calls on her cell phone. For whatever reason, your presentation just isn't having the effect you anticipated. What do you do? Should you just plow ahead as planned? Amazingly, many presenters do.

Presenters who ignore their audience are using cartoon logic. If a cartoon character walks off a cliff, he won't fall if he keeps walking and doesn't acknowledge that he's in midair. If your presentation isn't working, you won't "bomb" as long as you keep talking and don't acknowledge that your audience is drifting. But in real life, when you walk off a cliff, you fall. And when your presentation goes off a cliff, you don't sell anything.

Paying attention to audience feedback is critical for successfully adapting your presentation to meet the needs of your audience. They'll tell what they want to hear if you watch and listen for it. If they're staring out the window, looking away from you, and fidgeting, then *you* need to adapt. Ask a question to get them reinvolved. Or give them a dramatic statistic to wake them up. If someone keeps asking about a point you plan to cover later, skip ahead to it. Don't treat your presentation like it's set in cement. It's not.

So you've got to be flexible. You've got to be ready to instantly adapt to the situation based on audience feedback. And if that means abandoning your carefully prepared presentation — so be it. Get a sense of what your audience wants, and give it to them. (For more on gauging your audience's reaction, see Chapter 12.)

### Not following up

Sometimes, you're asked a question that you can't answer. The proper response is to say you'll get the information and get it to the questioner. But not everyone keeps this promise. Big mistake. If you don't follow through on a simple thing like getting information to people, they won't trust you to follow through on other promises — like your company's great customer service.

And if you didn't promise to get anything back to your audience, follow up anyway. Send them a thank you note for giving you the opportunity to make your presentation. It's just common courtesy, and it will make you stand out from all those sales presenters who don't send one.

# Energizing with a Motivational Presentation

Have you ever noticed that an oral presentation has a unique ability to inspire and move people? Think of great business leaders. These are executives who can capture their employees' hopes and dreams in a few well-chosen words that energize anyone who hears them. Let me put it another way: I've never come across anyone who got really enthusiastic about a memo or e-mail. But a presentation is another story. In this section, I show you how to construct a message to inspire the troops, lift their spirits, and cause dancing in the streets — well, maybe just in the cubicles.

# What is inspiring?

One thing that distinguishes people from animals is our need to be part of something bigger than ourselves. A successful motivational presentation makes people feel like they have a purpose; that their work makes a difference.

Veteran sales executive Joe DiNucci agrees. "People respond to leadership," he says. "They want to be uplifted. They want you to affirm to them everything is going to be okay. That they can do it." Corny? Absolutely. And absolutely true.

An inspiring presentation reinforces what your audience already feels. It reminds them of why they feel that way and encourages them to pursue common goals. It helps them break out of their normal mindset; to feel empowered and capable of great achievement. It restates the audience's beliefs in a way that's exciting.

# What should you include?

After you understand the beliefs and values of your audience, you can translate their feelings into words. That's the whole purpose of a motivational presentation. You've got to give voice to their yearnings with soaring rhetoric that transcends the humdrum of everyday life and transports them into a universe of great potential. Show a world of endless possibility in which each member of the audience can play a critical role. Does it sound too difficult? Stop worrying. Just make sure you include the following items in your presentation.

## An inspiring mission

Perhaps the most important part of a business-related motivational presentation is the mission. It must be clearly articulated. And it must be stated in a way that excites the audience. To succeed, a motivational presentation must describe a mission in terms that allow audience members to see their work as useful, important, and meaningful. They want to feel that they make a difference and that they're contributing to the greater good.

For example, say your start-up company makes digital cameras. You could say that the mission is to generate a hundred million dollars in revenue in five years. But that's not exactly inspiring. Instead, say that the company's mission is to help people preserve joy. Because your product doesn't require film, it encourages people to take more pictures and create a graphic record of their lives — to preserve joy. Now, that's exciting. This mission gives meaning to the daily grind beyond just making the numbers.

## *Encouragement that the mission is achievable*

After articulating an inspiring vision, the rest of a motivational presentation should show that the mission is achievable — specifically by the members of the audience. They want to hear words of encouragement. They want to know that they can do it. The following subsections go over some devices that can help you get this message across. Remember to tie them into the point you're making.

### *Tell success stories*

A success story is just what the name implies. Typically, it involves someone that the audience can identify with (the presenter or someone else) overcoming difficult obstacles (business or personal) in order to achieve a successful result (a sale, a promotion, an award, or whatever).

The success story is the building block of a motivational presentation. Consider it your proof that what you're saying is possible — that the audience can do it! You can almost reduce this to a mathematical formula. The longer the odds that the story's protagonist overcomes, the more motivating the story is. Let's face it. We love to hear about people worse off than ourselves who accomplish more than we've currently achieved. It gives us hope. If they could do it, we should be able to. (See Chapter 6 for more on using stories.)

### *Give quotes*

If success stories are the building blocks of a motivational presentation, quotations are the mortar that holds them together. No matter what you're talking about — success, perseverance, winning, teamwork — you can find an inspirational quote on the topic. Sure, quotes can be hokey. But most people like to hear them if you don't overuse them. So scatter some inspiring quotes throughout your presentation. You can find lots of them on the Web. Here are some starting points. (For more on quotations, check out Chapter 6.)

- ✔ www.motivationalquotes.com
- ✔ http://followyourdreams.com/food.html
- ✔ www.sperience.org/Weekender/index.shtml
- ✔ www.ideasandtraining.com/Motivation-Success-Quotations.html
- ✔ http://dmoz.org/Reference/Quotations/Inspirational/

 For added impact, use inspirational quotes from your customers. They're not that hard to find if you do business with Fortune 500 companies or other large organizations. Many executives at these companies have written books and articles that include good motivational maxims. For more information on finding this type of info, take a look at Chapter 3.

## Motivational thoughts

Need some inspiring quotes to drop into your next presentation? I've listed a few to get you started.

> Courage is about doing what you're afraid to do. There can be no courage unless you're scared. — Eddie Rickenbacker

> The dictionary is the only place where success comes before work. — Unknown

> It's not who you are that holds you back; it's who you think you're not. — Unknown

Winning is not everything, but the effort to win is. — Zig Ziglar

One hundred percent of the shots you don't take don't go in. — Wayne Gretzky

Vision without action is a daydream. Action without vision is a nightmare. — Japanese proverb

Life isn't about winning every battle; it's about winning the ones that count. — Jackie Chan

### Employ metaphors

Another staple of the motivational presentation is the extended metaphor. It helps your audience think about your message in terms they understand and, thus, remember more of it. Metaphors are often used by some of the best motivational presenters in the world: Sunday-morning television preachers. One of their favorites is the travel metaphor. "We are on a journey, and this life is only the first stop. So we've got to stock up on supplies to get us the rest of the distance. And what supplies do we need to get while we're here on earth? Kindness. Forgiveness. Tolerance. These are the fuels that will take us in the right direction on our journey."

Want to use the travel metaphor in a motivational business presentation? No problem. "Our digital camera company is on a journey. We want to help every person in the world preserve joy. That's our destination. How do we get there? Well, we've already got a great vehicle — this company. Fantastic pilots — all of you people. And a great map — our business plan. Now we need fuel — hard work, creativity, and so on."

Sports metaphors are still popular and still work. The big game. Running for a touchdown. We're in the ninth inning with two out and three men on base. We've got to take that final shot before the buzzer. Worried that these are too cliché? Use a less popular sport. "Our strategy is at a crucial point. We're one move away from checkmate. Now we've got to execute perfectly, and we'll win."

Check out Chapter 6 for information on analogies and Chapter 7 for more on metaphors.

### Use "we" a lot

Include yourself in the same boat as the audience. We can change the world. We can make things happen. We can do it. It sounds more encouraging to say "we" than to say "you." It also establishes a personal connection with the audience.

### Get personal

Use motivational examples from your own life. Hearing stories from the horse's mouth is always exciting. Ever wonder why so many former Olympic athletes are on the motivational lecture circuit? We want to know how they did it. And your audience wants to know how *you* did it. Not an Olympic athlete? Don't worry. Tell the audience how you overcame obstacles to achieve something, even if it wasn't winning a gold medal. In many cases, that's even more inspiring than hearing an Olympian. More audience members can probably identify with you than with a world-class athlete. And don't limit yourself to work-related stories. Did you overcome an impoverished childhood? Did you recover from a life-threatening illness? Any personal story can work in a business presentation if it makes a point, and it's not so personal that the audience becomes uncomfortable.

### Appeal to emotions

An emotional appeal speaks to the hearts of your audience members. Politicians use this appeal every time they talk about patriotism, the American way, and the American dream. An emotional appeal is supposed to tug at your heartstrings. It works best when your audience consists of people who like to take feelings, not just facts, into consideration when forming their opinions.

Say you're giving a presentation about the need to be a good corporate citizen and help the community get a traffic light at the busy intersection near your office building. You could point out that helpless toddlers have been among the accident victims there or that recovery time for an injured adult caused his family great financial hardship. Describing such loss or hardship can appeal to the emotions of your audience.

## Avoiding motivational mistakes

When you're sitting in the audience, it's hard to think of anything worse than a motivational presenter who doesn't motivate. You just want to run away. To keep your audience from experiencing this misery, avoid the following:

✔ **Talking in generalities:** Your audience wants information about how to do things. Tell them specific actions that they can take to be more motivated and inspired. The old-fashioned pep talk doesn't work anymore.

✔ **Using the same old examples:** You need to do extensive research and tailor your presentation to the needs and situation of each particular audience. Find out what motivates *them*. Your audience wants customized material.

✔ **Presenting without passion:** It's ironic, but not uncommon, for people to deliver an entire motivational presentation as if they're talking about widgets. Hey, you're supposed to appeal to the emotions. Get excited. Show some passion. You can't expect your audience to get worked up if you're bored to death.

✔ **Failing to adapt to current events:** If you're scheduled to give a motivational presentation on a day when layoffs were just announced, or the company's stock has tanked, or a customer just canceled the company's biggest order, throw away your script, because no one will be in the mood to hear a lot of optimistic platitudes.

# Chapter 18

# Tackling Technical and Financial Presentations

*A* college professor was discussing a very complicated and technical concept in finance. Suddenly, a student yelled, "I can't understand this. Why do we have to learn this junk?" The professor said, "To improve our country."

The professor continued his lecture. And the student yelled again, "How does studying finance improve our country?"

The professor replied, "It keeps people with your grades from getting into law school."

Whether or not you agree with the professor's assessment of the student, one thing is certain — it's difficult to explain technical information in a way that everyone will understand, especially when it involves financial concepts. But don't worry. In this chapter, I show you how to give technical and financial presentations that anyone can comprehend.

## Presenting Technical Information

Have you ever played the grade school game Telephone? You start with a simple sentence, and whisper it to the person next to you. By the time it goes around the room, the sentence comes out completely garbled. And that's *simple* information. When you present complex information, you don't usually have to do it through a chain of people. But the filtering takes place anyway. And that represents the chief challenge of making a technical presentation: how to simplify your information enough to make it readily comprehensible to your audience.

In order to get the inside track on communicating technical information, I spoke with someone who gives and listens to more technical presentations than most people — David Haussler. He's the director of the Center of Biomolecular Science and Engineering at the University of California at Santa Cruz. You may have heard of him before; Professor Haussler led the team that did the number crunching for the Human Genome Project. As you may imagine, his life is a whirl of scientific conferences where he's presenting or listening to technical presentations. He's even testified before Congress. So he knows how to simplify technical information to the point that even a politician can understand it. Many of his ideas are sprinkled throughout this chapter.

## Identifying your audience's level of understanding

A prime rule of presentation theory is that you don't want to talk over or under the level of your audience. This is especially true with technical presentations. If you blather on about the mathematical proof of an equation in Einstein's Theory of Relativity to a group of visitors to your telescope factory, they probably have no idea what you're talking about. And they probably don't care. One of the keys to a successful technical presentation is assessing the audience's level of knowledge and interest in your topic. Here are a few things to find out from the organizer of the event:

- ✔ Will I be presenting to experts?
- ✔ What does the audience expect to hear from me? Introductory material? An overview of the field? The latest developments?
- ✔ What does the audience want to do with the information I give them?
- ✔ What is the educational level of the audience?
- ✔ Has the audience heard similar presentations before?

One of the biggest problems faced by technical presenters is the mixed audience. No, not male and female. I'm talking about an audience made up of experts and laypeople. How do you pitch the level of your talk? If you make it too simple, the experts are bored. If you make it too complicated, the laypeople don't understand it.

Don't expect a pat solution. But one approach is to include information for both groups in your talk. You can start with the easy stuff and call it a "review" for the experts. Then, when you go over the more difficult material, the laypeople are more likely to understand some of it.

# Nice and easy: Simplifying your presentation

You're the expert. So most, if not all, members of the audience will know less about the information you're presenting than you do. "That's why you have to take extra steps to keep it simple," explains Dave. "You've got to make it much simpler than you think it needs to be, because you're looking at the information with a lot more knowledge and experience than your audience." This is true even if you're talking to an audience of experts. "No one is as expert in your exact topic as you are," observes Dave.

Don't assume that your audience knows the basic principles of your field. Whatever technical area you discuss — science, law, medicine — quickly review any basic principles that the audience needs to know in order to understand your presentation. Do it in a positive way that assumes they already knew the principle but may have forgotten it. For example, "As many of you will recall, the first law of thermodynamics states . . . " When you put things this way, no one is made to feel ignorant. And don't forget to tell them how the principle relates to what you'll be discussing and why they need to know it.

If you're not talking to experts, try to avoid including math in your presentation. Sometimes, you've got to put some in, but keep it to a minimum. Why? Many people are scared of math. The minute they hear numbers, their minds shut down. Then nothing you say registers with them.

# Using analogies

One of the most effective ways to simplify complex material is to express it in terms that the audience already understands, which is why scientists often use analogies to explain their work. An *analogy* is a comparison. If you're talking to laypeople, and you try to explain artificial-intelligence breakthroughs by comparing them to Einsteinian physics, you're probably not going to get too far. But if you can compare and explain artificial intelligence in terms of *The Simpsons*, then you've got something. (Homer is a looping algorithm. . . .)

Here's an analogy that Dave has heard used to explain what scientists accomplished by finding and sequencing 30,000 genes in the human genome:

> It's like obtaining a very detailed map of a city. Each of the genes is like a house and each one has an address. So when it's all worked out, you have a complete map.

## Don't read all about it: Presenting a technical paper

Technical papers are the currency of scientists. Writing them, publishing them, and presenting them at conferences wins them respect from their peers — not to mention raises and promotions. Unfortunately, while the papers may be Nobel Prize–caliber, the presentations usually aren't. Why? Because the presenters read the paper to the audience — literally.

Don't stand in front of your audience and read the paper! Sound obvious? It is. But scientists, particularly academics, do it all the time. I don't care how many awards your paper won. No one wants to hear you read it word for word.

Members of your audience can do that for themselves.

Your job is to *summarize* your paper in your presentation. Give the highlights. Don't swamp the audience with details. Even if you're talking to experts in your field, you've been thinking about your experiment or theory for months or years. No one else has a fraction of your familiarity with the material. They want *you* to explain it to them, simply and concisely.

If you can't present your paper without reading it, then don't expect your audience to pay much attention.

Create analogies and other comparisons by pretending that you're trying to explain a technical concept to little kids. How would you get them to understand it?

Check out Chapter 6 for more on analogies.

## Eliminating jargon

Most fields of specialized human endeavor have their own terms — better known as *jargon*. Jargon provides a communication shorthand for experts who must talk to one another all day. Their specialized vocabulary allows them to exchange information quickly and specifically. And jargon makes people who know it into insiders. The jargon serves as a secret code understood by people in the field and not by outsiders.

Neither reason justifies using jargon in a technical presentation unless you're talking to people in your field. In fact, the second reason — using jargon to be an insider — just insults your audience, because it makes them outsiders.

Jargon, by definition, won't be understood by your audience. So eliminate it from your presentation when you're speaking to laypeople.

The one exception to using jargon in a technical presentation to laypeople is when you explain the terms to your audience. Teaching them the secret language of your field makes them feel like insiders. However, your use of jargon in a presentation needs to be limited — if your talk is full of technical terms, explaining everything may take more time than you have.

## Connecting to real life

If you really want your audience to understand the technical stuff you're talking about, relate it to something in their lives. "You've got to connect with people on more than just a technical level," notes Dave. "Even if your audience is other technologists, you still have to make that connection with a real-world experience."

For example, Dave attended a technical talk about mathematical models used by the phone company in automated voice recognition systems. "The presenter had tapes of people calling in saying weird things," Dave recalls. "He showed us how hard it was for the system to recognize what the callers were asking for. That's an everyday experience that everyone can relate to — getting frustrated by calling up and getting an automated process instead of a real human being."

Most people aren't automatically interested in technical information. In fact, they often assume that it will be boring. So you've got to change that mindset at the outset of your presentation. Tell your audience why your information is important — specifically to them. How is it relevant to their lives? What can they do with the information you'll give them? How will their fortunes be poorer if they tune out your pearls of wisdom?

## Mind your manners: Being patient and polite

Yes, you're the expert. We know that already. That's why you're giving the presentation. So you don't have to impress us by showing off or putting down audience members. Your status as a "big brain" may automatically create a barrier between you and your average-intelligence audience before you even begin presenting. Don't make it worse by calling their questions or comments stupid. Or by stating, "It's obvious," when someone doesn't understand something. Or by purposely using a lot of big words to show how smart you are.

## Comparing apples and oranges

Have you ever made a brilliant argument for or against something, only to have someone say that you're comparing apples and oranges? All of a sudden, the momentum shifts. Everyone who thought you were a genius suddenly wonders if you know what you're talking about. Not anymore. Now you can say that your opponent is absolutely correct — you *are* comparing apples and oranges. Just use these lines from a presentation by Professor Paul Kennedy of Yale:

It's very easy to compare apples and oranges. When you look at an apple and look at an orange, you can see the great differences. You rarely note the similarities. But if you then put on your table an apple, an orange, and a banana, you begin to see how much the apple and the orange have in common as compared with the banana or the bunch of grapes.

In other words, apples and oranges are similar; they have a lot in common, and so on. I like these lines because you can use them to squelch anyone who disagrees with a previous comparison that you made.

You're supposed to be transferring information to us with your presentation, not humiliating us. So be patient. Help us along. Don't ridicule us. And think about how you like to be treated when you're in the audience listening to someone who's an expert in a field you know nothing about. Smiling once in a while doesn't hurt, either.

## Conveying enthusiasm

The stereotype of the technical presenter is a sober, logical, emotionless, left-brained, rational, no-nonsense type of scientist. Showing passion and enthusiasm? Maybe if you're a *mad* scientist.

Not so, argues Dave Haussler. "The most important thing is enthusiasm," he says. "You have to believe in what you're saying, and you have to convey that." Really? "Enthusiasm and belief in what you are trying to convey are more important than the technical details," says Dave. "You can be technically perfect, but if you're not enthusiastic about what you're saying, people will fall asleep or walk out. They'll never remember it."

## Crafting clean visual aids

Visual aids are a critical component of a technical presentation. When you have a lot of complex information, communicating it in a visual format is very effective. To put it another way: Showing a diagram is easier than describing it.

"It's very hard to do a technical presentation without visual aids," Dave agrees. "But you have to make those visuals clean. If you have too much detail, they look overcrowded." Unfortunately, he says that's a common mistake.

You can find suggestions for designing good visual aids and PowerPoint slides in Chapters 10 and 14. But here are some special things to keep in mind for technical presentations:

- ✔ Convey one idea clearly on every slide. "If you have multiple ideas, put them on one at a time," says Dave. "Don't give everybody too much at one time."

- ✔ If you write a caption under the axis of a graph, make sure that your audience can read it.

- ✔ Don't include slides of raw data. Instead, use charts or graphs that explain the relationships among the data.

- ✔ Don't use tables that contain a lot of numbers. No one will be able to read them. If you have to use numbers, display them as graphs.

- ✔ Use cartoons that illustrate your point. It's great way to bring some fun into a technical presentation.

- ✔ Unless they're essential, don't use equations. They're too difficult for most people to understand at a glance, and they bog you down.

# Focusing On Financial Presentations

An executive went to his doctor for an annual physical. The doctor said, "I've got bad news. You've only got a few hours to live." The executive couldn't believe it. He asked, "What should I do?" The doctor said, "Go listen to a CFO give a financial presentation." "Will that make me live longer?" asked the executive. "No," said the doctor. "But it will seem like it."

Let's be honest. Financial presentations aren't known for their riveting, emotional, exciting content. Too often, they're crammed full of data that no one understands except the person presenting it. But it doesn't have to be that way. If you think about it, financial presentations should be exciting. They tell the story of a company's success or failure in the marketplace. Has it vanquished economic obstacles through cunning strategy and precise execution? Or has it withered on the vine beneath blazing competition and poor management decisions? Financial information has all the makings of great drama: high-stakes conflict, all-too-human executives, and a cast of thousands.

So why are most financial presentations so boring? Maybe the people presenting them didn't read this book. Another reason may be that they don't tell their stories.

"Numbers can't speak for themselves," observes Les Wright. "You must tell the story behind them." He's right. And he should know. Les is a veteran Silicon Valley executive who has served as CFO at numerous high-tech companies. He's presented the numbers more times in his life than you'd want to count. His insights appear throughout this section of the chapter.

## *Talking finance to a general audience*

Do you have to give a financial presentation to nonfinancial people? Whoever they are, here are a few things to keep in mind:

- **Concentrate on basic financial measures and explain them.** You don't have to go into every financial metric ever devised. "Stick to the basics," advises Les. "Reviewing the company's balance sheet and profit-and-loss statement is probably enough. Just make sure you explain exactly what they are and what they measure."

- **Show why your company has value.** "The numbers tell the story, but they're not the story," says Les. "Talk about the company's opportunity, and back it up with examples of performance or potential."

- **Identify other metrics that can help them understand your business.** "Traditional financial measures may not tell the whole story," explains Les. "Discuss other benchmarks you use to measure progress in your business." For example, during the Internet boom, *page views* (the number of times a Web paged was viewed) were a key indicator for dot.com companies. In the cable television business, the number of households that subscribe to a particular cable service is a significant figure.

- **Go easy on the PowerPoint slides.** "No one reacts well to 40 slides of bullet-packed content," says Les. "Especially when you turn around and read them line by line from the screen." Les recommends using between 20 and 25 slides.

- **Don't overdo the numbers.** "If you're a publicly traded company, a lot of the standard financial information is available on the Internet or through press releases," says Les. "So you only need to show the numbers that you'll actually talk about." (An income statement and a balance sheet are always needed in a financial presentation.) He uses as few numerical slides as possible. "Fewer numbers lets me tell the story better," he observes.

# Presenting to analysts, bankers, and other financial experts

One of the most important financial presentations in the business world is the one given to analysts and commercial bankers. *Analysts* are the number crunchers from Wall Street investment firms who track the financial performance of particular companies and industries. Their opinions play a key role in determining the value of a company's stock. So when you present to them, both what you present and how you communicate are important. (You're most likely to be addressing these folks if you're a CFO, CEO, or marketing executive.)

Is there a secret to impressing them? "It helps to work for a company that's profitable and has an improving trend," says Les. How true. It also helps to have an organized, coherent presentation. Start with the tips for talking to a nonfinancial audience. Then factor in these special considerations:

- **Include traditional financial measures.** "Analysts expect to see some amount of trended financial information," says Les. "You've got to show trended profit-and-loss data, a balance sheet, revenue, operating-model information, inventory turnover, that sort of thing."

- **Tell your company's story.** "Analysts are sophisticated financial people," observes Les. "They can grasp the numerical part of your story pretty quickly. What they want to understand is the purpose of the story. They need to assess how the future looks for your company and decide whether to recommend buying your stock." How do you help them do this? Talk about things the company is doing that will expand its revenue and profit margin — for instance, new products that will position the company favorably relative to its competition or provide expansion into new geographic markets.

## Adding color

Just because the stereotypical financial presentation is boring doesn't mean yours has to be dull. Yes, the data is dry. But you can use quips, quotes, and anecdotes to make it more interesting. (For more on quotations, check out Chapter 6.)

According to Les, the best place to add color is when you're discussing your company's products and markets. "People like to hear customer stories," says Les. "Talking about how customers have used your products to solve problems or produce positive results is a good way to break up a financial data presentation."

Quips and quotes can be inserted anywhere in the presentation — as long as they make a point. Take a look at some ideas to get you going:

- ✔ **If your results were out of line with your guidance to analysts.** Say: There are three types of analysts in the world. Those that make things happen. Those that watch things happen. And those that wonder what happened. You're probably wondering what happened.

- ✔ **If you attribute a poor quarter to product development delays.** Say: If there is a fifty-fifty chance that something can go wrong, then nine times out of ten it will.

- ✔ **If you explain why you have to restate the last quarter.** Say: It's been said that there are three kinds of CFOs: those who can count and those who can't.

- ✔ **If you blame poor results on bad economic assumptions.** Say: The First Law of Economists states: For every economist, there exists an equal and opposite economist. The Second Law of Economists states: They're both wrong.

## Using charts and graphs to explain your numbers

Charts and graphs provide a way to show your audience the relationships among your numerical data. Drawn properly, they should be much easier to understand than boring rows of numbers. But don't overpack your presentation with them. They should be used to augment your important points, not to bury them.

And when you do use a chart or graph, make sure you can explain it. Imagine taking an audience question about a graph and realizing that you have no idea what the graph really means. If you don't know what a graph means, you have two outs: find out or take it out.

### Selecting a chart or a graph

Should you use a chart or graph? It depends. What kind of data are you presenting? What kind of relationships does it express? What effect on the audience do you want it to have? Take a look at some rules of thumb for using common types of financial charts and graphs:

- ✔ **Pie chart:** Pie charts are useful for showing the percentage of a whole. Want to show your company's share of the prune market? What about indicating how much of each dollar your company spends goes to advertising? These are classic pie-chart illustrations.

✔ **Bar chart:** Bar charts come in two varieties — vertical and horizontal. They're useful for showing comparisons. Want to show your company's revenue in relation to your competitors? How about comparing the profit margins of your two main product lines? These are classic bar-chart illustrations.

✔ **Line graph:** Line graphs are useful for illustrating changes over time — trends. Want to see how much your company's insurance costs have changed over the past five years? How about when your start-up can project profitability? These are classic line-graph illustrations.

(For more information on different charts and graphs, check out Chapter 10.)

Written financial reports often include numerous tables of data — rows and columns of numbers. Should you use them in your presentation? Not if you can help it. Even simple tables are hard to understand when you're sitting out in the audience. Charts and graphs are much easier to comprehend and have much more impact.

### Designing financial charts and graphs

When it comes to financial charts and graphs, less is more. The fewer lines, numbers, and pieces of text that are on the chart, the easier your graphic is to understand. Remember, a chart or graph is supposed to be *easier* to understand than a table of numbers.

Take a look at a few more tips for designing financial charts and graphs:

✔ Make sure your data is accurate. You lose a lot of credibility if it's not! It just takes one person in your audience to point out a discrepancy, and all your work may be down the drain.

✔ Make sure that your chart or graph accurately portrays the data. If a bar is labeled $5 million, it shouldn't touch the line indicating $6 million.

✔ Graphically distinguish data that is actual from data that's estimated or projected. (See Figure 18-1 for a line graph with projected data.)

✔ A chart or graph appropriate for one audience may be too complex for another audience. Ask yourself: Will the audience understand it or be confused by it?

✔ Don't turn a spreadsheet into a slide or overhead without modifying it. It's too crowded. No one can read it. And it makes you look ridiculous for doing so.

✔ Don't represent too many variables on one chart or graph. Try not to use more than three variables.

✔ Use a minimum amount of text. The more text you use, the longer it takes for your audience to mentally process your chart or graph.

✔ Keep text horizontal. It's easier to read. So if you have vertical bar charts, don't write text vertically in the bars.

You can focus audience attention on a chart or graph by building it one line at a time in a PowerPoint show. (See Chapter 14 for more on diagram builds.)

**Figure 18-1:**
Make sure that you clearly mark projected data in a financial line graph.

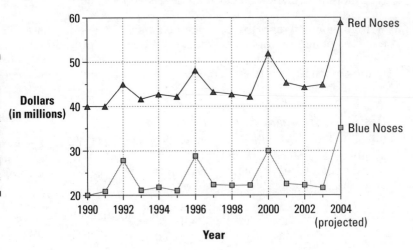

# Chapter 19

# Making Informational Briefings and Training Presentations

*B*riefings are one of the most common types of presentations in the world of business and government. Ever had to give a status report? That's a briefing. The main purpose of a briefing is to convey information. Many organizations schedule briefings on a regular basis — the weekly staff meeting is just one example. In this chapter, I provide some suggestions for making an effective briefing. I also discuss a specialized type of informational presentation: the training session. If you ever have to train anyone — and eventually, you may — you can find some useful tips for putting together a training presentation.

# Basic Rules for Informational Briefings

Anyone who has ever served in the military, worked in government, or had a job just about anywhere else has probably been exposed to an informational briefing. They're often the presentations that people try to miss. Why? They're routine. They're done so often that it seems nothing new is ever reported. And the brown-nosers in your organization often use them to advance their, well, brown-nosing — not a pleasant sight to watch. Be that as it may, the informational briefing is an entrenched part of corporate life. So you may as well make your briefings effective when you have to give them. Keep the following rules in mind:

✔ Keep your presentation as short as possible. Don't go into endless detail; provide only the essential information. That's why it's called *giving a brief*.

✔ Break your briefing into components so you can ask for audience questions or comments after each section.

✔ Keep the number of PowerPoint slides you use below three digits. We really, really, really don't want to see 100 slides, even if you think all of them are great. (See the first rule.)

✔ Start with a short introduction of your topic followed by your information.

✔ Your briefing is only as good as your information. If you have any concerns about the validity or quality of your information, make sure that you communicate that to your audience — for example, if you're presenting sales data that has not yet been verified.

✔ An informational briefing is traditionally limited to facts. Try to omit opinions and recommendations.

✔ Your briefing will be more interesting and informative if you use examples to support your points. Any applicable case studies usually work well — anything that can bring your information to life. (For more on examples, check out Chapter 6.)

✔ If you can tell your audience why the information you're presenting affects them and their jobs, they may actually pay attention.

✔ A clear and confident delivery helps to reinforce the importance of your information. Avoid terms like "maybe," "possibly," "it seems like," "could be," and similar phrases. These make you sound like you're hedging and don't have confidence in what you're saying.

✔ Be prepared to answer questions. In fact, a good conclusion to your briefing is to ask the audience if they have any questions. Make sure they understood everything you said. (For more on fielding questions, see Chapter 13.)

Think about *The Three Bears* when you're putting together your briefing. The papa bear's briefing has too much information. The mama bear's briefing doesn't have enough information. And the baby bear's briefing is just right.

# Special Rules for Training Presentations

Professional trainers have many names for the training presentation that you *don't* want to give. Mumble and stumble. Death by PowerPoint. And my personal favorite: the pour and snore. That's the one where the presenter pours out information as the audience snores away. Hey, you've probably been there — in the audience, that is. We all have.

In this section of the chapter, I give you some tips to make sure your audience soars instead of snores. To do that, I spoke with my old friend Paula Swanson. After a long career as a trainer for the U.S. government, she began her own consultancy. Based in Alameda, California, Paula Swanson Enterprises helps corporations train employees from different cultures to work together effectively.

## Using different learning styles

We all know that people learn through their senses: Our five senses are the way we receive information about the world. And some people claim to have a sixth sense. (That's how they receive information about the next world.)

Anyway, educational psychologists have long known that three senses — seeing, hearing, and touching — are the primary ways that we learn. Each of us has one of these senses as our dominant learning style. And your training audience will probably contain all three types. So you should understand the differences among them. Take a look at what you need to know:

- ✔ **Visual learners** respond to well-designed visual aids. That includes films and videos, as well as PowerPoint shows. You can identify them by their use of words and phrases dealing with vision. "I see what you're talking about.", "Show me what you mean.", or "I'm not getting the picture." For these people, seeing really *is* believing.

- ✔ **Auditory learners** respond to sound. They like lectures. They also pay close attention to your *paralanguage* — pitch, tone, rate, and so on. So if you drone on in a monotone, they climb the walls. You can identify them by their use of words and phrases dealing with hearing. "I hear what you're talking about.", "Tell me what you mean.", or "Listen to what I think."

- ✔ **Kinesthetic learners** respond by actually doing the things that you want them to learn. Because they learn by doing and practicing, they like "hands-on" and experimental types of learning. They're interested in any way they can get physically involved. You can identify them by their use of words and phrases such as "I can't wait to get my hands on that.", "I am excited about doing this.", and "When can I practice doing that?" They are the types of learners who would most enjoy a "ropes course." Your personal attention can be very important to them. They also tend to touch you when you're in close contact with them — a hand on your shoulder, that sort of thing. You know, touchy-feely.

In light of the three different styles of learning, it behooves you to include methods in your presentation that address each of them. Stimulate your audience with a mix of visual, auditory, and kinesthetic information. By using a variety of training approaches, you ensure that something gets through to everyone in your audience. And there's a side benefit — your session doesn't get boring. If people don't like lectures, you'll soon be asking them to engage in small-group exercises. If they don't like small-group exercises, maybe they'll like your group discussion.

## No kids allowed: Understanding adult learning preferences

Before you start developing your training presentation, remember that adults learn differently than children do. So a presentation that wows grade school students doesn't necessarily win applause if given to their parents. The following subsections go over some basic tenets of educational psychology that apply to training adults. Keep them in mind as you create your presentation.

### Tell me why: Keeping your presentation relevant

Adults want to know why your presentation matters to them. Is it work related? Does it further their goals? Does it lead to a promotion? If they can't see a practical application in your training, then they won't be a very attentive audience. And they won't learn much. That mea  you can't take chances. Don't assume they'll figure out why your information is good for them. Make the connection for them. Tell them very specifically.

### Build self-esteem

Adult egos come in many sizes, and not just people with big ones worry about being humiliated during a training session. Each person may be wondering: What if I give a wrong answer? What if I say something that everyone else disagrees with? What if I do something that makes me look silly? So the presenter has to tread very carefully. Keep the feelings of your audience in mind — especially when you ask them to participate. It's risky for them. They don't want to be the main topic tomorrow at the water cooler. Do your best to establish an atmosphere in which it's okay to take risks and fail.

How do you do that? Establish up-front exactly what will happen during your training session. Telling your audience what they can expect will relieve some of their anxiety. Also important is the way you describe your session. Tell attendees that you're there to help them improve, and that amnesty has already been granted if they do something wrong.

Trainer John Spafford suggests getting a cover letter from top management to give attendees before your session begins. The letter should emphasize the amnesty concept and encourage attendees to do whatever it takes to master the skills under discussion.

### Provide chances for exchanging experiences

An adult audience already has a wealth of knowledge and experience it can apply to the concepts and information you provide. Give your audience members an opportunity to do so. Let them exchange ideas and work together. They may learn more from one another than they do from you. That's okay. The whole point of your presentation is for them to learn stuff. (For more, see "Making your presentation interactive," later in this chapter.)

### Act as a facilitator

Adults like to be treated as peers. But the teacher-student relationship gives more power to the presenter. Don't take advantage of it. In fact, try not to use it at all. It just creates resentment in adults who "don't want to be treated like children" and "don't want to be told what to do." So instead of viewing yourself as the all-powerful, fountain-of-knowledge teacher, envision yourself as a facilitator. Playing that role will make you much more appreciated by your audience and more likely to help them learn — you're facilitating their acquisition of new skills and knowledge.

One of the simplest ways to perform a facilitator role is to ask questions. If attendees don't know something, don't just give them the answer. Ask strategic questions until the attendee can provide the answer.

## Planning do's and don'ts

Now you need to create your content — the material that you'll be presenting. The following subsections go over a few do's and don'ts to help you through the process.

### Do include a strong opening and closing

The opening and closing are the two most critical parts of a training presentation. The opening is when your audience members decide whether they're interested in what you have to say. And if they decide to pay attention, then the information in your closing is what they have the best chance of remembering.

Here's what you should tell your audience in your opening:

> ✔ State the learning objectives of your presentation. These objectives are the whole purpose of your presentation. Everything you do and say should be designed to support them. So think very carefully about what you want your audience to learn. "You need to know if they've learned what you wanted them to," says Paula. "So come up with very specific objectives."

✔ Tell them how they can benefit from the information you're about to give them and why your presentation is relevant to them. (For more on this, see "Tell me why: Keeping your presentation relevant," earlier in this chapter.)

✔ Provide an overview of the entire session, the various segments, and how they're organized. If you break up your information into organized segments, your audience has an easier time learning and remembering. (See Chapter 4 for more on organizing your presentation.) Breaking up information will also give you obvious times to provide breaks.

✔ Tell them what's expected of them after they've attended your training session.

✔ Do something to get their attention: do an opening exercise, play a game, ask a thought-provoking question.

Here's what you should do in your closing:

✔ Review all the major points that you've covered.

✔ Reiterate the relevance of the information.

### Do choose appropriate methodologies

There's more than one way to skin a cat and more than one way to train someone to skin a cat. But enough about taxidermy. The point is that you can use many methods to train your audience. Lecture, group discussion, debate, role-playing, and the list goes on. Choose the methods that best convey your content. And keep in mind that you're dealing with adult learners. Take a look at a few suggestions:

✔ Demonstrate a skill in front of the entire group and then have people practice it in small groups. Adults particularly enjoy working in small groups.

✔ Demonstrate a skill to a member of the audience who then demonstrates it to someone else in front of the entire group.

✔ Discuss a case study. Adults like case studies because they're realistic. Keep that in mind when you're creating them.

✔ Break the audience into small groups, and give them a problem-solving exercise. Have the solution require information that you've already discussed.

### Do customize your information for your audience

The more specifically you can make your content apply to your audience, the more relevant it becomes for them. And relevance is a big deal with adult learners. So if you're talking to accountants, don't use the same examples as when you're talking to engineers or doctors. Yes, it takes some work and research to keep changing the examples, but work and research make your presentation effective.

### Don't try to cover too much

A common mistake made by rookie trainers is trying to cover too much in one session. And you may fall prey to this same temptation when you put your training presentation together. Don't! Your audience will learn more if you cover a few things completely rather than a lot of things incompletely. They don't want to be overwhelmed with information. (For more on organizing your presentation, check out Chapter 4.)

Having trouble deciding what to cut out? Go back to your learning objectives, and match them against the material you're thinking about including. Does the material further any of the objectives? If not, cut it. And be honest with yourself.

### Don't go too long without a break

No matter how fascinating your presentation, your audience still needs a chance to move around every so often. We're wired that way. (Adults don't like to sit for long periods of time; it's tough on their aging backs.) So give your audience a break — literally. You think little kids make a fuss about going to the bathroom? They've got nothing on their adult counterparts. If you're facilitating a session that will last a few hours, give your audience time to go to the bathroom and get a drink of water. Try to give them ten minutes of break time for every hour of training time. You can also give people a chance to move around by strategically scheduling exercises throughout your session. Let me put it this way: No one wants to hear you drone on for hours. And if they start wiggling around in their seats, you've lost them.

## Making your presentation interactive

Another unique aspect of training presentations involves interaction with the audience. Training presentations are designed to encourage audience participation. The more the audience participates, the more successful the presentation is considered to be. In an ordinary presentation, you ask the audience to hold questions and comments until the end. In a training presentation, you welcome audience input whenever it comes and encourage it as much as possible.

Why the emphasis on interaction? A basic principle of learning theory holds that people who actively participate learn better and retain more of your message. And doesn't that sound like what you're trying to accomplish?

The key to a successful training session is taking the focus off the trainer and putting it on the learner. "Trainers tend to talk too much," says Paula Swanson. "They should really try to talk as little as possible." She says the trainer should try to create an environment where the audience has as much time as possible to discuss and experiment among themselves — using the trainer's information, of course.

Here are a few techniques to encourage audience interaction during your presentation.

### Ask questions

A question immediately involves the audience members, because it forces them to start thinking of an answer. Look through your presentation, and translate your content into questions whenever possible. Asking questions keeps your audience engaged and thinking. The ancient Greek philosopher Socrates taught by asking provocative questions, and his Socratic method is still famous today. But your questions don't all have to be provocative. You can ask audience members to guess the outcome of a demonstration, experiment, or exercise. You can ask them to brainstorm solutions to a problem. You can ask if they see any patterns based on what you've discussed so far. Just ask.

Here's a great tip from Paula Swanson for using questions when you're discussing good and bad examples of something — supervisors, for example. "If you start off by asking, 'What's an example of a good supervisor?' people will groan," she says. "But if you ask, 'Can anybody give me an example of bad supervisory practices?' every hand in the room goes up." Why? "People love to talk about how bad things are," she observes. "It's a great way to get them energized." After discussing the bad examples, she easily transitions to the good examples — the topic she really wants to talk about. So when you're asking questions, do worst first.

### Use small-group exercises

Remember that adult learners already have a lot of knowledge and experience to share. Putting them in a small-group setting allows them to exchange ideas and learn from one another. That's the type of interaction they probably enjoy most. Provide opportunities for your audience to work in small groups.

Have a spare exercise or two ready to use in case you need them. (Make them exercises that you can plug in anywhere in your session.) They come in handy if some of your segments run faster than you'd planned.

### Give plenty of feedback

One of the most powerful forms of interaction during your training session is the feedback that you provide to members of your audience. They want to know how they did on your exercises. And more important, they want to know if they're successfully acquiring the skills and information that they've come to learn.

But remember: Self-esteem is a big issue with adult learners. Egos are fragile. No one wants to hear that she's incompetent — especially in front of coworkers. So be very careful with your feedback.

Take a look at a few tips for making feedback helpful rather than hurtful:

- **Make feedback as specific as possible.** A general comment like "You didn't do that well" doesn't tell the audience member what to fix or how to improve.

- **Distinguish between people and performance.** If you criticize something done by an audience member, clearly point out that you're talking about an act or behavior he performed, not his personality.

- **Precede negative feedback with positive feedback.** Before you say what someone did wrong, say what she did right. C'mon, you can find something!

## Good times: Adding fun to your presentation

We live in an entertainment-oriented world. And people want to be entertained — especially during training sessions. That's why the word *infotainment* has come into prominence. "It's a cross between information and entertainment," explains Paula. "It really means that a training session will be lively and engaging as well as informative."

Does that mean you tell a lot of jokes during your training presentation? Not necessarily, particularly if you can't tell a joke. But you can use many other forms of humor to create rapport with your audience and gain their attention. (See Chapter 8 for more information on using humor.) Telling an embarrassing story about yourself is always a good icebreaker. For additional ways to use humor in training, check out *Laugh and Learn* by Doni Tamblyn (Amacom).

But fun isn't limited to humor. Here are some other ways you can inject fun into your training session:

- Stage a mock quiz show to review material that you've already discussed.

- Give candy as a reward to anyone who asks a provocative question.

- Bring hats and other props that you can use to emphasize points at appropriate times.

- Play games that reinforce the skills and information that you're presenting.

# Breaking the ice

When a training session begins, your audience may be uncomfortable, because they don't know each other. And if they do know each other, they may be even more uncomfortable. Worrying about looking silly in front of strangers is bad enough. But it's really scary if it can happen with people you work with every day.

That's why a lot of trainers use icebreakers, which can set a fun tone for your training session and get people feeling more comfortable. Yes, they can be corny. But they usually accomplish their mission — reducing stress and getting your audience in the proper mood to learn.

Here are a few to get you started:

- Ask each person to introduce herself and to describe the first work she ever got paid to do and what she learned from it.

- Tell each person to imagine that he is a corporation. Ask him to write a corporate slogan for himself and explain how he chose his slogan.

- Again, tell each person to imagine that she is a corporation. Ask her to draw a logo for herself and explain what it means.

- Ask everyone to tell the group his middle name and how he got it. You, the presenter, should go first.

- Ask everyone to tell the group a business buzzword or buzzphrase that she can't stand (and why she can't stand it).

- Pair off audience members, and have them interview each other. Then have them introduce each other to the group.

# Chapter 20

# Presenting a Business Plan to a Venture Capitalist or Your Boss

*A*lthough the saying "Time is money" can be applied to many of us, it doesn't apply to *venture capitalists* (people who invest in new businesses — also known as *VCs*). They've got plenty of money; what they don't have is time. So they get pretty cranky when forced to listen to an amateurish presentation of a *business plan* (a detailed description of how a new business expects to succeed). The same is true for high-level executives on the receiving end of internal business-plan presentations. They don't have any more time than venture capitalists. And they're not any happier to suffer through a poorly executed presentation.

In this chapter, I show you how to present a business plan in a way that will keep investors from frowning and screaming at you. Most important, if they throw anything at you, it will be money.

For more information on business plans, check out *Business Plans For Dummies* by Paul Tiffany and Steven D. Peterson (Wiley), and *Business Plans Kit For Dummies* by Steven D. Peterson and Peter E. Jaret (Wiley).

## Hints for Presenting a Business Plan to a Venture Capitalist

In order to uncover the secret of prying an investment out of a venture capitalist, I spoke with prominent Boston VC Charles Lax, cofounder of SOFTBANK Venture Capital and founder and managing general partner of GrandBanks

282 Part V: Checking Out Tips and Tricks for Common Presentations

Capital. His firm receives thousands of requests for funding every year. After most entrepreneurs are screened out through phone conversations and Web-site reviews, a select few are invited to present their business plans. "We give them 60 to 90 minutes," says Charley. Not much time if you're asking for millions of dollars. And some VC firms allow even less. But don't sweat it. You'll do fine if you follow Charley's advice.

## Recognize that you're selling

A business plan presentation is a sales presentation. You want to sell the VC on your plan and your company. And just as in any sales presentation, the key to success is preparation. "I'd find out everything there is to know about your 'customer' — the VC," advises Charley.

He's always amazed when people come to his office to seek funding who haven't looked at his Web site. "Any VC you're going to see will have a Web site," Charley observes. "On that Web site, they'll have a list of portfolio companies and a bio of everyone you'll be meeting with. So you can learn about what they've invested in, what successes they had, where they went to school, what their personal interests are." All very valuable information for you to use as part of your presentation.

Dress appropriately. "Some firms expect men to be wearing suits and ties," says Charley. "With others, you can be less formal. Call and ask an administrative assistant what clothes are appropriate." (For more on dressing for success, see Chapter 11.)

And definitely bring a business card. Don't worry if your new venture doesn't have a logo yet. Make some temporary business cards. You make some yourself with an inkjet printer. "You know how many meetings I have a week?" asks Charley. "I have a stack of 40 business cards from a meeting I went to yesterday. The only thing I may walk away with is a business card. If you don't have a card, how am I supposed to get in touch with you? How can I remember who you are?"

## Establish a connection

You receive a much better reception for your presentation if you first establish a connection to the VC. Do you have mutual friends? Do you know someone else who was funded by the VC? Did you do business with one of the VC's *portfolio companies* (companies that the VC has already invested in)? Do you have a sales lead for one of the VC's portfolio companies? "If you come in with a sales lead for one of my portfolio companies, you've got my attention," says Charley. "It also tells me that you're pretty sharp." So again, read the VC's Web site, especially the bios. Figure out some connectivity, and communicate it at the beginning of your presentation.

## Ask the VC what to focus on

You could talk all day about your company and why the VC should fund it. But you don't have all day. If you're lucky, you get an hour. You often get much less time. (Always make sure you know how much time you'll have well in advance.) So you need to know what information is important to the VC. How do you find out? Just ask.

"Walk in and say, 'We have a lot of data that covers who we are, what we're trying to create and how we're going to get to market,'" advises Charley. "'Having said that, we want to make sure that we cover what you need covered. What information do you want us to focus on so we can make it productive for you? We know we have a limited amount of time.'"

## Talk up your team

"The purpose of your business plan presentation isn't just to get us to understand the opportunity," notes Charley. You also need to let the VC know how you're going to make things happen according to the plan. And the people who make things happen are your executive team. Emphasize their knowledge and experience, including their college degrees, top companies they've worked for, and their specialties.

Don't worry if your whole team isn't in place yet. Tell the VCs who you'd like to hire and how much they cost. Not having a complete set of executives can sometimes work in your favor. VCs like to suggest potential executives to their portfolio companies.

## Show how you fit with the VC's investments

You may have the greatest product in the world, but if it doesn't fit with a VC's investing strategy, you won't get very far. Many VCs invest only in certain types of industries or certain geographical regions. Know what those are. And be able to show how your venture fits in. Look at the VC's portfolio companies, and find similarities to your business. If you can show how the VC's portfolio companies would benefit from working with your company, even better. Establish a connection between your proposal and the VC's existing investments as early in your presentation as possible.

## Know your assumptions about how much you want for how long

"People often ask for too little or too much," says Charley. "Rarely do they ask for the right amount." That's why he wants to hear very specific details about how much capital you want to raise, what you're going to accomplish with it, and how long it will last.

Isn't that usually covered in the financial PowerPoint slides? Yes, but not in the way that VCs want to hear about it. "Every entrepreneur knows that the company has to do $100 million in year five, or the VC won't look at it," Charley explains. "We automatically know that the revenue projections are wrong. And the entrepreneurs know that I know when they walk in. So we don't have to spend a lot of time dickering over the specific revenue numbers."

So what exactly does he want to know about the numbers? "We can spend time talking about the *assumptions* that went into creating those revenue numbers," explains Charley. "The assumptions are the important things. Timelines for getting the product to market. What percentage of companies testing the product will become paying customers? How many people will be in your sales force? What kind of revenue per employee? What kind of revenue per salesman? What is your proposed cash burn? Those are the things we want to spend time talking about."

He also wants to talk about how much money you plan to spend and what you plan to spend it on. "Those are numbers we have control over," he notes. "So we want to know exactly how you plan to use any capital you receive from us. How long will the money last?"

## Have an exit strategy

When will the VCs get their money back? Every VC that you approach wants to know the answer to this question. So if your company doesn't go public, who will buy it? "VCs are in business to get liquid," explains Charley. "I closed a deal a month ago, and I'm already looking to sell the company." He asks everyone who comes for funding who will buy his or her company. If they haven't really thought about it or don't know, they'd better have some amazing technology.

## Tell a story with essential slides

Anyone giving a business-plan presentation must have a set of PowerPoint slides detailing the opportunity for investors. I've listed some of the slides that VCs expect to see. (For the scoop on using PowerPoint effectively, check out Chapters 14, 15, and 16.)

✔ **Executive summary:** This is your venture at a glance. It needs to include all the essential information about your enterprise: what it does, who's involved, size of market, how big you'll get by when, how you're different from competitors. Show this slide first. It may be the only slide that the VC sees if things come up and someone has to leave. In other words, the executive summary is your most important slide. It must convey everything the VC needs to know in case you never get to show any others.

✔ **Management team:** Who are the key people? What expertise do they bring? This slide should answer those questions. You can also include the name of your legal counsel — something Charley always wants to know.

Want to really beef up this slide? Include an advisory board. "We like to see people with a lot of relevant knowledge associated with an opportunity," says Charley. "So get some successful people in your industry to be part of your enterprise on an advisory basis. That will help get VCs excited."

✔ **Solution:** What customer problem does your product solve?

✔ **Financials:** These should include the usual suspects: revenue, profits, expenses, cash flow.

✔ **Capitalization table:** Who is currently invested in your company? How much have they invested? And when and at what price?

✔ **Market:** Who's going to buy your product? How much will they pay? How many potential customers do you have?

✔ **Competition:** Who are your current and potential competitors? You can score extra points by showing who's funding those companies and how much capital they raised.

✔ **Value proposition:** What's the sales pitch to potential customers? Why should they buy your product?

✔ **Technology:** These slides explain your product. Try not to use more than three slides here. One is preferable. (Many presenters go into too much detail on this topic.)

✔ **Distribution:** How are you going to get your product to the market? Sales force? Distributors? Partnerships?

✔ **Potential partners and exits:** List companies that might partner with your venture. List companies that might purchase your venture.

✔ **Funding:** How much do you want?

In what order should you show your slides? Whatever order is most persuasive to your audience. "Tell the story of how you created the idea or concept and why this is an opportunity," advises Charley. Tell the story with your slides. Use them in a way that builds the story to its logical conclusion — that you should get funded.

## Show enthusiasm

VCs are investing in you as much as in your business plan. They want to see people who passionately believe in their ideas. They like people who project confidence, not desperation. Get excited while you're presenting. Err on the side of too much energy. Make sure the VC knows how enthusiastic you are about your plan. I'll put it this way: If you were investing your money, and two opportunities seemed equally lucrative, would you go with the entrpreneur who was ho-hum or the one who was enthusiastic?

Don't be a pain. The people investing in your venture will be working with you on a regular basis. They don't want to partner with a pain.

# Special Rules for Presenting a Business Plan to Bigwigs at Your Company

To get the lowdown on presenting to bigwigs at your own company, I spoke with veteran high-tech executive Neil Baron. A Harvard MBA who has spent most of his career at Fortune 500 companies, Neil has had the opportunity to present many business plans to top management.

The following sections go over a few rules that apply specifically to presenting a business plan within a corporate organization.

## Talk to customers

Just because you have some cool technology doesn't mean you have a product or a business. "People get so excited about the technology that they don't stop to think if anyone would buy it," says Neil. "You've got to talk to your existing customers, find out if they're interested, and figure out the size of your market." Although talking to one customer is better than talking to none, it's not a large-enough sample. "Even if your technology satisfies the needs of one customer," explains Neil, "that doesn't automatically justify a funding investment from top management."

Nothing spices up your presentation better than positive quotes from customers, according to Neil, especially if you have customer feedback on product prototypes.

## Be aware of office politics

Some say that a friend in the corporate world is someone who'll stab you in the front. That may be a little extreme, but sometimes, it does seem like you see more backstabbing in big companies than in an orthopedic surgery center. The point is that you'd better be able to identify your allies and enemies in regard to your business plan proposal. Who will it affect, and how will it affect them? Answering that question is a good starting point for assessing the political implications of your plan. In an ideal word, your proposal would be evaluated solely on its merits, without reference to office politics. But we don't live in an ideal world. If we did, you wouldn't have to pitch your proposal. You'd already be the boss.

Want to improve your plan's chances for approval? Presell it to key decision-makers one on one in the days before your official presentation. If you get each person to buy into your ideas beforehand, you'll have fewer political problems later. "You can find out their concerns in advance and address them," notes Neil.

## Define the customer problem properly

"You've got to state the customer problem you're solving in real-world terms," says Neil, "not in geek speak." Unfortunately, many business plan presenters are engineers and overdo the technical jargon. Does it really make a difference? You be the judge. Here's an example from when Neil worked at a database software company.

"We had a solution that gave a lot of useful information to police," he recalls. "When officers pulled someone over at 3 a.m., they could use our software to immediately learn if that person was a high or low safety risk." Naturally, it was a highly technical, complex solution. "We could have talked about the need to integrate heterogeneous databases and multiple operating systems across multiple hardware platforms," says Neil. But that probably wouldn't have sold very well. Instead, they talked about how the software made "police officers safer when they made arrests while reducing the cost of fighting crime." Which do you think sounds more persuasive?

## Speak management's language

Every company has its own culture — beliefs, values, and ways of expressing things. Tap into it. Show how your business plan furthers the company's mission. What goals did your CEO outline in your company's last annual report? Talk about how your plan fits in with those goals. Use the buzz phrases popular with top management to describe what you're proposing.

Don't go overboard with corporate language. Make sure that any terms you use are actually used by everyone in the company. Some departments and divisions have their own jargon that doesn't translate across the organization. You don't want to sound like a character out of the Dilbert comic strip.

## Emphasize the financials

"Articulate right up-front how your company will make money by investing in your proposal," advises Neil. "Too many presenters don't spend enough time thinking about the financials, and they ignore the expense side of things. Make sure you do your homework on costs and benefits. Your idea isn't brilliant just because it sounds great. It's brilliant because it will make money for your company."

## Practice, then practice some more

Neil also advises doing dry runs with trusted advisors and coworkers. "Get them to ask you tough questions," he says. "Then you'll have answers ready when you get those same questions from top management." He suggests practicing five or six times, particularly your introduction. "If you can grab them at the beginning, everything will go more smoothly," says Neil. "The first five minutes is the key." (For more on practicing, see Chapter 5.)

# Top Mistakes to Avoid During Business Plan Presentations

Investors receive thousands of business plans every year. They don't have enough hours in the day or days in the week to hear a formal presentation of each one. So most of them are filed and forgotten. A select few are chosen, and their creators receive an invitation to present.

So if you have a chance to present your plan, you've already survived a major weeding-out process. That's the good news. The bad news is that even having come this far, only a miniscule percentage of business plans presented get funding. The odds aren't in your favor. But you can increase your chances for success. Just avoid making these common mistakes — whether you're presenting to venture capitalists or a company's senior executives.

## Forgetting about the customer

Make sure you talk to some customers before you even put together your presentation.

"Don't confuse developer interest with customer interest," warns Neil. Just because engineers are interested in making a red widget instead of a blue widget doesn't mean any customers want one. "Lots of plans assume that something that's interesting and challenging for development people to make will pay off for the company," he says. "But there are much cheaper ways to improve developer morale than funding your business plan."

## Arriving late

VCs and senior executives are very time-sensitive. They plan their schedules to the minute, because they have no time to spare. Being late makes you look really, really bad. It also cuts into your already-limited presentation time.

Be on time, but be prepared to wait for the other person.

## Having too much information about the wrong items

Talking to potential investors isn't the same as talking to potential customers. Customers want a major discussion of product features and benefits. Investors don't. Investors want to know how the business will succeed, how much their investment will return, and when they'll get their money back. Yes, technology is exciting. But it's not as exciting to investors as it is to the engineers who developed it. Unfortunately, detailed explanations of technology are too often what gets presented to potential investors. "We see this all the time," says Charley. "They overplay the technology and the addressable market, but they underplay the people. You've got to spend some time selling VCs on the people who will be part of your company if you want to get us interested."

Neil agrees. "If you're presenting internally to top management, you've got to spend more time on the market and the financials," he says. "And you've got to be succinct in general. No one wants to sit through 600 PowerPoint slides, even though you worked very hard to create all that material. The executives end up with their eyes glazed over and falling asleep. Top management mainly wants to know how the business plan will impact the bottom line."

## Being unprepared for questions

Can you think on your feet? I hope so, because you're going to have to do a lot of thinking while presenting your business plan. "Many people can't deal with being asked questions out of the order they do their presentation," observes Charley, "or being asked questions about things they didn't put in their presentation." He tends not to invest in these people. "You've got to expect and be prepared to handle questions when you present to VCs," he explains.

The same is true when presenting a business plan internally to top management. "You can't just focus on the plan," says Neil. "You've got to anticipate the types of questions you'll be asked by a team of senior executives."

How do you do this? First, based on your knowledge of the people who will be in your audience, make a list of questions that you think they may ask. Second, when you practice your talk with trusted colleagues and family members, ask them to pepper you with any questions they can think of.

Be prepared for off-the-wall questions. These may come from investors who aren't familiar with your technology or business. They may ask things that are so stupid or ridiculous that you just want to cry. But you can't cry, or you won't get funded. You also can't tell them that they have no idea what they're talking about. Prepare to be patient, and be ready to explain.

Your attitude when answering questions can be as important as the substance of your answer. Are you defensive? Confident? Arrogant? Investors have lots of business opportunities to choose among. They don't want to work with a jerk. More important, they don't want to invest in someone whose attitude creates a barrier to successful execution of the business plan.

If you still have questions about fielding questions, check out Chapter 13.

If you get a tough question, pause to gather your thoughts by taking a sip of water before you answer.

## Failing with the demo

Murphy's Law says that whatever can go wrong, will go wrong. This is axiomatic for demos. They just never work when you need them to. So don't even attempt one during a business plan presentation. If your demo fails, you just countered any excitement you generated. Instead, use a simulation. Show a video of your product in action or a series of photographs.

## Not numbering PowerPoint handouts

This is one of Charley's pet peeves. "They print out their slides and give us a copy," he explains. "Then we take notes on each slide as they do their presentation." So far, so good. What's the problem? "At some point in the presentation, they'll say, 'Go back to page 16; I want to talk about the architecture of the software.' Twenty percent of the time, there's no number on the pages." (See Chapter 14 for more on numbering your slides.)

## Not confirming how much time you have

VCs and top executives are busy people. So don't plan on having the amount of time to present that you've been promised. If you don't verify how much time you have as soon as you get to the meeting, you're making a big mistake. "If the main decision-maker only has ten minutes, you'd better rearrange your presentation," advises Charley. "You've got ten minutes to say who you are, how much money you're looking for, what your large market opportunity is, and who is going to be interested in buying the business."

PowerPoint has a feature that allows you to show your slides out of order if necessary. To find out more, check out Chapter 15.

## Talking too much

If you talk too much and go over your allotted presentation time, you leave less time for questions. And the question period is when investors really form opinions of your abilities. In addition, talking too much can leave your audience dazed and unable to distinguish important information from fluff. And you definitely don't want to obscure the reasons they should invest in your plan. Remember: Don't overstay your welcome.

## Making unjustified assumptions

Every business plan makes assumptions about financial projections, market size, product development timelines, and many other aspects of the business. That's okay. But you must be able to defend your assumptions. That's the problem many business plan presenters run into. Under close questioning, their assumptions prove at best incorrect and at worst laughable. Recognize the assumptions that you're making, and give plenty of thought to how you will justify them.

Everyone knows that a financial projection for a business plan is an educated guess. But try to use more education and less guesswork. Inflated revenues and minimal expenses don't impress investors with anything except your lack of credibility.

## Ignoring audience feedback

If your audience looks bored or confused, do you just stick to your prepared talk? No. You've got to make adjustments based on their feedback. And that means you've got to look for their feedback. Are they shifting in their seats? Are they looking at their watches? Are they staring out the window? Don't pretend everything is okay. Ask if they'd rather hear about a different aspect of the plan. Ask if they have any questions. Get them back with you again. (For more about gauging audience reaction, see Chapter 12.)

## Not following up

Investors frown on presenters who don't follow up. "You're getting a gift of my time," says Charley. "It's just common courtesy to send a thank-you note. Send it in an e-mail." Or if you really want to impress someone, send a hand-written note. It doesn't have to be an opus. Just thank the VC or company executive for their time and the opportunity to present your plan.

Want to score extra points? When you send the follow-up note, congratulate the VC on something. Did she just close a major deal? Did she get mentioned in the media? You can find something if you look hard enough.

# Chapter 21

# Making Virtual Presentations: Phone, Video, Web, and E-Mail

*A* virtual presentation includes any kind of presentation where people don't meet face to face. They can be given via telephone, video, or over the Web. Virtual presentations sometimes include sharing audio and video data, documents, or other types of information. They can be highly interactive or primarily a one-way transmission. Quite often, there will be a few people in one location around a speakerphone or in a video room and a few people in another location. Other times, all the participants are sitting alone in their cubicles, interacting via e-mail.

In order to get the latest information on virtual presentations, I talked with Kare Anderson, an expert who has spoken at numerous virtual conferences. A former journalist, Kare is now a professional speaker who talks about specific ways to communicate and connect in order to create more opportunity with others. (You can find out more about her at www.sayitbetter.com.) She provided a lot of the information in this chapter.

# Identifying Which Virtual Presentation Is Right for You

Before we look at different types of virtual presentations, let's examine the pros and cons of giving one. Here are the pros:

✓ If you fear presenting while facing an audience, a virtual presentation may solve that problem. Are you great on the phone but terrible in person? You'll love giving virtual presentations. It may eliminate your stage fright.

✓ You can save a lot of time, money, and energy with a virtual presentation. Instead of presenting in person numerous times at different locations around the world, you can present once from where you're located.

✓ You can potentially reach a much larger audience than with a traditional in-person presentation.

✓ It may actually be easier to get audience participation during a virtual presentation than a face-to-face presentation. Many people who are reluctant to ask questions or make comments in a "real" setting have no such hesitation in a virtual environment.

✓ If your presentation is archived, anyone who couldn't attend when you gave it can view it later.

That all sounds pretty good, right? But there are also some cons. They include the following:

✓ You miss a lot of the audience feedback (body language and so on) available in a face-to-face presentation.

✓ You can't create the same level of energy and enthusiasm that's possible when the audience is physically in the same room with you.

✓ If the technology malfunctions, your presentation is over.

Now you need to decide which virtual presentation is right for you. Many criteria influence your decision regarding what type of virtual presentation best suits your needs.

Some factors you should consider are interactivity, number of people in the audience, and type of information to be discussed. You can choose which type of presentation best fits your needs by examining the following short descriptions of different types of virtual meetings:

✓ **Telephone conferencing:** In this type of meeting, attendees can hear one another, but they can't see one another or exchange nonoral data (although such data can be mailed or e-mailed ahead of time). Such meetings work best with smaller groups, are conducted over the telephone, and are useful if complicated visuals aren't necessary or if attendees are uncomfortable with more technical types of virtual meetings.

✔ **Videoconferencing:** Videoconferencing refers to a meeting in which attendees at various locations can see and hear one another. It allows the use of visual materials, such as charts and graphs. Videoconferences can be conducted in studios that are specially designed for that purpose. Many corporations and larger businesses with multiple locations have their own permanent videoconferencing setups. Such meetings are best if watching body language is important or you need to communicate complex data. Video is also preferable if you want to make sure that all attendees are paying attention.

✔ **Web conferencing:** Web conferencing commonly refers to a meeting conducted over the Web in which attendees can receive and transmit video, audio, and data such as documents and PowerPoint slides. A small number of people (about five to ten) can work on a project together, called *Web collaboration;* a large group of people (up to several thousand) can receive a one-way transmission of information, called *Webcasting;* or several people can log onto a Web site and view a seminar or other event, called a *Webinar.*

The ability to archive Web conferences is one of the reasons they're growing in popularity. They can then be played back on-demand at a time more convenient for people who could not attend the event. Some companies also break Web conferences into smaller segments and use them as training modules.

✔ **E-mail meetings:** An e-mail meeting involves the exchange of e-mails in real time among meeting attendees. It allows attendees to share documents, graphic files, and other information that can be attached to an e-mail message. E-mail meetings are useful for communicating information, but wide-scale interaction is difficult.

Just knowing what each type of meeting is doesn't factor in other important considerations, such as technology, budget, and meeting goals. See how those factors may impact the virtual presentation you choose by reading the following sections.

## *Avoiding technical difficulties*

The type of virtual presentation you choose depends on the technology you have available and the level of technology that you want to involve. Kare recommends choosing the lowest technology that will allow you to accomplish your presentation goals. "The more complex the technology, the more things can go wrong," she notes. "The lower the level of technology, the more people can participate." That makes the phone the technology of choice if it suits your needs. It's the most familiar technology available. (Even though e-mail is simple to use, many older people remain wary of it.)

Make the following considerations before you decide what type of technology to use:

- ✔ **Audience experience:** The human factor can play a major role in deciding what type of technology to use for a virtual presentation. If most of the audience is familiar with telephone conferencing but not Web conferencing, you need to take that into consideration. It doesn't automatically mean you shouldn't go with Web conferencing, but it does mean that you must provide much more guidance to audience members.

- ✔ **Bandwidth:** If you're planning to give a presentation over the Web, then bandwidth is a major concern. *Bandwidth* refers to how much information can be carried over a connection to the Web. Video requires more bandwidth than audio. And you've got to make sure that each audience member has the minimum bandwidth required to receive the Web conference properly. Otherwise, you may have some people who receive the communication clearly and others who receive nothing. Check with the person or department responsible for running the technological aspects of your presentation to make sure that bandwidth is sufficient.

Use a telephone line to connect audience members for the audio portion of the Web conference. This lowers their bandwidth requirements and provides clearer sound.

- ✔ **Connection:** The kind of connection each audience member has can make a major difference in connectivity. Dial-up connections are the worst and may prevent folks that are dialing in from also accessing the audio (if they only have one phone line to share between the computer and voice communications). DSL, cable-modem communications, and network connections are preferred.

## Fitting the presentation into your budget

If budget constraints drive your choice of virtual presentation, then an e-mail presentation is the least expensive. In fact, if all audience members have access to e-mail, then the presentation costs nothing. On the other extreme, a video presentation involving several locations can be quite costly, especially if you need to rent video facilities for each location. In between these cost extremes are telephone conferences and Web-based presentations supplemented by the telephone.

## Factoring in your presentation goals

The purpose of your presentation will play an important role in determining what type of virtual format to choose. Here are some common goals and factors to consider:

✔ **Helping a group of people make a decision:** Group decision-making requires a lot of interaction. Ideas are discussed, opinions exchanged, and consensus achieved. These types of activities usually require a lot of interaction. So make sure that you have at least two-way audio capabilities for your presentation. At a minimum, that means telephone conferencing. It could also include Web conferencing or videoconferencing. In this situation, presenting solely by e-mail would be too slow and frustrating.

✔ **Selling a product or service:** Many sales and marketing experts consider visual information to be an indispensable part of the sales process. Prospects want to see what they're getting and who they're getting it from. And salespeople want to "read" the expressions of their prospects. So full-scale videoconferencing is ideal for this type of presentation. An alternative is Web conferencing with two-way visual and audio communication.

✔ **Training people:** Training presentations are well suited for Web conferencing. The training information can be directed to audience members as both visual and audio data. Upon completion of training modules, audience members can ask questions via telephone or e-mail. An alternative is a unidirectional videoconference. The trainer performs in a studio and is broadcast to television monitors where audience members are located. Again, they can ask questions via telephone or e-mail.

✔ **Announcing information:** This presentation, centered on one-way communication, can be accomplished through e-mail. Just send the announcement to everyone who is supposed to get it. If the announcement is very important, and you want to be sure it's received properly, you can choose a format with greater interaction, such as a conference call.

# Preparing for a Virtual Presentation

The key to a successful virtual presentation is the same as the key to a successful face-to-face presentation: preparation. Consider the following guidelines to ensure that you're ready for *your* virtual presentation.

## Knowing which nonvirtual rules apply

Always remember that a virtual presentation is still a presentation. The following basic rules for making an effective presentation apply:

✔ **Identify the purpose for the presentation.** Make sure you know why you're presenting. No one wants to hear a presentation, virtual or otherwise, that has no real purpose. Identifying the purpose of your presentation is critical for knowing how to construct it and deliver it. (For more on determining what your presentation needs to do, check out Chapter 2.)

✔ **Know your audience.** Find out as much as possible about your audience. (For more information on audience analysis, see Chapter 2.)

✔ **Organize your presentation.** Choose a pattern that suits your topic (for instance problem and solution; past, present, and future; theory and practice; or whatever works). Make sure that your audience can easily follow your message. (See Chapter 4 for more information.)

✔ **Write an introduction and conclusion.** Just because a presentation is virtual doesn't mean it doesn't need an opening and a close. The introduction has to preview and lead into your talk. The conclusion has to wrap it up. (For more information, check out Chapter 9.)

✔ **Provide materials in advance.** This allows audience members to become familiar with the proceedings beforehand and get more out of them. You can easily distribute materials via e-mail. Consider giving out the following:

  • **Agenda:** The audience wants to know what will happen and when. That's the purpose of an agenda. So provide one. An agenda makes it easier for audience members to keep track of the presentations. For more on agendas and other handouts, see Chapter 10.

  • **Support material:** Providing support materials such as presentation notes and outlines in advance also helps attendees get more out of your presentation. These can be sent easily and cheaply through e-mail.

  • **PowerPoint slides:** For presentations given on the Web, it may be smarter to distribute PowerPoint slides beforehand rather than using PowerPoint during your presentation. (See Chapter 14 for more on designing PowerPoint slides.)

  • **Contact information:** A list of all audience members' names, phone numbers, and e-mail addresses should be distributed so that they can reach one another in the event of a technical problem. (For more details on providing contact information, check out Chapter 10.)

✔ **Check the room(s).** It's standard advice to check the room in advance of a presentation. You want to make sure that it meets your needs: Check to be sure that it has enough seats for the people participating in the meeting, that the room layout is conducive to discussion, and that the equipment you plan to use is in working order. In the case of a virtual presentation, you won't be able to visually inspect all the meeting rooms, but do check the one that you'll be presenting from. (For more details, check out Chapter 26.)

## Considering unique factors

Because of the differences between virtual presentations and face-to-face presentations, you need to consider the following special factors:

✔ **Timing:** Unlike an in-person presentation, a virtual presentation can span several time zones. You need to take this into consideration when scheduling the presentation. If possible, give the presentation during normal business hours for all audience members. Be aware of when audience members at various locations usually take breaks or eat meals. Try to plan a presentation time that is convenient for all of them.

If you have a regularly scheduled virtual meeting (weekly, monthly, and so on) that includes people from several time zones, rotate the starting time. That way, no one has to get up early or stay up late every time.

✔ **Technology:** Make sure that all audience members have the equipment necessary to receive your presentation and that they know how to use it. Test the equipment beforehand. Then test it again. If the equipment doesn't work, your presentation doesn't work. Have a backup plan ready in case the equipment fails during your presentation. (Will you call everyone? E-mail everyone? Shout out the window?) If audience members are using a phone to connect with others, they need to make sure the line doesn't have the call-waiting feature or that call waiting is temporarily disengaged.

✔ **Appearance:** If you appear on screen via a Web or videoconference, then you should consider how your appearance will affect your message. Here are a few ways to improve your electronic appearance:

- Wear a conservative outfit that doesn't draw attention away from your face.

- Wear pastel colors rather than bright colors, because pastels broadcast better.

- Avoid striped, checked, or patterned clothing.

- Make sure your clothes contrast with your background colors.

- Use a solid-color background.

- Remove objects from the background that may distract your audience, such as pictures, posters, and so on.

# Practicing Do's and Don'ts

Just because a presentation is virtual doesn't mean you don't have to rehearse. On the contrary, more things can wrong with a virtual presentation. Here are some rules for practicing (for more on rehearsing, see Chapter 5):

✔ **Do plan your ending.** How will you keep the audience involved after your presentation concludes? Will you take a survey or a poll? Will you offer a free report? Will you direct the audience to your Web site?

✔ **Don't wing the rehearsal.** Make it as close to the live event as possible. Same room. Same time. Same technology.

✔ **Do test the technology.** Test whatever you're using. Streaming video? Test it. PowerPoint? Test it. Lots of bandwidth? Test it. I think you get my point.

✔ **Don't ignore the audience side of the technology.** Test what it's like to "attend" your Webinar. Does the login work? Can you see and hear everything you're supposed to see and hear?

✔ **Do review your graphics.** Now is the time to make sure that any images in your presentation look okay when transmitted over the Web.

✔ **Do time your presentation.** This helps ensure you don't go over your allotted time. It will also let you decide whether to break your presentation into a series of short segments.

✔ **Don't ignore the Q&A session.** Determine exactly how audience members will get to ask questions after your presentation. Will they ask them over the phone? Through e-mail? To you? To a moderator? Make sure that you work out all the details when you practice. (For details on fielding questions, see Chapter 13.)

# Delivering a Virtual Presentation

Participating effectively in a virtual meeting means adapting to a situation where many of the people with whom you're interacting aren't physically present. That can seem strange if you're the type of person who likes to shake hands and slap backs. Here are a few rules and tips to ensure you perform well with your virtual comrades:

✔ **Keep it as short as possible.** Many people think meetings are a waste of time. And those are the meetings where you can actually see one another face to face. Virtual meetings have the added burden of requiring the use of phones, computers, or other technology. So keep your virtual meetings as short as possible. You can also break them into segments. Instead of watching a streaming video for 15 minutes, break it into three 5-minute segments.

✔ **Make it as interactive as possible.** Even large virtual meetings can achieve a relatively high degree of interactivity if you plan for it. Software that allows polling can provide instant votes from any number of attendees. Or just ask questions and tally e-mail responses.

   • **Encourage participation.** One way to increase interaction is to encourage individual participation. At smaller meetings, begin by introducing each attendee and asking that person to say hello. At a minimum, make sure that whenever people speak, they identify themselves.

- **Ask for responses.** The simplest way to encourage participation is to ask attendees for responses. This is also a useful way to find out what they really think. (Unless everyone in the meeting is simultaneously televised, you can't read everyone's body language. And during a telephone conference, you can't read anyone's body language.) To make up for a lack of visual cues, presenters should frequently ask attendees for responses, using questions such as "Is there anyone who doesn't understand?", "Does this make sense?", "Do you agree?", and "Would you like to hear more about this?"

✓ **Develop a protocol for questions.** Large virtual meetings often provide limited interaction by allowing attendees to phone in or e-mail questions to the presenter. However, only some of the questions can be answered. So how does the presenter decide which questions to answer? "The person running the meeting should provide a rationale," says Kare. "Otherwise, attendees will perceive the process to be unfair." She advises stating how many questions were received, how many will be answered, and how the decision was made. "You can say something like 'We tried to pick the most diverse ones so that there's one question from every type of category that was asked,'" Kare suggests.

✓ **Take time to build relationships.** People who attend face-to-face meetings can build relationships by arriving early or staying late and chatting with one another. This type of bonding is good for any group that meets on a regular basis. If the meeting is virtual, create rapport by encouraging interaction. Have attendees tell the group something about themselves. Use this to kill time when waiting for everyone to dial in.

# Using Tips and Tricks for Success

Want an extra edge to ensure that your next virtual presentation is highly effective? Here are a few tips and tricks.

## Tips and tricks for telephone conferences

One of the most common virtual presentations made today is over the phone in a teleconference. Your next teleconference presentation will be more effective if you use common courtesy as well as a colorful voice. So keep the following ideas in mind:

✓ Speak clearly.

✓ Keep your answers short.

✓ Put your phone on mute when you're not speaking.

- ✔ Identify yourself and your location when you speak.

- ✔ Indicate when you're finished speaking.

- ✔ Explain any extraneous noises (people moving around the room and so on).

- ✔ Repeat any questions you're asked before you answer them.

- ✔ Don't hog time.

- ✔ Pause so another person can speak.

- ✔ Reserve complex questions for e-mail unless you need an immediate response.

- ✔ Use emotion in your voice, rather than speaking in a flat tone.

- ✔ Use metaphors and similes to create word pictures for attendees. (For more on metaphors and similes, check out Chapter 7.)

## Tips and tricks for videoconferences

Videoconferences have their own set of advantages and challenges. And they're growing in popularity as companies look for ways to cut travel costs. Here are a few tips to help you sparkle the next time you're on the tube:

- ✔ Avoid extreme close-ups of participants. No one wants to see the pores on your face.

- ✔ Make sure the person on camera is centered on the screen.

---

### New words for new meetings

The rapid expansion of technology that has created new kinds of virtual meetings has outpaced our ability to describe these meetings. Old concepts just don't apply. Many of the situations that arise in meetings held over the Web or phone defy explanation with existing language. So as a public service, here are some new words to use for common virtual meeting problems and events.

- ✔ *Bandwither:* The Web connection dies because there's not enough bandwidth

- ✔ *F-mail:* An e-mail message that's laced with expletives

- ✔ *Interactuary:* A professional who predicts the level of interaction that a virtual meeting will achieve

- ✔ *Teleconspire:* When two or more people arrange in advance to gang up on someone in a teleconference

- ✔ *Virtualpha:* A dominant personality who takes over a virtual meeting by hogging time and not giving anyone else a chance to speak

- ✔ *Wetbinar:* First-time test of a marketing seminar delivered over the Web

✔ Show you're listening when other people talk by nodding.

✔ If you write on a whiteboard, use large letters that are easy to read.

✔ Don't include lights (from the ceiling or elsewhere) in the picture.

✔ Avoid sitting in front of a window during daylight hours. It will make you appear as a silhouette.

✔ Avoid fluorescent lighting if possible. It doesn't make anyone look good.

✔ If you can't avoid fluorescent lighting, bring in other lights to offset the effects of the fluorescent lights.

✔ Make sure you have the telephone number(s) of the other site(s) participating in the videoconference in case anything goes wrong.

## Tips and tricks for Web conferences

The explosive growth of the Web has made a host of new communication technologies available to the business world. One that is being embraced quickly is the Web conference. If you haven't participated in one yet, odds are that you will soon. Here are some tips that will help you when you make a presentation over the Web:

✔ **Maximize attendance with a reminder.** Experience has shown that a large percentage of people won't actually attend a Web conference without a reminder. So here's what to do: Send a confirming e-mail right after they register. Send a reminder e-mail about a week beforehand. And send another reminder e-mail a few hours before the Web conference. (Hey, you did a lot of work on your presentation; you may as well get a big audience.)

✔ **Don't present in solitary confinement.** When your audience is entirely virtual, you lose the energy that comes from direct, face-to-face feedback. This can hurt you as a presenter. So here's what to do. Ask a friend or colleague to stay with you during your presentation, and direct your remarks to that person. His presence will help you sound more enthusiastic and engaging.

✔ **Control the length of your answers.** When you answer questions in an in-person conference, you can look at the questioners and tell when they're satisfied with your answer. You can't do that in a Web conference. So presenters have a tendency to make their answers too long. Here's what you should do: Give the answer as concisely as possible. Then ask the questioner if any more explanation is needed.

✔ **Pay attention to audience feedback.** You won't get as much feedback as occurs during an in-person presentation, but you will get some. If audience members e-mail, instant-message, or call in to tell you that you're going too fast or they can't see your visuals, make appropriate adjustments.

✔ **Break your presentation into short segments.** It's even more difficult to pay attention during a Web conference than during an in-person conference. (And it ain't easy during an in-person conference.) So divide your presentation into short (five- or ten-minute) segments. This allows you to pause for questions or breaks.

✔ **Don't rush the visuals.** Whether you're displaying PowerPoint slides, Web sites, or anything else, give your audience enough time to see them. You already know what's on them. Your audience doesn't.

✔ **Don't use too many visuals.** How many is too many? There's no set number. But if you have to rush through the visuals to fit them in, then you've got too many.

✔ **Make sure everyone disconnects at the end of the conference.** Yogi Berra once said, "It ain't over till it's over." He was talking about a baseball game, but he could have been talking about a Web conference. If your conference includes telephone communication, make sure everyone has hung up before you make comments that you might regret later. And I think you know what I mean.

✔ **Follow up after your Web conference.** You can still get an audience *after* your presentation. Archive the conference on your Web site, and send an e-mail to anyone who couldn't attend the live version. Many people prefer to view Web conferences at a time of their own choosing. Let them know it's available on your Web site. Also, send a thank-you e-mail to everyone who attended the live version. And consider sending them a survey or poll to keep the "conversation" going.

# Chapter 22

# Impressing with International Presentations

· · · · · · · · · · · · · · · · · · · · · · · · · · · · · · · · · · · · · · · · · · · · · · · ·

*In This Chapter*

▶ Doing your homework on your audience's culture

▶ Preparing your international presentation

▶ Understanding rules for giving an international presentation

▶ Working successfully with an interpreter

· · · · · · · · · · · · · · · · · · · · · · · · · · · · · · · · · · · · · · · · · · · · · · · ·

*A* mother mouse was trying to teach her offspring the ways of the world when she found herself, and her family, face-to-face with a great big cat. Her children were terrified. But the mother remained calm and started barking like a dog. The cat heard the barking, turned tail, and took off. The mother mouse turned to her kids and said, "Now you can see the importance of a second language."

When the mother mouse spoke to the cat, she faced a challenge prevalent in today's global economy. She had to communicate with an audience from a different culture. And as multinational corporations continue to expand, more and more presenters face this challenge. Not to worry. This chapter tells you how to come across well no matter what language your audience speaks.

## Discovering Your Audience's Culture

Most people wouldn't drive a car if they didn't know what the controls were or how to operate them. Why? They could wreck and hurt themselves, the car, and the people around them. Common sense, right? But many people are willing to give a presentation to an audience from a different culture without knowing anything about them. And that can be dangerous, too.

If you know nothing about your audience's culture, you may unintentionally offend, insult, or upset them. When this happens, your talk crashes, and you hurt yourself, your cause, and your audience. Unfortunately, the damage to a relationship with an audience is sometimes harder to fix than a broken car.

## Don't fall for stereotypes

Don't assume you know about a culture because you know the popular stereotypes. Just watching television shows or movies doesn't give you an in-depth understanding. Find out what the culture is really like. You can spare yourself a lot of embarrassment.

## Ask for help

How do you find out about another culture? Ask a member of that culture. Most people are delighted to talk about their ethnic or national background. If you tell them what you plan to say, they can help omit anything potentially offensive. They can also provide a window into your audience's mind, so you can shape your talk in a way that your audience will enjoy and appreciate.

For example, several years ago, I gave a speech to Filipino insurance sales representatives in Manila. Fortunately, I had a friend from the Philippines who vetted my entire speech. He told me which references were too U.S.-centric and wouldn't be understood. And he provided a lot of information about the culture, history, and politics of the Philippines. So I was able to make some specific references to people, places, and current events that were relevant to the audience.

What if you don't have a friend who can guide you? Find someone who can. Do you know a local merchant who comes from the country where you'll be presenting? Buy something from her, and ask for help with your presentation. Do you know someone who works for a multinational corporation? Find out if he can get you in touch with someone from the country where you're presenting. Does your community have a society or association of people from that part of the world? Find out, and call them. And don't forget to ask the person who arranged your presentation to provide some cultural help.

## Find information on the Web

*International Business Etiquette and Manners* is deservedly one of the most popular Web sites for obtaining specific cultural information about specific countries. It provides free information about the appropriate dress, protocol, etiquette, and behavior in numerous countries and regions of the world.

The site is designed to help you find facts quickly and easily. A page for each country is divided into seven sections: Introduction, Fun Facts, Geert Hofstede Analysis, Appearance, Behavior, Communication, and Resources.

In particular, the Appearance, Behavior, and Communication sections of each country bear directly on your presentation. These sections include business etiquette do's and don'ts involving dress, clothing, body language, gestures, gift giving, and greetings. For example, the page on Hong Kong advises that a red tie will impress your business hosts because red is a lucky color, and that it's important to use titles with names whenever possible.

You can access all of this information at `www.international-business-etiquette.com`.

# Crafting Your Message

Presenting to an audience from a country or culture other than your own? This section goes over a few rules to keep in mind when you're preparing what you will say to them. If you're unsure of where to look for information on a particular culture, such as preferred organizational patterns or appropriate graphic symbols, check out "Discovering Your Audience's Culture," earlier in this chapter.

## Adapt your organizational pattern

Different cultures organize information in different ways. You need to take this into account when you organize your presentation. For example, North Americans favor presentations with a linear structure — information flows along a logical path from beginning to end. Other cultures prefer a less focused approach. (See Chapter 4 for more on organizational patterns.)

## Quote someone from the audience's country or culture

Every country and culture has heroes. Authors. Artists. Scientists. Statesmen. Pick a native admired by your audience, and quote that person in your presentation. This communicates that you went to the trouble of looking into your audience's culture. And it will be perceived favorably.

Don't just force in a quotation. Tie it into a point that you're making. Otherwise, you appear to be pandering to the audience. (For more on quotations, see Chapter 6.)

## Don't use examples only from your country

Do all the examples and references in your presentation come from your own country? If so, you risk appearing pompous and arrogant when you're presenting outside your country. Find some examples from elsewhere in the world. In an era of rising nationalism, audiences can be very touchy if they think you're implying that your country is superior to theirs. (See Chapter 6 for more information on examples.)

## Remember there's more than one America

People from the United States like to refer to themselves as Americans. This annoys people from countries in Central America and South America. They're also Americans. A presenter from the U.S. should just say, "I'm from the United States."

## Use the audience's numbers

If you're talking about money or measurements, convert your numbers to the system used by the nation where you're presenting. And remember, most of the world uses the metric system.

If you're giving a talk about money to a group composed of people from many nations, try devising a chart with several major representative currencies, such as U.S. dollars, euros, and yen.

## Be careful referring to holidays

A holiday in one country isn't necessarily a holiday in another. And some holidays have the same names but different dates and meanings. For example, more than one country has a Thanksgiving. But the stuff about Pilgrims and Native Americans applies only to the United States. And although every country has a fifth of May in its calendar, only Mexico celebrates Cinco de Mayo. It's *not* a holiday for other Latin American countries.

## Find out what to emphasize

In Japan and other Asian countries, relationships are very important. Your presentation should emphasize possible long-term goals and benefits of working together. In contrast, a North American business audience is more interested in short-term factors such as costs and immediate results. Emphasis on the appropriate cultural values will help ensure that your presentation receives a positive reception.

## Adapt substance and style to cultural needs

European audiences prefer more depth than a U.S. audience. This affects both style and content. "In the U.S., audiences prefer speakers who are passionate about their topic," says Allen Weiner, president of Communication Development Associates. "They like speakers who are energetic — move around a lot and use a lot of gestures. In Europe, audiences regard high energy as a sign of shallowness. That there's too much effort going into style and not enough substance. If you're too upbeat in Europe, you're perceived as not having enough depth."

The distinction also plays out in content. Europeans prefer more detailed evidence in a speech — numbers and statistics. In the U.S., audiences like anecdotal evidence. "Give them stories in the speech and numbers in the handouts," Allen advises.

## Keep it as simple as possible

The time for brilliant rhetorical flourishes, witty turns of phrase, and complex message structures isn't when you're addressing nonnative speakers of your language. Give them a break. Keep your sentences short. Keep your vocabulary as simple as possible. And provide very clear transitions that let them know when you're moving from one point to another. This increases your likelihood of communicating rather than confusing.

## Keep it as short as possible

You probably already know that listening to a presentation in your native language can be tiring. So imagine listening to one in a nonnative language. Keep your presentation as short as possible! If you have a lot of content to deliver, consider scheduling break periods for your audience.

## Lose the idioms

Every language has colloquial expressions that cause confusion if translated literally. Avoid them. Search for them in your talk, and eliminate them.

Take the phrase "born with a silver spoon in his mouth." A speaker of American English understands that the phrase refers to a person who was born into a rich family. But speakers of other languages may think it refers to something rather odd and uncomfortable.

Even among English speakers, idiomatic expressions can cause confusion. If a British woman says to "knock her up" at nine o'clock, a British man knows she means to wake her up at nine. A U.S. male would think she wants him to impregnate her at nine.

## Lose the jargon and acronyms

Jargon and acronyms are confusing enough when you're talking to native speakers of your language. They're even worse when you're talking to non-native speakers. Make sure you define jargon for the audience, and explain what acronyms stand for. But avoid both whenever possible.

## Don't use unfamiliar sports metaphors

Baseball metaphors are great in the U.S., Japan, and a handful of other countries. But most countries in the world don't play baseball. If you're going to use sports metaphors, use them from sports that are popular in the country where you're presenting. Hint: Soccer is probably the most popular sport in the world (and it's called football in some countries).

## Watch out for double meanings

Expect and look out for other ways of referring to things. For example, when British managers agree to *table* a document, they include it in the agenda. When their colleagues from the United States agree to *table* a topic, they exclude it. If you catch a word in your talk that may be misunderstood, just change the word or make sure that the word's meaning is clear.

## Emergency laughs

When Martin Gonzalez Bravo worked as a marketing executive for Hewlett-Packard, he gave speeches to audiences around the world. And he'd always begin the same way: "I'm glad to be here. I've only been here a few days, but I'm already picking up your language." Then he'd say the following phrase in the language of his audience: "A life vest is located beneath your seat in case of emergency."

"No matter where I went, they always laughed," says Martin. "It was a great way to break the ice."

Everyone knows the line from the safety card on an airplane. And that's how Martin would learn it. "The safety card is always written in several languages," he explains. "So on the plane to wherever I was going, I'd memorize the line in the language of that country." He'd also write it down and ask coworkers to make sure he was pronouncing it correctly after he arrived at his destination.

Martin agrees that using humor when speaking to an audience from another other culture can be risky. But he says his line works because it transcends cultural boundaries. "Anyone who has ever ridden in a plane will get it," he notes. And that's no joke.

## *Don't assume your humor will work*

What makes something funny? Although one could write a dissertation on this subject (and many have), the short answer is that much humor is rooted in cultural values. So something considered funny in one culture may not be even remotely humorous in another. Unless you're very familiar with the culture, using humor is usually a mistake. The audience may not get your joke, or even worse, they may find it offensive.

## *Don't assume your graphic symbols will be understood*

It may seem like a good idea to use visual aids with lots of graphic symbols when you're presenting to a foreign audience. But often, it's not. Although some symbols are used most places around the world (men's and women's restroom symbols, for example), many are culture specific. For example, a piggy bank means savings to a U.S. audience. But in some countries, it indicates a disgusting animal. And a thumbs-up image — meaning approval in some countries — is offensive in others. So make sure that the graphic symbols you use mean what you think they mean to your audience.

## Be careful with colors

Another potential pitfall with visual aids is color. The problem is that different cultures assign different symbolic meanings to colors. For example, in Western cultures, white is associated with purity and weddings. In Asian cultures, white is associated with death and funerals. Red symbolizes rage in the United States, but it indicates happiness in China. So find out what colors symbolize for your audience before you make your visual aids. (And you won't paint yourself into a corner.)

## Make sure your handouts have been edited for cultural gaffes

Handouts are good when you're presenting to people who aren't native speakers of your language. A written summary of your remarks helps them understand and recall more of your message — especially if the handouts are in their language. But make sure the translation is correct, and that it doesn't offend any of the cultural sensibilities of your audience. Ask someone from that culture to review your handouts before you give them out.

Here are some things to watch out for:

- ✔ **Dates:** Use the format of the country where you're presenting. In Europe, 12/8/90 means August 12, 1990. In the United States, it means December 8, 1990.

- ✔ **Phone numbers:** Don't forget to include the country code as part of any phone listing. And remember that 800 numbers that provide toll-free calls in the United States don't usually work in other countries.

- ✔ **Money symbols:** The $ sign is used in connection with several different currencies. For example, do you mean Canadian dollars or U.S. dollars?

# Following Basic Rules for Delivery

When you're speaking in the international arena, a carefully prepared message isn't enough to ensure success. You also have to deliver your message properly. That means adapting your style to the cultural requirements of your audience. The following subsections go over some general rules to keep in mind. (If you don't know where to find specific information on a certain culture, see "Discovering Your Audience's Culture," earlier in this chapter, for help.)

## Get there ahead of time

Not just to the room where you're presenting (although that's a good idea). Get to the country where you're speaking far enough ahead of time (at least a day, if possible) to compensate for jet lag and to adjust to the time zone.

## Dress appropriately

Conservative business attire is always safe. Women must pay particular attention to clothes in countries where bare arms and legs or skirt length may be a cultural issue. And if you're going to dress in the traditional native garb of a country, make sure you do it accurately, or you'll look like a dork.

## Make sure your equipment works with foreign voltage standards

If you're planning to use visual aids such as PowerPoint, make sure that your equipment conforms to the electrical standards of the country in which you're presenting. It sounds obvious. But a lot of presenters forget.

If you're presenting in a developing country, anticipate problems with electricity. Brownouts are common. That may mean presenting without a microphone or computer. Be ready to deal with it. Also, have hard copies of your slides ready to distribute as handouts if necessary and a flip chart on an easel available in reserve.

## Follow protocol

Outside the United States, protocol often assumes a much more important role in the presentation process. Presenters are sometimes expected to give and receive gifts or to recognize dignitaries in the audience. And you may be expected to recognize dignitaries in a particular order and by their official titles. If you don't want to risk offending your audience, find out the traditions and rituals that they expect you to follow.

Give careful consideration to the person who will introduce you. It may have a direct impact on your status and credibility. In many countries, the higher the rank of the executive who introduces you, the more status you have as a presenter. In many Asian cultures, age is also a factor. The older the person who introduces you, the more status you receive.

## Project humility

The best way to win over audiences from any culture is to make it clear that you care for them and are really interested in them. That's a cultural universal. Just say you're really happy and honored to be there with them. In contrast, the opposite approach — arrogantly communicating that the audience has lucked out by being in your presence — is a big turnoff (and a common mistake).

## Don't greet the audience in their language if you don't speak it

It's almost a cliché for a presenter addressing an audience that speaks a different language to start by saying a few words or a sentence in that language. (Typically, it's something like "I'm happy to be here today" in the audience's native language.) The common knowledge is that this gesture shows that the presenter tried to learn a little of the audience's language.

If you're going to learn only one line, save it for the end. If you've established a connection with the audience, ending with a line in their language really cements the relationship. End by saying, "Thank you for being here with me today" in their language.

If you want to open with a line in the audience's language, find out how to say, "I'm sorry for not knowing how to speak your language." It's much more effective than a greeting like "I'm happy to be here today." (See the preceding rule regarding humility.)

## Eat the food

If you're presenting at a lunch or dinner meeting, or any other event where food is involved, you must eat. You can tell people of another culture that they're great, you love them, and they're wonderful. But if you don't eat their food, they won't believe you. You have to eat what they're eating. (That's why politicians always get themselves photographed shoveling in souvlaki, burritos, or matzo ball soup when they speak at events held by various ethnic groups.) So unless you have a specific dietary restriction due to health or religious reasons — *bon appétit*.

## Speak slowly

Slow down. If you're not presenting to native speakers, don't speak at your normal rate. Give them some time to mentally translate what you're saying.

(But don't slow down so much that you're insulting. You're not talking to children.) Elongate your pauses between sentences.

## Be aware of culture-related audience reaction

Don't assume you're doing well or badly based on your own culture's typical reactions to a presenter. Different cultures react quite differently. For example, in the United States, when an audience takes notes, the presenter is doing well. But in Japan, the audience takes notes to be polite — even if the presenter is terrible. Some cultures show approval of a presenter by applauding; others show respect by remaining silent.

## Be aware of differences in nonverbal communication

Be very careful with the body language you use in your presentation. A harmless gesture in one culture can be highly offensive in another. See Chapter 11 for specific examples.

## Use your own title to your advantage

In countries that equate status with a job title and the reputation of your employer, emphasize those items. For example, an audience in Japan will perceive you as more important if you say that you're an executive at a large multinational corporation than if you say you have an extensive education.

# Working with an Interpreter

While he was governor of California, Ronald Reagan occasionally gave speeches in Mexico on behalf of the United States. One time, he spoke to a large audience. But when he finished speaking, there was only a little unenthusiastic and scattered applause. Embarrassed and self-conscious, he thought he'd done something wrong. He was even more embarrassed when the next speaker, speaking in Spanish, got enthusiastic applause almost every other line. Although he didn't speak Spanish, Governor Reagan decided to hide his embarrassment by clapping louder and longer than anyone else. After a few minutes of that, the U.S. ambassador said, "I wouldn't do that if I were you, Governor. He's interpreting your speech."

The following sections go over a few rules that will help you avoid embarrassment the next time you work with an interpreter.

## Meet with the interpreter before you present

Want to increase your comfort level? Meet with your interpreter well before your talk. This allows the interpreter to get a sense of who you are and how you speak. Give the interpreter your script or notes and any handouts that you plan to provide the audience. (This includes PowerPoint slides and any other visual aids.) When an interpreter becomes familiar with your talk ahead of time, she can do a better job do when it counts — in front of your audience.

## Introduce your interpreter to the audience

This makes you look good. It's like when a star singer acknowledges the orchestra conductor. The recognition is also appreciated by the interpreter, who will then be motivated to do an even better job for you.

## Make your presentation easy to interpret

Use short sentences. Avoid jargon, acronyms, and colloquial expressions. And speak slowly. Make it as easy as possible for interpreters to do their job.

## Give your presentation to the audience

You'd be amazed how many presenters give their presentations to the interpreter. Don't. Direct your remarks to the audience, even if no one speaks your language. They can still make judgments about your body language and physical demeanor. And they're the ones that you want to influence.

# Chapter 23

## Dealing with Impromptu Presentations, Panels, and Roundtables

*W*hen people think about presentations, they usually picture someone standing alone in front of an audience, delivering a carefully prepared talk that covers a few major points. But presentations can take other forms. You may have to give a presentation "off the top of your head." Or you may have to speak as a member of a panel or a roundtable. In this chapter, you find out how to successfully handle these situations.

## Saying a Few Words: Impromptu Presentations

"Say a few words." This phrase can strike terror into the hearts of the bravest souls. But you should view it as an opportunity. Really. Everyone knows that you had no time to prepare, so no one expects you to deliver a presentation on the level of Lincoln's *Gettysburg Address* or Martin Luther King's *I Have a Dream*. You're held to a much lower standard. So if you say anything remotely well organized and intelligent, you're perceived as a genius.

## Be prepared

Yes, the whole idea of an impromptu presentation is that you don't know that you'll be asked to speak. But that doesn't mean you can't *anticipate* the possibility. Watch the Academy Awards some time. Only one person wins best actor, but five nominees have acceptance speeches sticking out of their pockets.

How can you anticipate when you may be asked to vocally bestow your wisdom? Use your common sense. Are you going to a business meeting? What's on the agenda? It may suggest topics that you need to be prepared to discuss — even though you're *not* a scheduled presenter. Think about the issues that may arise. Would you need to respond to any of them?

## Try to buy time

The time between when you're asked to "say a few words" and when you start talking can go by faster than a prayer at an atheists' convention. Yet this time is crucial to the success of your impromptu remarks. This short period is when you must plan and organize your entire presentation. Your goal is to lengthen this time period as much as possible. Use the following ideas to get started.

### Pause thoughtfully

When someone asks you to say a few words, you're not required to immediately start talking. You can pause and think. This technique actually increases your credibility. The audience assumes that your words are now carefully considered, rather than the first thoughts that flew into your head. (Little do they know.)

### Repeat the question

This technique is the traditional stalling device, but you should know another good reason to use it. Put the question in your own words. Then get confirmation that you've stated it correctly. You won't impress anyone when you give a fabulous impromptu presentation when it turns out to be on the wrong subject.

### Be ready with an all-purpose quote

It doesn't hurt to memorize a few all-purpose quotes — lines that you can use to begin *any* impromptu presentation, even in a workplace setting. Quoting someone makes you sound smart, and you get a little extra time to think about what you really want to say. Keep the following quotes in reserve:

> To paraphrase Richard Nixon, "Let's get one thing perfectly clear." In this case, I mean your question.

To paraphrase Robert Frost, "The brain is a wonderful organ; it starts working the moment you get up in the morning and doesn't stop until you get asked to make a speech."

# Organize your thoughts

Samuel Johnson once said, "When a man knows he is to be hanged in a fortnight, it concentrates his mind wonderfully." Well, when you know you have to give a presentation in 20 seconds, you may feel like you're about to be hanged, and you definitely need to concentrate your mind.

### Make a quick decision

The big myth about impromptu speaking is that your mind goes blank as soon as you're asked to speak. Actually, the opposite is true. Most people get an overwhelming number of ideas, and almost any of them can do the job. You need to pick one idea and stick with it. That's the secret. Commit to one main point — quickly.

### Pick a pattern

After you select your main point, you have to organize your presentation. What are your subpoints? How will you support them? Do you have examples or anecdotes? You need to pick a pattern of organization — something that allows you to quickly sort out your information. The following are two popular approaches:

- ✔ **Organize around the conclusion.** Decide on a conclusion. Organize all your information so that it supports your conclusion. Then start speaking. Everything you say should be designed to move your message toward the conclusion you select.

- ✔ **Organize around a standard pattern.** Pick one of the standard presentation patterns — past, present, future; problem, solution; cause and effect — and quickly fit its structure to your message. Many presenters find the chronological pattern easiest to use. (For more on presentation patterns, check out Chapter 4.)

### Find an opening

You can begin an impromptu presentation in many ways. But if the audience members don't know that you're presenting impromptu, then you have only one way to begin — tell them. Make absolutely sure that they know. Otherwise, they apply a higher standard to your remarks. And when you're presenting off the cuff, you don't want to be judged as if you had months to prepare.

Usually the audience realizes that your presentation is impromptu. In that case, how do you begin?

✔ **Tie into previous presenters.** This is probably the easiest opening. You just react to what's already been said.

✔ **Be candid.** If you really don't know much about the subject, admit that you're not an expert. Say something like "I'm not an expert on this issue, but what I know about it is this." Then offer any information you can contribute to the discussion. If you're completely clueless, offer to gather information and provide it in the future.

✔ **Tell a personal anecdote.** Think of a war story relevant to the issue at hand (that helps make your point). "That reminds me of the time I worked at Company X. We faced a similar issue. . . ."

✔ **Switch the topic.** This method is popular with executives at companies under attack by analysts. They pick up on something in a question and give a related answer. For example, when they're asked for their opinion on the company's poor performance in the past quarter, they give their opinion on why the company will do great in the current quarter.

One final word of advice on openings: Never apologize. What would you apologize for anyway? Not having a carefully polished talk ready? You're making an impromptu presentation! By definition, it's off the cuff.

### Stop talking

Stop when you're finished. It sounds obvious — but most people don't do it. The most common mistake related to impromptu speaking is rambling. The way to avoid this problem is to know where you're going. Make sure that you think about a conclusion in the short time you have to organize your thoughts. Then stick to your plan. When you get to the conclusion — stop.

# Being on a Panel

Many people who don't enjoy making solo presentations say they would rather speak as part of a panel. (Misery loves company.) Panelists can share ideas; work out problems; and provide information for colleagues, superiors, vendors, stockholders, and so on. They usually don't have to speak for the same length of time as a sole presenter, and they can pass tough audience questions on to other panelists. That's the good news. The bad news is that the panel format has its own unique set of challenges. If you're ready for them, you can shine. If you're not ready, you may look pretty foolish.

# Winning the inevitable comparison

Compared with a sole presenter, panelists have much less control over their message and image. Why? The audience *compares* panelists to one another as they speak. So how a panelist is perceived depends on who else is on the panel, which means that your presentation — which may be considered good if the audience hears no one else — can come off poorly if you're on a panel with high-powered presenters. You need to be aware of the factors that affect the comparison, and figure out how to control them. You don't necessarily want the other panelists to look bad; you want to make sure that *you* look good. To strategize for your panel session, ask yourself the following questions.

### Who else is on the panel?

Finding out who else is on your panel sounds pretty basic, and it is. But many people don't bother to do it. They're invited to be on a panel. They say, "Okay." And a few days, weeks, or months later (whenever the panel is held), they show up. They never ask for any details. You must find out who else is on your panel. How can you influence the audience's comparison if you don't know whom you'll be compared to?

Find out everything you can about the other panelists: their names, their qualifications, their jobs or departments, their knowledge of the topic, their reputations as presenters, and so on. And don't forget to ask about the moderator. Is there one? If so, you want to know everything about this person, too.

Sometimes, the entire panel hasn't been selected when you agree to serve on it. Maybe you're the first person invited. Fine. You still need to find out who else is on the panel. Wait a few days, weeks, or months (whatever is appropriate), and call the organizer. Get an update. Ask who else is on the panel. (If you're still the only panelist, then expect to get a new title — keynote speaker.)

Try to arrange a meeting with the moderator and other panel members well in advance of the program. That's when you can coordinate what each panelist will discuss and eliminate potential overlaps. The meeting can be held over the phone. This is also a good time to discuss exactly how the panel will operate.

### What are the rules?

Every panel operates within some set of rules. (All right, once in a while you see a panel that doesn't, but it's not very pretty.) You need to know those rules. Does everyone on the panel make his or her remarks before the audience asks questions? Or does the audience ask questions after each panelist speaks? Are the panelists even expected to make formal remarks? How much time is allotted for the entire session? How much time is given to each panelist? Do panelists get to choose their speaking order, or is it assigned? Is there a moderator, or is it a free-for-all? What's the physical setup? Does each panelist have a microphone, or do the panelists have to pass one around? Whether you want to follow the rules, bend the rules, or break the rules, you have to *know* the rules.

The rule-making power usually rests with the moderator. If you don't like some of the rules, talk to the moderator about changing them. It never hurts to ask.

### What is the speaking order?

The order in which panelists speak is a major factor in determining how you are perceived. Think about these factors:

- **First speaker:** The advantage of going first is that you can't be compared to anyone — yet. So if you're on a panel with several strong presenters, going first makes a lot of sense. Another advantage is that the first speaker can set the tone for the entire panel. Go first, give a well-structured presentation, and you set the standard. The audience now expects the other presenters to do at least as well as you did.

  The disadvantage of going first is that you can't react to the other panelists. They haven't said anything yet.

- **Last speaker:** The biggest advantage of going last is that you can comment on what all of the other panelists have said. This allows you to have the final word in defining the discussion. Going last is also the best position if you're not prepared. You can formulate your remarks while the earlier panelists are giving their presentations, and you can just comment on what they said.

- **Middle speakers:** The advantage of going in the middle is that you can comment on any panelists that spoke before you, and you can still shape the discussion of the panelists that go after you. The disadvantage is that you may get lost in the shuffle. A basic principle of psychology is that people most strongly remember things that come first or last. In a panel situation, that's the first speaker and the last speaker.

### What other things should you consider?

How big is the panel? What time of day does the session occur? The answers to these questions may affect your choice of when you want to speak (if you have a choice). A large panel with many presenters increases the chance that the audience is burned out by the time the last presenter gets a turn. Similarly, a panel held in the late afternoon means that the audience won't be focused on the last presenter (except for wondering when she will end so that everyone can go eat dinner). With an early-morning panel, the audience may still be waking up while the first panelist is presenting.

# Maintaining control of your message

Panel discussions create special obstacles to getting your message across. Many of these obstacles are beyond your control, so it's even more important than usual to identify your goals clearly and construct your message carefully. You want to maintain as much control as possible. Paying attention to the following factors helps you achieve that goal.

### Knowing why you're on the panel

Why am I here? This question has haunted philosophers for centuries. Now *you* have to answer it. (Fortunately, you just need to figure out why you're on the panel — not why you exist.) Your answer to this question shapes your message strategy. Are you on the panel as a favor to the moderator? Are you there to showcase yourself and your ideas? Are you there to gain recognition for your company or department? Who, if anyone, are you trying to impress? Your boss? The company president? You need to know what you want to accomplish.

### Preparing your message

Any presentation requires you to decide how you plan to get the audience to remember your key messages. This goal is even more challenging in a panel presentation, because there's a lot of "noise in the channel." The audience is bombarded by messages from your co-panelists. And the audience itself may offer statements or questions that provide further distraction from your key ideas. Your messages have a lot of competition, so you have to make them powerful, persuasive, and to the point.

Start by learning who the audience members are. What departments or companies do they represent? What are their jobs? What positions do they hold? Are they stockholders or vendors? You can involve them in your remarks by speaking directly to their interests, and then they don't have to wait for the Q&A period to get involved. (For more on question-and-answer sessions, see Chapter 13.)

Anticipate where you may be challenged on particular issues. You don't need co-panelists or audience members sinking your entire message by torpedoing you on one point — especially if you know it's coming. Defuse the issue by addressing it in your remarks before the Q&A period.

And listen to the other panelists. I mean really listen. Take notes as they're presenting, and be prepared to refer back to specific things they said. This tip is especially effective if you get the panelists' names right. ("As Heather and Amy said earlier . . .")

### Getting the timing right

Panelists get many opportunities to present information, such as when they make their remarks, answer questions from co-panelists, answer audience questions, and even when they tag statements onto the end of co-panelists' answers to audience questions. (For more on tagging onto others' answers, see "Answering questions when you don't get any," later in this chapter.) But not all opportunities to present information are created equal. Depending on what you want to say, certain times are better than others.

If you have important information for the audience, don't convey it right away. Let them settle down first and get used to the panelists. And don't wait until the end. You may run out of time, or the audience members may be distracted by their preparations to leave. Key information is best presented after the audience has heard you for a few minutes or a few times.

Another aspect of timing has to do with who gets the credit for an idea. It's not always the panelist who said it first. More often, it's the panelist who talks about an idea second who takes the idea and runs with it. This second panelist expands the idea, puts it into new words, and makes it her own. The audience never remembers that someone else mentioned the idea first. Keep this in mind when you toss your gems into the discussion. If your comment is a diamond in the rough, don't wait for a fellow panelist to polish it. They'll be polishing off your credit.

Timing also applies to how much you speak. If you speak every time a question or issue is raised, you seem pompous, and your answers lose their impact. People stop listening to you. But if you never speak up, you seem weak and irrelevant — if the audience even remembers you're there. So monitor yourself. Be aware of how much time you spend speaking. Assert yourself but don't go wild.

To deal with a co-panelist who wants to do all the talking during a discussion, simply look to the moderator for help.

### Planning your delivery

It's easy to forget about the audience if you get into a debate with another panelist. That's a mistake. The majority of your eye contact and "face time" should be with the audience. Focus on different sections of the room as you answer different questions. Make everyone feel like you're talking to him.

And don't become a victim of microphone placement. If there's only one mike for all the panelists, make sure that you have access to it. And please, don't lean forward to use it. Lift it up, and bring it close to your mouth. Too many presenters seem like they're bowing at the altar of the microphone. It's not a deity. You should control it — not the other way around.

### Interacting with other panelists

Your interaction with other panelists has a major effect on how the audience perceives you. Everyone assumes that panelists will have disagreements. It's *how* you disagree that's important. So here are two words of advice: Be diplomatic.

If you want to point out an inaccuracy stated by another panelist, say something like "I understand how Matt's experience could lead to his conclusion. However, I have found that . . ." Don't say that Matt is an idiot. The audience will get the idea.

You should also know where to turn for help (before the panel discussion even takes place, if possible). Which panelists are your allies? Which of them support your positions? Communications guru Barbara Howard calls this "knowing your second." In other words, who will "second" your motion? She suggests two methods for making "seconds" provide confirmation of your position. Nonverbally, you can turn to your "second," establish eye contact, and put him on the spot to offer support. Verbally, you can do this by saying something like "Matt, haven't you found what I've said to be true?" The main point: Don't leave it up to chance. Don't just make your statement and hope someone jumps in to support it. Make them jump in.

### Answering questions when you don't get any

Answering questions from the audience is your chance to shine. But what if the other panelists get all the questions? What if no questions are directed to you? Don't worry. Just play tag. As other panelists finish their answers, you can tag on your own statement: "I'd like to add one thing to what Sam just said. . . ." Is it aggressive? Yes. But it's better than sitting around after the session is over wishing someone had asked you something. If you want to make an impression, you need to have your say.

### Dealing with a moderator

A good moderator can make the panel a pleasure. The bad news is that many moderators are clueless. They see their function solely as introducing the panel members. When hassles occur — inappropriate questions from the audience, fistfights among the panelists — the moderator is nowhere to be found. And sometimes, they even screw up the introductions.

Assume that moderators will be incompetent, and celebrate if they're not. That means you must be prepared. Prepare to reintroduce yourself to the audience. Prepare to take charge if other panelists hog your time. Prepare to grab the microphone. And if you get a good moderator who runs a tight ship, be prepared to finish on time.

Want to improve the chances that the moderator will run the panel appropriately? Speak to the moderator beforehand — even if it's only a few minutes before the panel begins. Discuss your expectations, and see if they match what the moderator has in mind. Even if they differ, at least you know what to expect.

### Having a secret weapon ready

Smart panelists carry a secret weapon in reserve — the *sound bite,* which is a short line or phrase designed to capture audience attention. The sound bite gets its name from the radio and television news business. A reporter interviews someone for an hour. That night on the news, you hear the person for 30 seconds. That's the sound bite.

As a Sony Electronics executive, James Harris III always had sound bites ready for panel presentations. If the discussion involved products and product futures, he'd mention the "*Field of Dreams* engineering vision — if we build it, they will buy." Another line that stirred up the audience was "People win business, not products. Products enable you to get in the door."

# Participating in a Roundtable Discussion

Another speaking format closely related to the panel is the roundtable discussion. And no, you don't actually have to have a round table.

## What exactly is a roundtable?

Like a panel, a roundtable has multiple participants and a moderator. But a roundtable discussion is less formal, encourages interaction among participants, and doesn't require an audience.

A roundtable discussion is best described as a guided conversation. Participants, selected for their expertise, discuss a particular topic or set of topics. They discuss problems and come up with solutions. And as the term "roundtable" suggests, participants are seated so that they all face each other. (Often at a rectangular table. The point is that they can all see one another easily and take part in the discussion.)

The conversation is guided by a moderator who facilitates the discussion and keeps the agenda moving. (Either the moderator or a separate organizer can set the agenda.) The moderator's responsibilities include beginning and ending the discussion on time, making introductions, keeping the participants on topic, and summarizing the discussion. The moderator also makes sure that each participant gets an opportunity to speak.

"The major difference between a panel and a roundtable is that participants in a roundtable are expected to ask each other questions," notes Scott Fivash, CEO of Seattle-based CEOMedia. And he should know. As the publisher of *Washington CEO* and *California CEO* magazines, Scott often sponsors roundtable discussions for business executives.

"A moderator introduces the issue under discussion," he notes. "Then we go around the table. Each person introduces themselves and makes a comment." Scott gives out the agenda in advance so participants have time to think about it.

The other big difference between a panel and a roundtable is in the structure. Panelists direct semiformal remarks to an audience. Roundtable participants direct their remarks to each other and may not even have an audience, because the purpose of a roundtable is for experts to have a conversation that can yield insights into the topics under discussion.

## How to be a star in a roundtable discussion

Although roundtable participants are usually chosen for their expertise, the term "expert" is relative. You don't have to be a brain surgeon or rocket scientist to be an expert. Roundtable discussions can cover everything from marketing strategy to employee recruitment practices. When you're asked to participate, here some tips that Scott Fivash suggests you keep in mind:

✔ **To prepare yourself, get as much information as possible from the person who asked you to participate.** Why is the roundtable being held? What is it supposed to accomplish? What topics will it cover? Would any books or articles make good background reading? Why were you selected to participate? Why were the other participants selected?

✔ **Have a few talking points prepared.** "It's often the people who are most prepared who get to participate most in the discussion," observes Scott. That's why he suggests writing down three or four points to make before the roundtable begins. Then you can make them as the opportunity arises.

✔ **Tell stories.** "Everyone likes short anecdotal data," says Scott. "But keep your stories very short and to the point."

✔ **Be prepared to ask questions.** Roundtable participants are expected to ask questions; it's one of the advantages of participating in a roundtable. "Participants in our executive roundtables come expecting to get answers too," notes Scott. "As they discuss various business topics, they'll ask each other, 'How did your company handle that situation?'" If you know who the other participants will be, you can prepare specific questions for them. (To learn about the other participants, just ask the moderator or the roundtable organizer.)

✔ **Find appropriate openings for your questions.** The best time to ask a question about a particular topic is when that topic is under discussion. But what if you never get a chance or the topic doesn't come up? "You can create your own opportunity to ask a specific question to a specific participant," Scott explains. "Just conclude one of your comments by saying, 'Well, I'd really like to hear from Mr. So-and-So about how his company did it.'"

✔ **Recognize networking opportunities.** A roundtable provides more than an opportunity to state your ideas. It also allows you to develop valuable relationships with the other participants. "You can really get to know them just by discussing issues together," notes Scott. "And you can continue to cultivate those relationships after the roundtable has ended." So instead of just exchanging business cards and letting it go at that, do some follow-up after the roundtable. Call or e-mail people you met, and give them some additional ideas or information related to what was discussed.

# Part VI
# The Part of Tens

# In this part . . .

*I*n this part, I show you lots of comeback lines to use when things go wrong, and I tell you what to check before you present. I also tell you how to make effective presentations to your city council or school board, or at any other public meeting.

# Chapter 24

# Ten (or So) Comeback Lines to Use When Things Go Wrong

As the late comedy coach John Cantu once observed, "Ad-libs work best when they're written down." The time to think of a witty line to deal with a problem is before the problem occurs, because more than likely, you'll be too nervous at that moment. Using humor shows your audience that you're not upset and that you're still in control. Staying on your toes at all times is important, because unfortunately, lots of problems can occur when you're giving a presentation. In this chapter, I give you some lines for dealing with them.

## Visual-Aid Problems

Those pesky slides and overheads never seem to work right when you want them to. (For more on working with visual aids, check out Chapter 10.) Take a look at some distracting problems and what you can say in response:

✔ A slide or overhead is projected upside down.

- I'll get another one; this one must be defective.

- It looks good no matter how you look at it.

- For those of you sitting on your heads.

✔ Someone points out a spelling error on a slide.

   • As a famous author once said, "I never respected anyone who couldn't spell a word more than one way."

✔ You're writing on a flip chart, and the highlighter runs out of ink.

   • Obviously, I've come to the dry part of my presentation.

# Distracting Noises

Loud noises have a way of occurring just when you're in the middle of an important point. Take a look at some distracting noises and things you can say in response:

✔ Your microphone emits an ear-busting squeal.

   • It must have been something I ate.

✔ A police, fire, or ambulance siren disturbs your presentation.

   • [Name of someone the audience knows] is late again.

   • I told them not to pick me up for another hour.

✔ A cell phone rings in the audience.

   • Tell them I'm busy right now.

# You Make a Mistake

Nobody is perfect. Unfortunately, many of us realize this truth while giving a presentation. Take a look at some possible mistakes you can make and things you can say in response:

✔ You make a point that no one understands.

   • I can explain your difficulty understanding my (last point, chart, plan, whatever): In my previous job, I wrote instructions for putting together children's toys.

✔ You mispronounce a word or say something stupid.

   • I feel like the javelin thrower who won the coin toss and elected to receive.

# Chapter 25

# Ten (or So) Tips for Presentations at Public Meetings

● ● ● ● ● ● ● ● ● ● ● ● ● ● ● ● ● ● ● ● ● ● ● ● ● ● ● ● ● ● ● ● ● ● ● ● ● ● ● ● ● ● ● ● ● ● ●

*In This Chapter*

▶ Making your point clearly and effectively

▶ Ensuring that you don't offend public officials

● ● ● ● ● ● ● ● ● ● ● ● ● ● ● ● ● ● ● ● ● ● ● ● ● ● ● ● ● ● ● ● ● ● ● ● ● ● ● ● ● ● ● ● ● ● ●

*T*here's an old saying that you can't fight city hall. That may be true, but no one ever said you couldn't talk it into submission. And it seems like more people than ever before are trying.

You can now find more opportunities than ever before to voice your opinion at public meetings. Whether you're presenting to a city council, school board, planning commission, or any other public body, this chapter shows you how to state your position in a way that maximizes your effectiveness, or at least in a way that prevents getting a gavel thrown at you.

## Sign Up to Speak

Although every board, council, and commission has its own rules, most of them require you to sign up before the meeting if you wish to speak. Signing up allows the board to identify you in the agenda and the meeting's official minutes, and the advance notice allows a board to schedule speakers fairly (in the order they signed up) and to plan an efficient meeting.

This process of signing up typically involves filling out a speaker's card or similar form that requests your name and address. Sometimes, you just sign a list. The information you provide allows the board to identify you in the agenda and the meeting's official minutes.

The Rolling Stones may have had time on their side, but speakers at a public meeting don't. A quick survey of city and county Web sites reveals that most boards and councils limit speaker comments to two to five minutes. The most common time limit is three minutes. Some boards enforce their limits with a timer that buzzes when your time is up. Others just turn off your microphone.

Don't even assume you'll get a full allotment of time. If a lot of speakers turn out for a meeting, the board or council may limit you to one minute — or less, which makes sense from the board's perspective. It wants to give as many citizens as possible a chance to speak. (Even if it means cutting your brilliant insights down to 60 seconds.)

# Talk into the Microphone

Does talking into the microphone sound like an obvious tip? It is. But lots of presenters don't do it, especially people who are emotionally charged up about the issue they've come to present about. Or some people start by talking into the microphone and then forget as they get worked up. If you don't speak into the microphone, many people may not hear you. And in areas where public meetings are broadcast over cable television, any time you don't speak into the microphone, no one in the home audience knows what you're saying. And the home audience may be bigger and more influential than the audience in the meeting room.

# Identify Yourself and Your Position

Start by telling the board or council who you are and where you live. (This information is needed for the public record of the meeting.) Then tell them why you've come to speak and your position on the issue: "I'm here to speak about the proposed new traffic light at the corner of Main and Woodge. I'm against it."

# Start with Something Positive

If you want to talk people into your point of view, start by showing where you agree with them. By showing that you have some points of agreement, you establish a positive relationship with the board or council members. "Don't go right into your complaint," says Rich Johnson, a member of a school board in Sierra Madre, California. "If you start with something positive, it tells the board that you want to be constructive. You don't want to destroy the school. You just want to make it better." That makes your listeners much more receptive to your arguments.

# Present New Information

Boards or councils who refuse to see things your way commonly use the phrase "We've been over this a million times." The board or council has already evaluated certain arguments and rejected them. You need to offer *new* information. Present a new study, new data, or a new statistic that supports your view — that's what interests the board and council members.

To make sure you don't rehash old information the board already knows, review previous board meetings' minutes to see which arguments have already been made.

# Tell the Members What You Want

Are you trying to persuade a board or council to do something? Provide funding for your project? Agree with your position? Endorse your idea? Well, tell them. This advice sounds obvious, but you'd be amazed at how often this crucial step is omitted. In sales, it's called asking for the order. Ask the board or council members for the order. Don't assume that they know what you want them to do. Tell them clearly and precisely. And remind them of what you want them to do when you conclude your remarks with a statement, such as "And that's why I suggest you vote no/yes."

# Give a Clear Alternative

Have you ever reached a point in an argument where you said to your opponent, "So what do you want me to do instead?" Suddenly, this person falls silent. After all the objections to your behavior, your opponent has no alternative course of action to offer. The same principle applies to board or council meetings. Simply arguing against something isn't persuasive. If you want the city council not to raise a sales tax, tell them about another source of revenue. Always provide a clear alternative.

# Provide Handouts

Most boards and councils appreciate handouts that contain relevant information. Remember to bring enough copies to give to each board or council member. And if there's an opposing side to your issue, bring a copy for that person or group. "It's not fair for the opposing side not to be looking at the same information that the council has been given," says Patty White, a former mayor of Piedmont, California. You can also bring some extra copies in case any members of the press want one.

# Don't Repeat Yourself

Put yourself in the board or council member's shoes or ears. Would you want to listen to the same thing over and over again? No way. And neither do they. That means they don't want to hear you repeating yourself or previous presenters. So what do you do if Mr. Smith makes your point before you get to present? "When it's your turn, just say you agree with what Mr. Smith said and then sit down," advises school board member Rich Johnson. "Just repeating the arguments won't help your case and may turn board members against you."

# Always Be Prepared

Time is in short supply at board and council meetings. Agendas are crowded. Many tough issues need to be aired. And lots of people have done lots of work getting ready for the meeting. So no one wants to hear someone who is unprepared. Not only does it turn off board and council members, but it also makes you look bad. And it suggests that you don't really care that much about your issue — otherwise, you would have prepared. That means you should be familiar with the issue that you're going to talk about, have given it some thought, and have something to say about it.

Whatever problem or project has motivated your trip to a council or board meeting, the council or board members have probably dealt with a similar situation in the past. Really, you're not the first person to oppose budget cuts to your kid's school. Find out the history of your issue. Go to your local library and review archived copies of your local paper. Or find information on the Web. You need to know the history so you don't propose old ideas and arguments that have already been rejected.

After you put the history in perspective, double-check the current status of your issue. Has the situation changed since you did your research? Get your facts straight. Make sure you know what you're talking about before you start talking. Just because your neighbor down the street told you something doesn't make it true.

If you're speaking on behalf of an organization, remember that one speaker is much better than three, four, or five people saying the same thing. If you're representing an organization at a meeting, organize people to come and show support. (Assure them that they don't have to speak.) When you begin your presentation, ask those people whom you represent to stand. Showing a governing body that 50 of your neighbors took a few hours off work in the middle of the day to stand up and be counted scores points.

# Stay Cool and Calm

Although many issues facing boards and councils are highly emotional, the most effective presenters are those who come across as rational and businesslike. "Too many presenters regard board meetings as therapy sessions," observes Rich Johnson. "If you just want to vent, do it to your family or friends." He suggests a calm and cool demeanor. "If you come in with blustery charges or emotional tirades, you get written off immediately."

# Don't Be Rude

There's an old saying that you don't make yourself look good by making other people look bad. But lots of people try anyway — especially in board and council meetings. It doesn't work. "You don't get anywhere being rude or condescending to someone you don't agree with," says Patty White. "Point out why their position is incorrect, but don't belittle the other person."

She also suggests that you refrain from insulting board or council members. "I don't know why people think that calling a council member an idiot will produce a vote in their favor," White wonders. So keep calm and remember the golden rule: The council has the gold and makes the rules. So be nice to them.

# Don't Be a Professional Complainer

Professional complainers are easy to recognize if you frequent board or council meetings. These people sign up to present at every meeting. They love to hear themselves talk. And they just complain a lot. Most boards and councils have to deal with professional complainers. And you don't want to be one if you want to be taken seriously. "If you're at every meeting, and you're always complaining, your credibility disappears," observes Rich Johnson. "The board will metaphorically pat you on the head, compartmentalize you, and ignore you."

# Chapter 26

# Ten (or So) Things to Check Before You Present

**W**ant to maximize your chances of giving a successful presentation? Take care of the following items *before* you start talking.

## How to Get There

Do you know exactly where you're giving your presentation, how to get there, and how long it takes to get there? Well, find out. It's amazing how little consideration people give to these basic concerns. You knock yourself out preparing a killer talk, and then you blow it by going to the wrong ballroom. You need to know the *exact* location. Why? Because by the time you get to the correct room, you're frazzled and possibly even late. The time you were going to spend getting used to the room and psyching yourself up is gone forever.

Related concerns are traffic and parking. Don't plan your timetable on some general notion of how long it takes to get to the meeting site. Plan specifically for your travel time. Maybe it generally takes 30 minutes to get there. If you have to travel during rush hour, it's going to take longer. Plan for it.

Then you have the whole parking thing. Is it my imagination, or is it taking longer and longer to find a place to park? (Except for certain parts of California, where people are into creating their own space.) You need to know in advance where to park. Hey, you're the presenter. Tell them to give you a special parking spot at the meeting site. You deserve it.

On the day of your presentation, arrive at least one hour before you're scheduled to begin, which leaves enough time to correct any mistakes and still get mentally prepared.

# Room Layout

Always find out about the room long before you present. Several days ahead of time is preferable. If you can't do it in person, send someone you trust. At a minimum, pump your contact — the person who arranged for you to present — for information and details. Will you be in a banquet room? A conference room? A large meeting room? An auditorium? The room establishes important parameters for your presentation: how many people can attend, what type of audio-visual equipment you can use, whether you need a microphone, and so on.

Assessing the room in terms of potential distractions is also important. If you're presenting at a restaurant, hotel, or office building, chances are there's a nice view out the window of the meeting room. That's bad news, because you want audience attention focused on you, not the view.

What can you do? First, try to present in a room that has no windows. If that's not possible, make sure that the windows are covered with draperies or curtains. What if they have no curtains? Improvise. I've seen people hang table-cloths over the windows — anything to eliminate the competition of the view.

# Seating Arrangements

One of the most important aspects of the room where you speak is the seating arrangement. It affects your entire relationship with the audience. Done correctly, the audience members will sing your praises. Done incorrectly, they'll tell you to . . . sit on it. When it comes to seating, three basic considerations apply to any type of presentation in any type of setting.

- **First, and most important, can everyone see you?**

  You don't want any architectural features to block your audience from seeing you. Arrange the seating so no columns, folding walls, or other features prevent you from making eye contact with your audience.

- **Is the seating comfortable — both physically and psychologically?**

  The psychology of seating can have a tremendous effect on how your audience perceives your presentation. (Maybe that's why psychiatrists make patients lie down on a couch.) If your audience is 25 people in a room with 50 chairs, both you and your audience will perceive a small crowd. In contrast, if you set out 15 chairs and add 10 more as people arrive, everyone perceives a bigger turnout.

  Why does this matter? Because the first situation — 25 people in a room of 50 chairs — is a horrible setting for making a presentation. Everyone wonders why more people didn't show up. Your audience thinks that maybe they made a mistake in coming — which is a major strike against you before you even begin to speak. Even worse, you have to deal with the "energy" problem. When people are scattered throughout a room, you don't receive as strong a response as when they're seated together. You feel much less energy coming from the audience. Twenty-five people sitting together and laughing sound a lot louder than 25 people scattered through the room.

The general rule: The more densely packed the audience (in terms of seating, not intelligence), the better. When the audience members are seated together, it makes them feel more like a group. It also makes maintaining eye contact with them easier. Most important, it maximizes the energy of their response, and that energy is vital to your success.

✔ **Is the arrangement of chairs suited to the size of the room, the size of the audience, and the purpose of your presentation?**

Within the boundaries established by the room and furniture, you can arrange seating based on the size of the room and your purpose. Chairs arranged in a semicircle provide a more informal atmosphere. This arrangement puts you directly in front of each audience member. If the audience is more than 30 people, the group is probably too large for a single semicircle. In that case, you can stagger a second row of chairs behind the first row. Now you have a double semicircle where the second row looks between the shoulders of the people in the first row. For large groups or a more formal atmosphere, I recommend classroom-style seating in rows.

Here's the secret to getting the audience members placed to your liking: Arrange the seating *before* they arrive. (All right, so it's not such a big secret, but it's amazing how many people ignore this simple truth.) After the audience shows up, it's too late to mess with the seats. People hate being told to move after they've plopped their fannies into the chairs — that's just human nature.

The most important thing to remember is that seating arrangements aren't set in cement, and neither are the seats. Don't be afraid to move things around. Ask your contact for help.

# Human Equipment

If people can operate equipment for you, make sure that they know what they're doing. You don't need an Einstein to work a slide projector, but it does require a minimal level of competence. Also, make sure that you know whom to contact for help with minor and major catastrophes — a light bulb burns out, a microphone breaks, or a UFO zaps your notes. Better yet, bring your own backup solutions — spare light bulb, hard copies of your slides, and so on — in case the equipment operator never shows up. And for that same reason, make sure you know how to operate the equipment yourself.

# Audiovisual Equipment

You can't check slide or overhead projectors too many times. After you get your slides or overheads focused, walk around the room while one is projecting on the screen. Can it be seen from everywhere in the room? Overhead projectors often block the view of people seated in line with them. If that's the case, try to project your overhead higher up on the screen — closer to the ceiling. And definitely use a screen. It shows your slides or overheads much better than a wall. Also, bring spare projector light bulbs and an extension cord in case you need them.

# Sound System

If you need a sound system, is one available, and does it work? Make sure that the volume is adjusted so that everyone in the room can hear you. Different microphones pick up and broadcast your voice in different ways.

*Test the microphone in the location where you'll actually use it.* I discovered this lesson the hard way. Just before a speech to a group of Defense Department managers, I tested the microphone while standing in the front of the room. It worked fine. But I didn't go behind the podium where I'd actually be speaking. Big mistake. When I started my speech, the microphone erupted in screeching feedback. Great way to begin, right? Turns out the culprit was a metal sprinkler nozzle in the ceiling over the podium.

Make sure that you know how to work the microphone. Do you know how to turn it on and off? If you have a microphone stand, do you know how to adjust it? Different microphones pick up and broadcast your voice in different ways. Play with the microphone until you get a good idea of its range.

# Electricity

Where are the electrical outlets in the room? Do you have enough of them to run your equipment? Are they two-prong or three-prong? Do yourself a favor. Always bring an adapter and an extension cord. You'll be glad you did.

# Podium

Is there a podium or lectern if you need one? And is it the right size? The *right size* is whatever suits your purposes. Do you want the audience to see you? Then make sure you're taller than the podium or that you get a box you can stand on behind the podium. Are you afraid the audience will throw things? Get a podium that's high and wide. In either case, make sure that the podium has a light that's in good working order — especially if you're going to darken the room for slides. You can't get the audience to see the light if the podium leaves your notes in the dark.

# Lighting

Test the "house lights" to see if they work and how the light fills the room. Find out if you can adjust their level of brightness. If they're adjustable, take advantage of this feature — especially if you're using slides.

# Restrooms

Definitely check the restrooms. Where are they located? Do they have paper towels available? Is there an adequate supply of toilet paper? Do the toilets work? This may sound trivial now, but it can become very important. You never know when you need a restroom in a hurry — especially if you're nervous.

# Temperature and Ventilation

Mark Twain once said that everybody talks about the weather, but nobody does anything about it. When it comes to the "weather" in your meeting room, nobody even talks about it, but maybe *you* should do something about it. The "weather" — temperature and ventilation — can have a greater effect on your audience than anything you say. Ever had to sit through a presentation in a hot, stuffy room? Or a chilly room? It ain't fun. And it's certainly not conducive to listening to the presenter. If the room is hot and stuffy, get a maintenance person to turn up the air conditioning. If it's too cold, turn up the heat. Don't make the audience wait for your hot air.

# Index

• *J* •

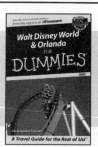

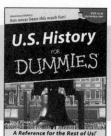

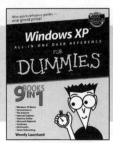

# FOR DUMMIES®

## Plain-English solutions for everyday challenges

## HOME & BUSINESS COMPUTER BASICS

0-7645-0838-5

0-7645-1663-9

0-7645-1548-9

### Also available:

Excel 2002 All-in-One Desk Reference For Dummies (0-7645-1794-5)

Office XP 9-in-1 Desk Reference For Dummies (0-7645-0819-9)

PCs All-in-One Desk Reference For Dummies (0-7645-0791-5)

Troubleshooting Your PC For Dummies (0-7645-1669-8)

Upgrading & Fixing PCs For Dummies (0-7645-1665-5)

Windows XP For Dummies (0-7645-0893-8)

Windows XP For Dummies Quick Reference (0-7645-0897-0)

Word 2002 For Dummies (0-7645-0839-3)

## INTERNET & DIGITAL MEDIA

0-7645-0894-6

0-7645-1642-6

0-7645-1664-7

### Also available:

CD and DVD Recording For Dummies (0-7645-1627-2)

Digital Photography All-in-One Desk Reference For Dummies (0-7645-1800-3)

eBay For Dummies (0-7645-1642-6)

Genealogy Online For Dummies (0-7645-0807-5)

Internet All-in-One Desk Reference For Dummies (0-7645-1659-0)

Internet For Dummies Quick Reference (0-7645-1645-0)

Internet Privacy For Dummies (0-7645-0846-6)

Paint Shop Pro For Dummies (0-7645-2440-2)

Photo Retouching & Restoration For Dummies (0-7645-1662-0)

Photoshop Elements For Dummies (0-7645-1675-2)

Scanners For Dummies (0-7645-0783-4)

## Get smart! Visit www.dummies.com

• Find listings of even more Dummies titles

• Browse online articles, excerpts, and how-to's

• Sign up for daily or weekly e-mail tips

• Check out Dummies fitness videos and other products

• Order from our online bookstore

Available wherever books are sold. Go to www.dummies.com or call 1-877-762-2974 to order direct